# CASTING LIGHT
# ON THE SHADOWS

# CASTING LIGHT ON THE SHADOWS

*Canadian Perspectives on*
*Special Operations Forces*

Edited by

## COLONEL BERND HORN
### AND
## MAJOR TONY BALASEVICIUS

Foreword by

## COLONEL DAVID BARR

CANADIAN DEFENCE ACADEMY PRESS
KINGSTON

THE DUNDURN GROUP
TORONTO

Editor: Michael Carroll
Copy-editor: Nigel Heseltine
Design: Bruna Bucciarelli
Index: Yves Raic
Printer: University of Toronto Press

Library and Archives Canada Cataloguing in Publication

Casting light on the shadows : Canadian perspectives on special operations forces / [edited by] Bernd Horn, Tony Balasevicius.

Co-published by Canadian Defence Academy Press.

Includes bibliographical references and index.

ISBN-10: 1-55002-694-1
ISBN-13: 978-1-55002-694-8

1. Special forces (Military science)--Canada. 2. Canada--History, Military. 3. Special forces (Military science). 4. Military art and science. I. Horn, Bernd, 1959- II. Balasevicius, Tony III. Title: Canadian perspectives on special operations forces.

U262.C37 2006          356'.160971          C2006-905402-9

1   2   3   4   5      11   10   09   08   07

Conseil des Arts du Canada   Canada Council for the Arts   Canada   ONTARIO ARTS COUNCIL CONSEIL DES ARTS DE L'ONTARIO

We acknowledge the support of the **Canada Council for the Arts** and the **Ontario Arts Council** for our publishing program. We also acknowledge the financial support of the **Government of Canada** through the **Book Publishing Industry Development Program** and **The Association for the Export of Canadian Books**, and the **Government of Ontario** through the **Ontario Book Publishers Tax Credit** program and the **Ontario Media Development Corporation**.

Care has been taken to trace the ownership of copyright material used in this book. The author and the publisher welcome any information enabling them to rectify any references or credits in subsequent editions.

*J. Kirk Howard, President*

Printed and bound in Canada
www.dundurn.com

Canadian Defence Academy Press
PO Box 17000 Station Forces
Kingston, Ontario, Canada
K7K 7B4

| Dundurn Press | Gazelle Book Services Limited | Dundurn Press |
|---|---|---|
| 3 Church Street, Suite 500 | White Cross Mills | 2250 Military Road |
| Toronto, Ontario, Canada | High Town, Lancaster, England | Tonawanda, NY |
| M5E 1M2 | LA1 4XS | U.S.A. 14150 |

# CONTENTS

# FOREWORD

It has become a cliché to state that the world changed dramatically in the aftermath of the terrorist attack against the World Trade Center in New York City on 11 September 2001. However, it did, and that heinous act has had dramatic repercussions around the globe. Canada has not been exempt. The cataclysmic event and its consequences altered how we look at the world. It was also important in determining the type of military forces we as a nation required to defend Canadian interests domestically and internationally.

Not surprisingly, as the Canadian Forces continues to undergo a major transformation, a key component of its reconfiguration is the establishment of a Canadian Special Operations Forces Command (CANSOFCOM). This new command provides the nation with agile, high-readiness Special Operations Forces capable of conducting special operations across the spectrum of conflict at home and abroad. However, as effective as SOF has proven to be worldwide, it remains poorly understood by the conventional military, politicians, and the public at large.

For that reason, I am delighted to introduce *Casting Light on the Shadows: Canadian Perspectives on Special Operations Forces*. This seminal book opens a window on Special Operations Forces. In short, it provides an authoritative examination of SOF theory, history, and current issues, as well as provocative views on the future.

Significantly, contributors who are recognized specialists in their fields have written this book from a distinctly Canadian perspective. In essence, they have prepared a primer that serves as a solid foundation for an understanding of SOF, which in light of the current and future security environment have become the forces of choice.

Colonel David Barr
Commander CANSOFCOM

# ACKNOWLEDGEMENTS

A s with any endeavour of this magnitude, the product is the result of hard work by many hands. As such, the editors wish to acknowledge the contribution of all those who provided assistance, both directly and indirectly, to this project. First, we wish to thank the contributors for their in-depth research and insights into this very important subject area. Furthermore, we greatly appreciate their agreement in allowing us to use their material for this volume. Next we would like to thank the *Canadian Army Journal* and the *Canadian Military Journal*, particularly its editor, David Bashow, and its publication manager, Monica Muller, for their assistance in providing material for this book.

We also owe a debt of gratitude to the academic and research staff at Library and Archives Canada, the Directorate of History and Heritage, and the Royal Military College of Canada. In addition, we wish to thank Ann-Marie Beaton of Canadian Press for her assistance in obtaining permission to use the photograph that graces the front cover.

Finally, we wish to thank all those who have taken the time to share their experiences, insights, and comments, which have made the book all the richer. We remain indebted to all of you for your contributions.

# INTRODUCTION

## Bernd Horn and Tony Balasevicius

Special Operations Forces (SOF) have never been an integral element of Canada's military capability. Although units have existed periodically throughout our history, they have always been in the shadows, and barely tolerated. In this context, Canada has not been much different from other countries. Not surprisingly, special and unique organizations are usually viewed suspiciously by the conservative, conventional military that embraces and takes great comfort in uniformity and standardization.

However, the tragic terrorist attacks against the United States on 11 September 2001 changed much of that. In the aftermath of 9/11, SOF became the force of choice. Their inherent responsiveness, small footprint, cultural and regional awareness, and impressive suite of capabilities made them a force multiplier with an impact on operations far in excess of the numbers actually employed. Their influence in both political and real terms has forced even their greatest detractors to reconsider their value.

The Canadian case is a perfect example. In the wake of 9/11, when the United States was busy conducting Operation Enduring Freedom, later to evolve into the war on terrorism, Canada's defence minister found himself consistently under fire from the Canadian press and public for a seemingly inadequate national military contribution to the American efforts in Afghanistan. One day, almost in frustration with the constant harassment, he revealed that Canadian "commandos" were in fact deployed in support of the U.S. efforts. Canadians met the revelation with complete surprise. Although very few even realized such a force existed, all seemed completely satisfied, even proud, that Canada was evidently doing its part. Thereafter, the defence minister mentioned the involvement of the formerly ultra-secret and little-known Joint Task Force Two (JTF-2) at every opportunity. Predictably, he immediately pushed the military chain of command to double the size of the unit. After all, it seemed almost too good to be true. The small and highly capable force earned credibility and political capital from allies, appeased the Canadian public, yet represented a relatively small commitment in personnel and resources. It fit perfectly with the Canadian way of war.

SOF's time has clearly come. As war, conflict, and peace continue to evolve, the role and requirement for SOF will likewise evolve and grow. They have become a critical component of any nation's military capability. It is for this reason that Canadian Forces (CF) transformation has resulted in an integral SOF capability. The limited original hostage rescue capability housed within the context of JTF-2, which was taken over from the Royal Canadian Mounted Police Special Emergency Response Team (SERT) in 1992, has grown to become the Canadian Special Operations Forces Command (CANSOFCOM). This new formation consists of a number of distinct units and capabilities that are already in place or in the process of being established. These include the JTF-2; a Canadian Special Operations Regiment; a special tactical aviation squadron; a joint nuclear, biological chemical (JNBC) company; and the requisite formation headquarters, support functions, and organizations. CANSOF missions include counterterrorism, counter-proliferation (i.e., weapons of mass destruction [WMD]), special reconnaissance, direct action, non-combat evacuation, and defence diplomacy and military assistance (DDMA).

However, despite the growth, SOF is not well understood. Most individuals, whether in uniform or out, will not understand the CANSOF organizations and tasks listed earlier. Nor will they necessarily comprehend the rationale for the establishment or expansion of these special units. The perennial question is inevitable: why establish new organizations for those roles when we could just assign the tasks to existing units?

It is for this reason that this book has been produced. It consists of a series of essays on SOF-related issues and topics. Some essays are previously published articles, while others were written specifically for this volume. Each, however, is a stand-alone chapter that speaks to a specific SOF topic or issue. All are authored by individuals with specialized knowledge and expertise in the field. Together the essays provide a complete compendium of information and knowledge on Canadian SOF-related issues. As such, this volume should provide readers, whether military or civilian, with a solid foundation.

The book itself is divided into three distinct sections. The first provides theoretical background. It covers the theory (e.g., definition, selection, and training requirement), as well as many of the current issues important to understanding the dynamic nature of SOF. The second part offers historical perspectives on the evolution of SOF both internationally and in the Canadian context. This is fundamentally important as it explains the origin and evolution of SOF. It also reveals the timeless institutional hostility and barriers that SOF have endured. Finally, the third section affords views on the future requirement of SOF with specific emphasis on the Canadian case.

In essence, this book is a primer for Canadian Special Operations Forces. It is intended to fill a void. It should serve to inform, educate, and create discussion and debate on the evolving role of SOF in the Canadian military. As the war on terrorism continues, and Canada maintains its role in supporting coalition operations around the world, SOF will remain on the leading edge of Canada's contribution. To ensure the greatest effectiveness can be achieved, a deep-seated understanding of all aspects of SOF, by both operators and those who would employ them, must be achieved. Hopefully, this volume helps achieve that aim.

# PART I

*Theoretical Foundation to Understanding Special Operations Forces*

# 1

# Special Operations Forces:
## *Uncloaking an Enigma*

### Bernd Horn

We shall go
Always a little further: it may be
Beyond that last blue mountain barred with snow,
Across that angry or that glimmering sea.
— James Elroy Flecker, *The Golden Journey to Samarkand*

The war against terrorism, specifically the ground campaign in Afghanistan that began in the fall of 2001 after the catastrophic attacks on the World Trade Center towers in New York City, achieved in a very short period what over 50 years of lobbying and activities on the fringes of military operations failed to do — namely, convince military commanders and decision makers that Special Operations Forces (SOF) are not only a viable force but may in fact be the force of choice for the future. Even in Canada, the concept of SOF, at least initially, met with great support. Representing our initial contribution to the ground war, the Joint Task Force Two (JTF-2) was lauded by the minister of national defence (MND) as our elite commando unit. Overnight, this ultra-secret unit was heralded as a national strategic force. Its ability to deploy rapidly, operate with coalition forces, and quickly adapt to a foreign and very hostile environment earned it the respect of the public in general.

Its perceived success, utility, and relevance also earned it ministerial approval for expansion to twice its size!

It was the initial frenzy and hype, almost a convulsive reaction towards what appeared to be yet another wave of incantations of how conflict had changed that triggered another scramble for the establishment of an SOF capability in the Canadian Forces (CF). That initial wave was subsequently stalled by a defence review, as well as an entrenched institutional bias against such forces. Nonetheless, it is difficult to stop a concept whose time has come. Although CF transformation has been underway for years, it received dramatic impetus from General Rick Hillier upon his appointment as chief of the defence staff (CDS) in 2004. An integral part of that transformation was the creation of a Canadian Special Operations Forces Command (CANSOFCOM).

And so Canada, much like its allies, has become a believer and is investing in SOF. This is not surprising. After all, during those trying days following the 11 September 2001 tragedy in New York when pictures of heavily armed, albeit uniquely dressed SOF operatives were flashed on CNN and in magazines worldwide, the public and many in the military were introduced for the first time to the concept of Special Operations Forces and their inherent strength and relevance to the modern battlespace. Reporters often used colourful and highly dramatic imagery to describe SOF. For instance, one theme repeated by journalists described SOF as "the toughest, smartest, most secretive, fittest, best-equipped and consistently lethal killers...."[1] Yet a clear, comprehensive definition or understanding of what these forces really were was never fully addressed. It was generally accepted that everyone knew what the term meant. But do they?

Even today, after cataclysmic events, the subject of SOF never fails to elicit emotion. Far too often the debate is marred by the polarity between the two sides, that is those who support the concept and those who see SOF as pampered prima donnas representing an incestuous elite, that are far too specialized and devour far too many scarce resources. This has resulted in a continual struggle to objectively analyze the value, utility, and relevance of SOF. The controversy over the significance of SOF begins with their definition. Quite simply, SOF means different things to different people. Moreover, there is often confusion over concepts, entities, and terms such as *SOF, Special Forces (SF), Airborne, reconnaissance units, elites, counterterrorism, counter-insurgency, actions behind enemy lines, unconventional warfare,* and *guerrilla warfare.* In fact, much of the literature in this field often either assumes an

20

understanding of the different terms and/or uses them interchangeably. The most common misuse is the transposing of SOF with SF and vice versa. Further confusion is evident as many use Special Forces correctly to refer to such forces as the American "Green Berets," while other use the term to refer to forces that are simply "special" (i.e., unique or different). Although all Special Forces (e.g., Green Berets) are by nature Special Operations Forces, not all SOF organizations are necessarily SF. This reality must be factored in when discussing the larger issue of SOF.

The genesis of this confusion is readily apparent when one examines the historical roots of the debate. Colonel Aaron Bank battled with the vagaries of the concept of SOF operations and organizations in his struggle to establish the U.S. Special Forces, as noted above, commonly referred to as the "Green Berets." He observed that the term *Special Operations*, as it was interpreted by others, was a catch-all that "included cold-weather operations; mountain warfare; and amphibious, airborne, Ranger, and commando operations."[2] Bank commented that it was "too damn broad and all inclusive!"[3] Colonel J.W. Hackett reinforced this prevailing vacuum of in-depth thought on SOF. He nailed down their role as "to hinder the most effective application of the enemy's resources in war and to secure advantages in the employment of our own."[4] Adding to the confusion, M.R.D. Foot, a wartime intelligence officer for the Special Air Service (SAS) and British historian, attempted to define SOF by the activities they undertook. As such, he asserted that special operations "are unorthodox coups ... unexpected strokes of violence, usually mounted and executed outside the military establishment of the day."[5] Finally, American Lieutenant-General William E. Yarborough professed that "special warfare is an esoteric art unto itself."[6] He once described the Special Forces soldier as "a man who could be dropped by himself into the wilderness with nothing but a knife and his own devices, and emerge sometime later, leading a fully trained and equipped fighting force."[7] Needless to say, there was a profound lack of clarity.

But to many, special operations and the forces tasked with their execution represented a very narrow scope. General Collins, the U.S. Army chief of staff in 1951, was representative of a common military perception. He defined Special Forces operations as those "carried on within or behind the enemy's lines."[8] This constricted view was echoed by numerous academics and scholars as well. A study of commando (special) operations from 1939 to 1980 rendered the observation that special operations were "self-contained acts of war mounted by self-sufficient forces operating within hostile territory."[9] Dr. Terry White reinforced this idea. "Special Forces," he explained, "are personnel who receive specialized training to execute tasks behind the enemy's lines in support of conventional military operations or a counter-insurgency campaign."[10] Major-General Julian Thompson, a former Royal Marine Commando and author of *War Behind Enemy Lines* agrees. He believes that Special Forces, usually raised because of enthusiastic backing from a very senior military commander, was all about actions behind enemy lines. However, he also defined SOF by function, namely: Offensive action, the gathering of intelligence, and operating with indigenous resistance.[11]

But other schools of thought also emerged. James Lucas, a well-known author on military subjects, particularly the Second World War German units and organizations, set three criterion for special forces: units from a conventional arm of service that have been grouped to form a unique fighting detachment, units that conduct operations using tactics or weapons of an original nature, and units that are raised to conduct a specific type of military operation (e.g., a guerrilla group such as Werewolf).[12] Lucas also notes that Special Operations Forces "carry the nimbus of success ... recruit discreetly and accept only those few who attain the unusual standards that are set."[13] He added, "Theirs is a reputation for iron-hard toughness."[14] Similarly, author and military analyst James Dunnigan boils SOF down to "the most capable troops sent to take care of the most difficult missions."[15] For this reason, Dr. Terry White argued that "Army SOF includes elite light infantry units such as rangers, commandos and paratroops used for shock action: strikes, raids, ambushes and temporary seizure of bridges, road junctions and strongpoints."[16]

Along those lines, retired U.S. Colonel John M. Collins, also a former senior specialist in national defence with the Congressional Research Service, explained that:

> SOF help shape the international security environment, prepare for an uncertain future, and respond with precision in a range of potential crises. Unique training and skills enable them to operate in situations where conventional units cannot be used for political or military reasons. Moreover, they place a priority on applying finesse rather than brute force and possess overt, covert, and clandestine capabilities not found elsewhere within the Armed Forces.[17]

Complicating the issue and further adding to the quagmire of perceptions and fallacies is yet another interpretation that describes and defines the realm of SOF within the context of elitism. Eminent scholar Eliot Cohen, in his seminal work *Commandos and Politicians*, used the term *elite units* to describe SOF operations and organizations. The concept of elite was central to his interpretation and description of SOF activities and membership. Cohen developed specific criteria that defined elite units. "First," he wrote, "a unit becomes elite when it is perpetually assigned special or unusual missions: in particular, missions that are-or seem to be extremely hazardous. For this reason airborne units have long been considered elite since parachuting is a particularly dangerous way of going into battle. Second, elite units conduct missions that require only a few men who must meet high standards of training and physical toughness, particularly the latter. Third, an elite unit becomes elite only when it achieves a reputation-justified or not-for bravura and success."[18] But strategist Colin Gray insists that "elite, as a quality, refers directly to the standard of selection, not to the activity that soldiers are selected to perform." He asserted, "Special operations forces must be elite forces but elite forces generally are not special operations forces."[19]

Conversely, military historian, Douglas Porch, believes that conventional measures of elite status are such benchmarks as "battlefield achievement, military proficiency, or specialized military functions."[20] Eric Morris, also a historian, agrees. He described Special Operations Forces as elite units by virtue of the fact that they were required to demonstrate "a prowess and military skill of a higher standard than more conventional battalions."[21] Canadian defence reporter David Pugliese concurred. He defined SOF as "the most elite, most skilled and certainly enigmatic of military fighters."[22]

In its purest form elites represent "the choice or most carefully selected part of a group."[23] Sociologists and political scientists have tended to define elites as a cohesive minority in any given group or society which holds the power of decision making. They further assert that the chief strength of a given elite is its autonomy and cohesiveness that are borne from an exclusiveness that is protected by rigorous entrance standards. Elites are extremely homogeneous and self-perpetuating.[24] In short, the term *elite* connotes a select minority within a group or society that holds special status and privilege. Traditionally, this meant those who held political, administrative, and economic power within a society.[25] Although some of the components are representative of SOF, it still falls short of a comprehensive explanation.

23

Somewhat related to this approach, is that of military analyst and writer Mark Lloyd. He insists that SOF-type forces, which he also described as elite, have become increasingly more specialist and secretive in the second half of the twentieth century. He in turn divided SOF into three categories: Special forces capable of operating in any theatre in the world, special purpose forces designed and trained for a single type of warfare, and units of special designation, trained and equipped for a single operation, which he describes as a wartime phenomenon.[26]

Australian historian D.H. Horner took a comparable tack. He believed that SOF referred to a combination of Special Action Forces "which perform operational roles that are not normal for conventional forces" (i.e., SAS and commando, and special force signal units) and Special Forces, which included "military personnel with cross-training and specialized military skills, organized into small multiple purpose detachments with the mission to train, organise, supply, direct, and control indigenous forces in guerilla warfare and counter-insurgency operations and to conduct unconventional warfare operations."[27] Strategist Colin Gray agreed. He observed that SOF "undertake missions that regular forces either cannot perform or cannot perform at acceptable cost."[28]

Numerous other military analysts, researchers, and scholars have applied a similar approach. Basically, they recognized that some units, by virtue of the quality of personnel, training, or mission, were not representative of their conventional brethren. As a result, they were automatically labelled as SOF organizations, and they were also automatically bequeathed with de facto elite status.[29]

A number of recurring themes have become evident. First, is the emphasis on SOF as those who operate behind enemy lines. Second is the concept of elite organizations and third is the idea of special training and expertise. As such, defence correspondent Christopher Bellamy described "special [Operations] forces" as "small, highly motivated volunteer units with special training or expertise ..."[30] Correspondingly, Tom Clancy, the respected American military analyst and writer, wrote, "They [SOF] are specially selected, specially trained, specially equipped and given special missions and support.... By creating superbly trained specialized units for specialized tasks, roles, and missions, particular problems that prove beyond the capabilities of general purpose forces can be handled by smaller more focused units."[31]

Ongoing analysis and study on SOF has created additional dimensions that although embracing the recurring themes have also began to capture the evolving nature of SOF from a Second World War commando raid mentality to the use of these forces for political, economic, or informational objectives in a very risk-averse political environment. Naval Captain William H. McRaven, a former Sea Air Land (SEAL) force commander and author of *Spec Ops*, defined special operations as those "conducted by forces specially trained and equipped, and supported for a specific target whose destruction, elimination, or rescue (in the case of hostages), is a political or military imperative."[32]

He maintained a somewhat limited direct action orientation that emphasized that all special operations are conducted against fortified positions.[33] This approach places emphasis on training and drills to penetrate defences. Former Royal Marine Commando, journalist, and author Robin Neillands explained that the SF or SOF member (he treated them incorrectly as one and the same):

> Is defined by his role and his training. He is a soldier who tends to operate in small groups, often at night, behind the lines or in the amphibious or parachute assault role. He uses technology appropriate to the task in hand.... He is highly skilled in the necessary military techniques, though his training is mainly directed towards irregular warfare, reconnaissance and raiding operations.... The Special Force soldier is, first and foremost, a well-trained fighting man.[34]

In essence both definitions follow a technical orientation focusing on training and organization. This approach, as with the others already mentioned, can apply to many forces both SOF and conventional. However, it must be noted that Neillands begins to cast light on the crux of SOF, namely the individual soldier. This will fall out shortly.

There is one approach to defining SOF that must be addressed. This is an oft favoured approach to quote official definitions, normally those of the U.S. military or the North Atlantic Treaty Organisation (NATO). The weakness, however, is that most official definitions are broad and inclusive because they are often more concerned with getting consensus of the respective working group or policy makers and avoiding disagreement, than they are in compiling a definitive concise definition. Nonetheless, they do provide a doctrinally and politically accepted perspective on SOF. For instance, one definition, written for a hand-book for Congress and the American Special Operations Panel defines SOF as:

> Small, carefully selected military, paramilitary, and civilian units with unusual (occasionally unique) skills, which are superlatively trained for specific rather than general purposes, and are designed to undertake unorthodox tasks that ordinary units could accomplish only with far greater difficulty and far less effectiveness, if at all.[35]

The official NATO definition given in *AJP-1(A) Combined SOF Concept 3200* (March 1997) explains that SOF are:

> [Forces that provide] a flexible, versatile and unique capability, whether employed alone or complementing other forces or agencies, to attain military-strategic or operational objectives. Special operations, in contrast to conventional operations, are generally small, precise, adaptable and innovative, they may be conducted in a clandestine, covert or discreet manner.[36]

The former commander of the United States Special Operations Command (USSOCOM) asserted that "today's SOF offer special skills; unconventional tactics; small, rapidly deployable units; and unique capabilities that set them apart from conventional forces."[37] Similarly, the commander of U.S. Army Special Operations Command (USASOC) wrote that "Special forces ... are specially trained and prepared to conduct foreign internal defense, unconventional warfare, special reconnaissance and direct action missions."[38] The focus of these official definitions is clearly the non-conventional capability and/or skill set.

The official U.S. definition for special operations, given in *Doctrine for Joint Operations*, casts light on the corollary concept of SOF work:

> [Special] operations conducted by specially organized, trained, and equipped military and paramilitary forces to achieve military, political, economic, or psychological objectives by unconventional military means in hostile, denied, or politically sensitive areas. These operations are conducted during peacetime competition, conflict, and war, independent or in coordination with operations of conventional, non special operations forces. Politico-military considerations fre-

26

quently shape special operations requiring clandestine, covert, or low visibility techniques and oversight at the national level. Special operations differ from conventional operations in the degree of physical and political risk, operational techniques, modes of employment, independence from friendly support, and dependence on detailed operational intelligence and indigenous assets.[39]

Furthermore, the doctrine highlights eight major roles that define American SOF by function:

- *Direct Action* — "Operations of an overt, covert, clandestine or low visibility nature conducted ... in hostile or denied areas." (e.g., raid, ambush, direct assault, sabotage, stand-off attacks from air and ground).
- *Strategic Reconnaissance* — Intended to collect specific, well-defined, and time-sensitive information of national or theatre-level significance (depends primarily on human-intelligence agents).
- *Unconventional Warfare (UW)* — May replace, complement, or supplement conventional military operations. It involves covert, clandestine, or low profile assistance for insurgents. Raids, sabotage, deception, and survival techniques are key to UW.
- *Foreign Internal Defence* — Strategic defensive counterpart to UW. In essence assistance to foreign powers to forestall or defeat selected insurgencies, resistance movements, and lawlessness.
- *Counterterrorism* — Counterterrorism may attack terrorists before they can strike or be reactive. It emphasizes passive protection for personnel and installations — but the passive element is not considered an SOF function.
- *Combat Search And Rescue (CSAR)* — The recovery of service personnel in distress on land or sea in trying conditions.
- *Psychological Operations* — The purposeful use of information and actions to influence the emotions, attitudes, and behaviour of target audiences in ways that expedite the achievement of security objectives in peacetime and war.
- *Civil Affairs* — The support of humanitarian and civic action operations.

Equally, one can look at a Canadian adopted definition of special operations to glean their doctrinal approach to SOF, which is in accordance with NATO policy:

> military activities conducted by specially designated, organized, trained, and equipped forces, using operational techniques and modes of employment not standard to conventional forces. These activities are conducted across the spectrum of military operations independently or in co-ordination with operations of conventional forces. SOF units are strategic assets that lack the size and equipment for direct involvement in major battles. They are built around carefully selected and highly trained people and rely o the use of intelligence, stealth, surprise and operational flexibility to achieve their objectives.[40]

Lastly, the Australian Defence Force view of SOF provides yet another doctrinal example:

> as specially selected military personnel, trained in a broad range of basic and specialist skills, who are organised, equipped and trained to conduct Special Operations ("measures and activities conducted by specially trained, organised and equipped forces to achieve military, political, economic or psychological objectives by, means outsides the scope of conventional forces"). These operations may be conducted during, peacetime, conflict and war, independently or in conjunction with conventional forces and other government departments.[41]

The doctrinal definitions given, including the clarifying roles, echo many of the former concepts, specifically the notion of specialized training and organization, unusual techniques and employment, and the idea of specialized areas of operation. But they also place emphasis on the political element, as well as the sphere of their use as in peacetime, conflict, or war. Moreover, they specifically introduce the idea of political oversight and approval, and establish the idea that the risk of employment in itself defines SOF as "special."

As such, the evolution of the definition of SOF emerges — highlighting, in particular, the complexity and uniqueness of SOF. Colin Gray correctly sought a more expansive way of looking at SOF when he wrote, "in order to secure a sufficiently holistic understanding of special operations, it is useful to think of them in terms of three things: a state of mind, forces and a mission."[42] In this vein, U.S. Defence Secretary William Cohen in his *Annual Report to the President and Congress, 1998*, wrote that SOF:

> are the forces of choice in situations requiring regional orienta-
> tion and cultural and political sensitivity, including military to
> military contacts and non-combatant missions like humanitar-
> ian assistance, security assistance, and peacekeeping operations
> [and are] warrior-diplomats capable of influencing, advising,
> training, and conducting operations with foreign forces, offi-
> cials and populations.[43]

Together these definitions begin to portray a component beyond the traditional paradigm. Although there is no argument that SOF is partly defined by the fact that they contribute special skills and unique capabilities beyond the capacity of conventional units and that they are rapidly deployable in times of peace or war, the true nature of SOF is found in the operators that conduct the missions. What sets them apart goes beyond special skill-sets that can be taught to conventional units such as parachuting, counter-insurgency, or close quarter battle drills. Rather, the heart of SOF pertains to their intellectual and philosophical capability — their distinct way of thinking.

It is for this reason that selection is such an important component of SOF. Military historian James Ladd noted from the beginning that the foundation of SOF success was the high standard of selection and metic-ulous training. He stated that the aim was to select and produce individ-uals capable of carrying through a mission on their own when others in their group were killed or put out of action.[44] Now more than ever, SOF warriors are also required to be able to operate effectively and successful-ly in volatile, uncertain, complex, ambiguous, and dangerous environ-ments, whether in peace, conflict, or war, often with minimum direction and supervision. Therefore, it is not surprising that selection has become a major identifier and definer of SOF. For example, Charles Heyman, the editor of *Jane's World Armies*, is now one of many who classifies SOF on selection processes.[45] Major-General Miroslav Stojanovski, deputy chief of the general staff, Macedonian Army SF, agreed. "The human factor is key," he argued, "Without the right soldier, the best equipment is useless."[46]

As such, a universally accepted three-tier system for SOF has been developed that roughly corresponds to both the rigour of the selection standards, as well as the respective role equated with each level. For example, "Tier 1" SOF consists of primarily "Black Ops," or counterterrorism hostage rescue operations. Normally, only 10 to 15 percent of those attempting selection are successful. What makes this number so impressive is that a large percentage of those trying are already second- or third-tier SOF members. Organizations that fall into this category include the U.S. 1st Special Forces Operational Detachment — Delta; the German Grenzschutzgruppe-9 (GSG 9); the Canadian Joint Task Force Two (JTF-2); and the Polish commandos — Grupa Reagowania Operacyjno Mobilnego (GROM, Operational Mobile Response Group), to name but a few.[47]

"Tier 2" SOF reflects those organizations that have a selection success rate of between 20 and 30 percent. They are normally entrusted with high value tasks such as Strategic Reconnaissance and Unconventional Warfare. It is at this level that selection is separated from training because the skill sets are considered so difficult, that the testers are looking only for attributes that cannot be inculcated. The actual skills required can be taught later during the training phase. Some examples include the American Special Forces (Green Berets); the American SEALs; and the British, Australian, and New Zealand SAS.[48]

The final grouping, or "Tier 3," consists of those units, such as the American Rangers that have a selection success rate of 40 to 45 percent, and whose primary mission is Direct Action. At this level selection is mixed with training. However, the quality control line is drawn here. Generally units below this line are not considered SOF.[49] It is for this reason that airborne forces are most often not considered SOF as contemporary airborne success rates are approximately 70 percent.[50]

So, in the end, how do you define SOF? It is generally accepted that modern SOF are organizations specially selected, organized, trained, and equipped military and paramilitary forces that conduct high-risk, high-value special operations to achieve military, political, economic, or informational objectives by generally unconventional means in hostile, denied, or politically sensitive areas, in peace, conflict, or war.[51] Furthermore, SOF, as described above, are further defined internally by a three-tier system based on selection standards. In essence, however, the SOF soldier is defined by his role, intellect, and philosophical approach to warfare. In the end, its all about the individuals and teams that ensure success.

NOTES

1.  William Walker, "Shadow Warriors — Elite Troops Hunt Terrorists in Afghanistan," *Toronto Star*, 20 October 2001, A4.

2.  Aaron Bank, *From OSS to Green Berets: The Birth of Special Forces* (Novato, CA: Presidio Press, 1986), 167.

3.  *Ibid.*, 167.

4.  Colonel J.W. Hackett, "The Employment of Special Forces," *Royal United Services Institute (RUSI)*, Vol. 97, No. 585 (February 1952), 28.

5.  Colin S. Gray, *Explorations in Strategy* (London: Greenwood Press, 1996), 151.

6.  Frank Barnet, B.H. Tovar, and Richard H. Shultz, eds., *Special Operations in US Strategy* (Washington, DC: National Defense University Press, 1984), 299.

7.  Robin Moore, *The Hunt for Bin Laden: Task Force Dagger* (New York: Ballantine Books, 2002), xviii.

8.  Alfred H. Paddock, *U.S. Army Special Warfare: Its Origins* (Washington, DC: National Defense University Press, 1982), 122. He stated that special forces operations could encompass the organization and conduct of guerrilla warfare; sabotage and subversion; evasion and escape; Ranger and commando-like operations; long-range or deep penetration reconnaissance; and psychological warfare.

9.  E.N. Luttwak, S.L. Canby, and D.L. Thomas, *A Systematic Review of "Commando" (Special) Operations, 1939–1980* (Potomac, MD: C and L Associates, 24 May 1982), quoted in Gray, 147.

10. Dr. Terry White, *Swords of Lightning: Special Forces and the Changing Face of Warfare* (London: Brassey's, 1997), 1.

11. Julian Thompson, *War Behind Enemy Lines* (London: Sidgwick & Jackson, 1998), 6-7.

12. James Lucas, *Kommando — German Special Forces of World War Two* (London: Cassel, 1985), 7.

13. *Ibid.*, 9.

14. *Ibid.*, 9. Historian Charles Messenger wrote, "publicity given to him [commando] during the war tended to make him out to be some form of cutthroat, highly individualistic and with little regard for the niceties and discipline of ordinary military life." Charles Messenger, *The Commandos 1940–1946* (London: William Kimber, 1985), 410.

15. James F. Dunnigan, *The Perfect Soldier: Special Operations, Commandos and the Future of US Warfare* (New York: Citadel Press, 2003), 3.

16. Terry White, *Fighting Skills of the SAS and Special Forces* (London: Magpie Books, 1997), 12.

17. John M. Collins, "Special Operations Forces in Peacetime," *Joint Forces Quarterly* (Spring 1999), 56.

18. Eliot A. Cohen, *Commandos and Politicians* (Cambridge: Center for International Affairs, Harvard University, 1978), 17 and 15–28.

19. Gray, *Explorations in Strategy*, 158.

20. Douglas Porch, "The French Foreign Legion: The Mystique of Elitism," in *Elite Formations in War and Peace*, eds. A. Hamish Ion and Keith Neilson (Westport, CT: Praeger, 1996), 117.

21. Eric Morris, *Churchill's Private Armies* (London: Hutchinson, 1986), xiii.

22. David Pugliese, *Shadow Wars* (Ottawa: Esprit de Corps Books, 2003), 3.

23. David Guralnik, ed., *Webster's New World Dictionary* (Nashville, TN: The Southwestern Company, 1972), 244.

24. John Porter, *The Vertical Mosaic: An Analysis of Social Class and Power in Canada* (Toronto: University of Toronto Press, 1965), 27 and 207; Robert Putnam, *The Comparative Study of Political Elites* (Englewood Cliffs, NJ: Prentice-Hall, 1976), 4; Geraint Parry, *Political Elites* (New York: Praeger Publishers, 1969), 30–32; Sylvie Guillaume, ed., *Les Elites Fins de Siècles — XIX-XX Siècles* (Editions de la Maison des Sciences de L'Homme D'Aquitaine, 1992), 27; and M.S. Whittington and Glen Williams, eds., *Canadian Politics in the 1990s* (Scarborough, ON: Nelson Canada, 1990), 182.

25. Hervé Bentégeant, *Les Nouveaux Rois de France ou La Trahison des Élites* (Paris: Éditions Ramsay, 1998), 19.

26. Mark Lloyd, *Special Forces: The Changing Face of Warfare* (New York: Arms and Armour Press, 1996), 11.

27. D.H. Horner, *SAS: Phantoms of the Jungle — A History of the Australian Special Air Service* (Nashville, TN: The Battery Press, 1989), xiv.

28. Gray, *Explorations in Strategy*, 149 and 190.

29. See D.R. Segal, Jesse Harris, J.M. Rothberg, and D.H. Marlowe, "Paratroopers as Peacekeepers," *Armed Forces and Society*, Volume 10, No. 4 (Summer 1984), 489; and Donna Winslow, *The Canadian Airborne Regiment in Somalia: A Socio-Cultural Inquiry* (Ottawa: Commission of Inquiry into the Deployment of Canadian Forces to Somalia, 1997), 128–138. Roger Beaumont stated that parachutists "created elitism through an ordeal that tested a man's courage and earnestness before combat." Roger Beaumont, *Military Elites* (New York: The Bobbs-Merrill Coy Inc., 1974), 101. In a similar vein Gideon Aran stated that "Jumping can be viewed as a test which allows those who pass it to join an exclusive club, to be initiated into an elite group." Gideon Aran, "Parachuting," *American Journal of Sociology*, Vol. 80, No. 1, 150.

30. Christopher Bellamy, *Knights in White Armour: The New Art of War and Peace* (London: Pimlico, 1997), 77.

31. Tom Clancy and John Gresham, *Special Forces: A Guided Tour of the U.S. Army Special Forces* (New York: Berkley Books, 2001), 3.

32. William H. McRaven, *Spec Ops: Case Studies in Special Operations Warfare: Theory and Practice* (Novato, CA: Presidio Press, 1995), 2.

33. *Ibid.*, 3.

34. Robin Neillands, *In the Combat Zone* (London: Weidenfeld and Nicolson, 1997), 4.

35. See J.M. Collins, *Green Berets, Seals and Spetsnaz: US and Soviet Special Military Operations* (London: Brassey's, 1987); and Terry White, *Fighting Skills of the SAS*, 11.

36. NATO, *AJP-1(A) Combined SOF Concept 3200* (March 1997).

37. General Henry H. Shelton, "Special Operations Forces: Looking Ahead," *Special Warfare: The Professional Bulletin of the John F. Kennedy Special Warfare Center and School*, Volume 10, No 2 (Spring 1997), 3; *Defense 97*, Issue 3, 34.

38. Lieutenant-General Peter J. Schoomaker, "Army Special Operations: Foreign Link, Brainy Force," *National Defense* (February 1997), 25.

39. Joint Chiefs of Staff, *Joint Publications 3.05: Doctrine for Joint Special Operations* (Washington, DC: Office of the Joint Chiefs of Staff, 1990). Direct action missions are "designated to achieve specific, well defined and often time-sensitive results of strategic, operational, or critical tactical significance."

40. Colonel W.J. Fulton, DNBCD, "Capabilities Required of DND, Asymmetric Threats and Weapons of Mass Destruction," Fourth Draft, 18 March 2001, 16/22.

41. Australian Defence Force, Report A87-14356, HQSO 97, "The ADF Commando Capability."

42. Gray, *Explorations in Strategy*, 156.

43 Glenn W. Goodman, Jr. "Regional Engagement Forces," *Armed Forces Journal International* (May 1999), 69.

44. James Ladd, *Commandos and Rangers of World War II* (New York: St. Martin's Press, 1979), 166. British Commando instructors embedded the belief that "it's all in the mind and the heart." *Ibid.*, 168.

45. Charles Heyman, "Special Forces and the Reality of Military Operations in Afghanistan," *Jane's World Armies*, online, accessed 26 September 2002.

46. The "Wolves," the elite SOF unit of the Army of Macedonia selected 22 individuals from 700 applicants — a 2 percent selection rate. See Ann Rogers and John Hill, "Operations in Iraq Point the Way for Macedonian Military Reform," *Jane's Intelligence Review*, April 2004, 20–21.

47. See Colonel C.A. Beckwith, *Delta Force* (New York: Dell Publishing Co., 1985), 123 and 137; interview with Major Anthony Balasevicius, former SOF standards officer (and recognized expert on SOF selection and training theory and practice); Leroy Thompson, *The Rescuers: The World's Top Anti-Terrorist Units* (London: A David & Charles Military Book, 1986), 127–128; General Ulrich Wegener, presentation to the RMC Special Operations Symposium (5 October 2000); and Victorino Matus, "The GROM Factor," *www.weeklystandard.com/content/public/articles/000/000/002/653hsdpu.asp*, accessed 18 May 2003.

48. Actual selection pass rates vary somewhat between different sources. However, even with the variances, the groups all fit into the Tier 2 range. See Judith E. Brooks and Michelle M. Zazanis, "Enhancing U.S. Army Special Forces: Research and Applications," *ARI Special Report*, Vol. 33 (October 1997), 8; General H.H. Shelton, "Quality People: Selecting and Developing Members of U.S. SOF," *Special Warfare*, Vol. 11, No. 2 (Spring

1998), 3; Marquis, 53; Commander Thomas Dietz, CO Sea Air Land (SEAL) Team 5, presentation to the RMC Special Operations Symposium (5 October 2000); Leary, 265; Dunnigan, 269 and 278; and Michael Asher, *Shoot to Kill: A Soldier's Journey Through Violence* (London: Viking, 1990), 205.

49. See Colonel Bill Kidd, "Ranger Training Brigade," *US Army Infantry Center Infantry Senior Leader Newsletter* (February 2003), 8–9.

50. This can be problematic as airborne units generally share some attitudinal, cultural and philosophical traits (i.e., tenacity of purpose, no mission too daunting, disdain for those outside the group, et cetera). In addition, many early airborne units also had rigorous selection and training standards that would easily fall into the Tier 3 and sometimes Tier 2 levels.

51. This definition is not original. It takes its root from Thomas K. Adams, *US Special Operations Forces in Action: The Challenge of Unconventional Warfare* (London: Frank Cass, 1998), 7, and adds other critical components drawn from the remainder of the chapter.

# 2

---

# Finding the Right Stuff:
## *Special Operations Forces Selection*

### Tony Balasevicius

Two of the "fundamental truths" consistently espoused by those employed in Special Operations Forces (SOF) are that SOF cannot be mass-produced and competent SOF cannot be created quickly after emergencies occur.[1] This can be easily understood. The level of training needed by SOF is extremely demanding and few who consider attempting the arduous SOF selection and training process will ultimately succeed. By way of example, the average failure rate on the American Ranger course is 42 percent,[2] while the attrition rate at the Fort Bragg Special Warfare School for their Special Forces (Green Berets) is about 70 percent,[3] and the same is true for the Sea Air Land (SEAL) forces.[4] This high failure rate is significant as the cost of training each soldier is extremely expensive both in terms of money and resources.

It takes about three years from the time a SEAL is selected into the program until he is combat ready and it costs approximately $800,000 (U.S.) to train a SEAL during the first year alone.[5] This prohibitive financial outlay has forced many militaries to develop sophisticated procedures that are able to quickly assess a candidate's suitability to undertake the rigorous training requirements.

This initial filtering mechanism has proven extremely cost-effective and ensures a higher rate of success on training, which ultimately saves scarce resources. However, over the years various myths have developed regarding the SOF selection process and what it is designed to accomplish. Even to those who have successfully gone through the process it is viewed as little more than an exhausting "bag drive" and more important, a "right of passage." This lack of understanding, about what the process is designed to accomplish, has been exacerbated by its secretive nature and stories that circulate, which are largely based on the perceptions of candidates. The purpose of this chapter is to examine SOF selection. Specifically, it will look at how the process was developed and scrutinize some of the underlying philosophies used to govern its organization and conduct.[6]

Despite extensive advances in the area of personnel selection since 1945, the make up of the contemporary soldier that is sought and so highly prized by SOF organizations has changed little since the inception of the first modern SOF units in the early stages of the Second World War. Many of the first SOF units used a rudimentary process that included basic fitness testing and a series of interviews. The real selection of the individual was based on selection by training attrition that was little more then a candidate's ability to complete a physically demanding training period or course such as that used by the British Commandos. Although this type of selection was effective, it could not drive candidates to their physical limits and teach them highly specialized skills at the same time. As a result the process produced a product that was little more then a highly trained soldier. The first organizations to see a need for a separate and extensive multi phase selection program were the American Office of Strategic Services (OSS)[7] and its British counterpart the Special Operations Executive (SOE).[8]

The Americans created the OSS during the Second World War to conduct clandestine operations in Axis-occupied countries. In order to carry out these operations they required agents that could be trained to operate behind enemy lines for extended periods with little or no supervision and they wanted to ensure that they were getting the right type of candidates. Rather then using the standard military training package as part of the selection process, which was a common practice at the time, William J. Donovan, the founder and wartime head of the OSS, asked a group of prominent American psychiatrists to develop a method of screening and selecting candidates that was based on the specific requirements of the OSS.[9]

Due to its unique mission and the fact that the OSS had not started operations there was no institutional knowledge on which to base the specific requirements of work to be done by the agents. As a result, much of the research carried out by the psychiatrists was both innovative and groundbreaking.[10] The research team looked at two possible approaches to assessment — organismic and elementalistic.

According to Major Sam Young, former deputy inspector general for inspections, U.S. Army Special Operations Command, "the organismic approach assesses an individual's performance on an assigned task or in a difficult situation. For example, an individual is given an axe and a set of climbing spurs and is instructed to retrieve an object from a tree. The way the individual accomplishes the task reveals much about his personality and behavior."[11] He explained, "while the organismic approach requires assessors to develop situations that will allow them to evaluate behavior, the elementalistic approach, which was in its infancy during the early 1940s, identifies personality traits through written tests. For instance, a series of questions can reveal behavioral or personality traits about an individual when he answers in a particular fashion or pattern."[12] Over time the researchers concluded that the best method of evaluating a candidate's capabilities and a better method of predicting performance outcomes was to use a combination of the two approaches.[13]

Eventually, the researchers were able to come up with a job description of what the agent was likely to do when deployed. This work resulted in a list of requirements, on which all candidates were assessed and included such things as motivation for assignment, energy and zest, practical intelligence, emotional stability, social relations, leadership ability and security.[14] The research team also developed methods to test candidates for each of these specific requirements. Although ratings were made on each of the dimensions, the OSS selection process was based on the concept of the "whole person" and that each part of the process is mutually dependent on each other."[15] In order to get an appropriate assessment, candidates were required to undergo three days of evaluation at the OSS's main assessment centre (Station S) located in Fairfax, Virginia.

An assessment centre is a facility where the testing is done under the observation of staff responsible for the process. This allows a standardized assessment of behaviour to take place, which is based on multiple evaluations including job-related simulations, interviews, situational tests, paper-and-pencil examinations, psychodrama, and casual observation and/or psychological tests.[16] Assessment centres allow judgments on behaviour to be made, which are then pooled among assessors or by using some type of averaging process.[17] In Fairfax, tests were developed so that each activity could assess a number of individual traits. For example:

> One of the many tests administered was a leaderless group situation called the "Brook Test" during which the candidates, in groups of six, would be taken to a shallow, quiet stream whose banks were eight feet apart On one bank was a heavy rock, on the other a log. Various materials, such as logs, rope, a pulley, and barrel were available. The candidates were told to move a delicate piece of equipment (the rock) across this stream, leaving all materials on the opposite side when done. Candidates were assessed on individual traits such as leadership, energy, initiative, leadership, and physical ability.[18]

Other tests included giving the candidates a diagram and telling them to build a structure without themselves constructing it. At the site, two workers, who were directed beforehand by the testers not to be very helpful, greeted the candidates when they arrived. The idea was to see whether the candidate could provide the necessary leadership and diplomacy to get and keep the workers focused on the task. In addition, there were a number of elementalistic tests that included psychological, memory, and interrogation testing as well a number of group discussions.

Over time the OSS researchers were able to use these comprehensive psychological evaluations of candidates to develop a profile of the person whom they felt would be needed to perform the hazardous missions. The criteria of compatibility, integrity and stability were given great weight throughout the assessment process and many of these procedures were changed or modified based on experience.[19] Although there is some debate as to how good the assessments were at predicting the eventual success of the volunteers, there is no question that the work carried out by the OSS researchers had a profound effect on the development of personnel selection after the war.

Despite its significance, the contributions of the OSS on personnel selection did not have an immediate impact in the SOF community. This may be partly due to the fact that historically SOF organizations tended to develop in an ad hoc manner and outside the military's institutional rules of governance. As a result, they generally started their existence based on sponsorship by a key military or political champion, but do not always enjoy full institutional support.[20] This has always left SOF units stretched for both personnel and resources as they try to set up their internal organizations and remain focused on their first priority, which is the operational mission. As a result, they tend to stay with what they know works and in this regard they generally used the concept of selection by training attrition.

Although selection by training attrition has proven to work, it can be extremely wasteful. By the late 1980s, the American Special Forces (SF) realized this and they were looking for ways to streamline their selection and training processes and this search resulted in significant changes to the way they carried out both. Using the principles established by the OSS selection and training became clearly separated but closely related activities, primarily to reduce training time and resources by increasing the overall efficiency of the process.[21]

This decision was based principally on the high attrition rates being experienced on the American Special Forces Qualification Course (SFQC). Failures were forcing the American SOF organization to pay the costs of moving the candidate to and from the training location. In an effort to find a better way of predicting a candidate's success on the course and save financial resources, the Special Warfare Center and School (SWCS) developed Special Forces Assessment and Selection (SFAS) courses.[22]

SFAS allowed the centre to bring candidates to the process on temporary duty and if it was determined the candidate had potential to pass they were then posted to the SWCS. "The new temporary-duty program" explained Lieutenant-Colonel Marrs, "afforded Special Forces a cost-effective means of assessing a candidate's physical and mental abilities. At the same time, the screening effect of SFAS limited attrition in the SFQC."[23] The process of change started in 1987, when SWCS began working with researchers from the American Army's Research Institute to determine desirable personality traits needed by successful candidates and then to develop effective methods of assessing those traits. Work progressed rapidly, and by the following year, it had advanced to the point where SWCS was able to carry out the first Special Forces Assessment and Selection course.[24] The development of this approach not only saved money but, more important, provided the Americans with a number of other benefits.

The flexibility of having a separate but sophisticated selection process allows SOF organizations to move the difficult physical and other high failure requirements up front. It also allows continuing research that links changing operational requirements to training and directly back to the selection process, and this lets units evolve the selection of their people relative to the changing requirements of operations. In fact, this process creates a more learning orientated environment that remains flexible and adaptive, a concept especially relevant since future SOF tasks are likely to remain both diverse and complex.

Despite the high skill levels eventually attained by SOF soldiers to deal with these diverse and complex situations, their selection is governed by the same basic principles that prevail in the selection of many other civilian organizations seeking people for a specific job. What makes the selection of SOF stand out from others is the high physical and the increasingly high cognitive requirements needed to do the job. Selection procedures for SOF, like all other selection processes, are designed to do nothing more then predict future job performance on the basis of the applicant's ability to perform specific tasks.[25] The ability to predict job performance cannot be properly measured unless the job the soldier must do is fully understood. Therefore, before a selection process can be developed SOF organizations must carry out what is commonly called — in the field of personnel psychology — a job analysis.

The job analysis is a process of "breaking down the complexities of the job into logical parts that include specific duties and tasks. This analysis helps identify and organize the knowledge, skills, and aptitudes required to perform the job correctly. This is accomplished by gathering tasks, activities, and requirements through observation, interviews, or other recording systems."[26] Getting the job analysis completed is an extremely important first step of the process for SOF. Research has shown that "both the selection and training process designed for SF are inextricably linked to the requirements of the job that SF must accomplish."[27] Findings emphasize that the job analysis accomplishes three important objectives:

- Identifying what soldiers are expected to do. That is, it specified the dimensions of the SF job performances and identified tangible examples of successful and unsuccessful performance on each dimension or category
- using this information to construct behaviourally anchored rating scales that could be used to assess SF job performance, and
- Identifying attributes that were the best bet predictors of SF job performance.[28]

42

Identifying these critical predictors and criterion measures for SOF organizations is another important aspect of the selection process. In the case of the American special forces, unclassified research acknowledges that there as many as "11 SF roles that cover 26 basic performance categories and these are linked to 29 attributes that are deemed critical to effective performance."[29] From these results, researchers identify selection instruments that are the most likely to correlated with performance for the specific job. Multiple assessment methods are normally used in a selection process, as one technique is unlikely to assess all attributes.

When multiple assessment methods are used, it becomes extremely important to determine what is to be tested and how many times the test needs to be done during the process. The wrong decision at this stage will result in wasted time and resources. For example, researchers Zazanis, Kilcullen, Sanders, and Crocker found that American special forces view communication attributes as important. However, "results of the SME surveys indicate that SFAS provides a high level of assessment regarding the set of physical-fitness attributes, a moderate level of assessment regarding the cognitive and personality attributes and a low level of assessment regarding the set of communication attributes."[30] They explained, "results also suggest that culture/interpersonal adaptability, although rated as one of the top 10 attributes, is not required until Phase III [well into the training process] of the SFQC."[31]

Generally, these types of omissions are precisely what the selection process attempts to avoid, as incompatibilities between training and selection create difficulties and, more important, inefficiencies because candidates who will ultimately fail required attributes are allowed to move on. This becomes especially important when training is complex and spread over an extended period. The ability of the system to determine failure at the early stages of the process is the key to its efficiency. In this respect, what is important to know at the beginning of the process is what attributes are necessary to successfully carry out the training.

Attributes that are needed and tested during the selection process are generally broken down into broad areas that include physical fitness, cognitive, personality/interpersonal, and communication. Each of these categories is further broken down into sub-categories with between three and 11 specific attributes. Lieutenant Sam Simpson, a former member of the Australian Special Air Service (SAS), provides a good perspective on where the emphasis should be placed when researchers and assessors are considering important personnel attributes within these sub-categories. "Technical efficiency can be taught," he observed, "the personal qualities required for long-range, long-term operations in enemy territory however are part of a man's character and, although they may be developed over a period, they must be learnt in child-hood."[32] He added, "These qualities are: initiative, self-discipline, inde-pendence of mind, ability to work without supervision, stamina, no fear of height, patience and a sense of humor."[33]

Attributes are designated for testing during the selection process because they are needed to meet the job requirement specified by the SOF unit. Once this has been established all designated attributes must be looked at several different ways using various tests, as in the case of the OSS examples. The philosophy behind many of these checks is straightforward. The "no fear of heights," attribute is a good example. If the operational requirement is for the SOF team to cross an obstacle using a rope bridge up to 500 metres above the ground, the soldier must have the technical ability to traverse the rope. Therefore, that ability becomes a teaching requirement during the later training phase. However, to cross the rope 500 metres above the ground demands that a candidate not have a fear of heights. As a result, "no fear of heights," is designated as an attribute needed for the training, and must be evaluat-ed during selection.

Once an attribute has been designated for evaluation during selec-tion, the next step is to determine the best methods to carry out the test. The most effective means to evaluate an attribute is to develop the test to mirror the actual operational requirement, having them actual-ly cross an obstacle 500 metres above the ground, for example. If this cannot be done, having them look over the side of a 500-metre cliff (tied to a rope) or having them climb a very tall obstacle will quickly ascertain if fear is present. It is understood that putting a candidate in a position of danger will likely cause them to become nervous; as a result, standards are normally established to differentiate between what constitutes nervousness and what represents fear. Each attribute that is designated is reviewed in this type of detail and is based solely on the job requirement.

Selection processes are designed to evaluate most designated attrib-utes a number of times and when necessary, under various circum-stances and conditions. This allows the SOF organization to get the broadest and fairest possible assessment of each candidate. Once the specific areas have been selected and the tests developed they are reviewed to determine when they will be sequenced into the assessment process to achieve the necessary results. In most cases, assessment problems are designed to find a balance between conducting versions of the same tests as many times as possible, the cost of administering the test, and when the test needs to be sequenced during the process for optimal results. In order to get the necessary quantity of evaluations, most SOF organizations have introduced a number of pre-screening phases into their processes.

These pre-screening phases can be grouped together or separated both in time and by location. Regardless, of how they are organized or how many pre-screening phases there are, each phase is linked to the operational requirements of the unit and is designed to weed out inappropriate candidates as early in the process as possible. Despite formatting differences between organizations the basic instruments used for testing during the process are relativity consistent and well established.

These include such things as medical screening, the gathering of biographical data, general info briefing, interviews, physical abilities test, psychological testing, personality test, cognitive ability tests, work sample tests, physical and abilities test, and self/peer assessments.[34] Most SOF organizations also use some type of assessment centre at the end of the process where they bring and closely observe the candidates. However before going to an assessment centre candidates must normally initiate the process by requesting permission to apply for selection.

With this request the candidate enters the pre-screening or initial screening phase. This first phase serves two purposes, it indicates to the SOF organization that the person is interested, and it provides potential candidates with an opportunity to get some idea of what they can expect in terms of the intensity and the level of difficulty of the selection and training process. It also provides soldiers with an idea of what the working conditions in the unit are like should they be successful. To this end, many SOF organizations have developed Internet sites, phone centres, or recruiting locations where candidates can go to find basic recruiting information.

Should the candidate prove interested they will be required to get a medical examination to certify they meet the specific requirements outlined in the prerequisites. The most important event during this phase is the candidate's ability to complete a physical fitness predictor test, which will include a combination of aerobic endurance (running or rucksack marching), upper body strength (pull-ups and push-ups), and abdominal strength (sit-ups) tests. Many SOF units tend to use their

Army's standard fitness test but at a much higher cut off mark because SOF researchers find it quite easy to tie physical performance levels on their selection process to these commonly used tests.

To better illustrate this point, the U.S. Army research institute, found that candidates having achieved a score of 226-250 on the American Army Physical Fitness Test (APFT) had a 42 percent possibility of passing while candidates achieving a 276 or higher had better then 78 percent chance of passing.[35] Tying physical performance levels on their selection process to commonly used military tests gives SOF units the ability to test physical predictors locally and this is one reason why they are generally included in the pre-screening process.

Once the candidate has passed the physical predictors test their request along with the results of other pre-screening requirements, their service file and a commanding officer's recommendation are forwarded to a selection or processing centre for review. At this point candidates may receive an initial interview and carry out some additional (inexpensive) testing. The interview is a face-to-face conversation between the candidate and a member of the selection staff. The purpose of the interview is to give candidates a realistic preview of the role, task, and mission of the unit as well as the working conditions they can expect and to answer any question the candidate may have. The initial interview also allows additional information to be gathered by the SOF organization including the candidate's service background, an assessment of various personal attributes, personal circumstances, known phobias, athletic activities, proven ability to cope with stress, language ability, and motivation. Finally, a preliminary appraisal and recommendation on the suitability of the candidate is developed based on the information collected.

Depending on the sophistication of the process information on candidates will likely be entered into a database for future reference. The candidate's service file and commanding officer's recommendation will be closely evaluated as most SOF organizations want to get a good overview of the candidate and his work history as it is generally accepted that past performance is a good predictor of future performance. This information and the initial assessment are also important if the unit has a large pool of candidates and a limited number of vacancies for their selection phase at the assessment centre. Candidates who meet the requirements will then be rated, based on the information already provided. A cut-off line may be designated and anyone above the cut-off line will be given an opportunity to advance to the next phase.

The next phase of the process is normally carried out at the assessment centre and depending on the type of SOF organization, these assessment centres can keep a candidate from anywhere between 10 and 30 days. The U.S. Army tells soldiers wanting to attend the Special Forces (Green Berets) selection process that, "Soldiers attend SFAS on a temporary duty status" and "should plan to be at Fort Bragg, North Carolina for up to 30 days."[36] Staff at the assessment centre will evaluate all attributes needed for the effective performance of the SOF soldier.

During the first part of this phase candidates will go through most of the initial psychological, personality, and cognitive ability testing. This stage also includes the use of written and oral tests, interviews, and possibly some other types of job simulation tests. Much of this initial assessment will be done in a classroom, small office, or in the area near the main camp. Tests such as phobias are usually completed in a series of stands that are similar in concept to those used by the OSS. However, the main focus during this initial period is skills training and physical conditioning in order to get candidates ready for the physical fitness attribute testing.

Historically, physical fitness has been an important attribute for the SOF soldier and it is a key aspect of the SOF selection process. More important, fitness is not an attribute that can be viewed in isolation and must therefore be put into its context within the overall job requirement. In this regard, the personal qualities and skills required for long-range, long-term operations in enemy territory dictate that, among other things, soldiers must be able to navigate while carrying heavy loads over long distances. Consequently, carrying heavy loads and navigating must be tested together under the physical fitness requirement because the soldier must remain sufficiently alert to effectively navigate during periods of significant physical fatigue. However, navigation is a skill, and if testing is going to be fair, training on navigation will have to occur to bring everyone up to the same standard prior to assessment.

The need to provide skills training, such as navigation, prior to the actual testing phase forces designers of the selection process to incorporate an instruction phase that also includes a series of workup exercises so that candidates are not starting off with 30-kilometre marches. Unfortunately, this also extends the length of the process. In the case of selection course for Britain's Special Air Service (SAS) the process begins with 10 days of fitness training and map-reading where candidates perform their tasks in small groups. This stage is followed by another 10-day phase where candidates are expected to carry out marches alone.[37] This initial training and work-up period allows candidates to get a feel for what will be expected, and it allows the assessors to determine whether the candidate has the ability to move on to the next phase.

During the testing phase candidates are expected to travel significant distances, over a period of days or weeks with little sleep and few days off. They generally do so by moving from checkpoint to checkpoint, which is designed to achieve a number of things. Checkpoints allow staff to monitor the overall progress and to check the condition of the candidates as they move through. They also serve as "assessment stands," which test different attributes that must be assessed during periods of fatigue and stress. Tasks at checkpoints are based primarily on projective and situational tests. For instance, candidates may be required to perform an unexpected task, such as stripping and reassembling a weapon that they are not familiar with, or they may have to answer questions concerning the terrain they have passed to test powers of observation.[38] These tests are nothing more then a continuation of the testing that started during the pre-screening phase and in fact, some may be the same tests that were administered earlier but under different circumstances.

This phase of the assessment is extremely important because the physical and mental stress candidates will go through, as an SOF soldier, can never be underestimated. According to researcher Martha L. Teplitzky, who worked on physical performance predictors for SF assessment: "Special Forces soldiers are distinguished by many characteristics, among them, their physical endurance and ever present rucksacks. Deploying without the logistical support available to conventional forces, Special Forces soldiers carry on their back what they need to survive and fight. A fully loaded operational rucksack can easily weigh up to 100 pounds and for many missions this load must be carried long distances over difficult terrain."[39]

Like many aspects of the selection process, the conditions and standards expected for SOF rucksack marches during the selection process are classified. This is due to two factors. First, it provides part of the physiological uncertainty the candidates must be evaluated on, but more important, if the selection process is a true reflection of the job requirements then the distances and conditions will be very close to the operational requirements of the particular organization. To put the overall physical fitness requirements into better context, assume the operational requirement is for the SOF soldier to complete a tour of 20 days behind enemy lines navigating on average 20 kilometres a day carrying 100 kilograms of kit, the selection process testing for this event must by necessity be very close to this requirement. This is one reason why the process is carried out over an extended period.[40]

Apart from the gruelling physical requirements, one of the most difficult aspects of the selection process for candidates to deal with is the fact that they are never told how they are doing. The reason for this lack of feedback is simple, According to Carl Stiner, A former SF commander:

> Special Forces soldiers, who must operate in environments in which every kind of support is minimal, absent, or transitory. Some soldiers have the spirit and will to handle that situation, but many others don't. The Special Forces sensory-deprivation training program is designed to find who has what it takes. Soldiers are not told the goals or the standards they are expected to reach, or whether they're doing well or badly ... He is not told whether he has passed or failed, or if he made the journey in the correct time. Success in this exercise comes not only from accomplishing a difficult task, but from doing it totally out of his own internal resources.[41]

In addition to proving they have the required level of physical fitness and that they can work in sensory-deprivation, candidates must also show they possess those other attributes such as initiative, self-discipline, independence of mind, ability to work without supervision, stamina, patience, and a sense of humour, while experiencing high levels of fatigue and coping with significant physical and mental stress.[42] At some point the combinations of stressors begin to have an effect. According to author Tony Geraghty, "As the course continues, the volunteer finds his judgment is becoming eroded by a lack of sleep. Each day begins at about 4 am and ends with a briefing at 10.30 pm or later for the next days exercise. The effect is cumulative over the whole twenty-one days."[43]

However, having the necessary physical ability is not enough. Many candidates believe, incorrectly, that if they complete the process they have passed. They could not be more wrong. Completing the process means simply that the candidate has demonstrated the needed physical attributes. To be successful, individuals must show that they have all of the necessary attributes needed by the SOF organization. A soldier can be the fittest person in the world but if psychological testing indicates criminal tendencies, or if cognitive capabilities are not adequate to meet the pace of training, or personality test shows the candidate cannot work with different cultural groups they will not be accepted into the SOF community. Confusion in the candidate's mind about where they stand in the process is compounded by the fact that security and or legal requirements, as in the case of psychological testing, may prevent a full debrief of the candidates weaknesses.

In the end, acceptance into the SOF community means being able to prove that you have all of the "right stuff." Not surprisingly, few are capable of reaching the high standards needed by these units and for many Western SOF forces shortages in manning will continue to be an ongoing problem. This difficult situation has become worse as the SOF have taken a lead role in the war on terror after the 9/11 attacks, and is compounded by the fact that the number of potential candidates has been dropping. According to Marrs, this situation is the result of a number of factors: "The personnel strengths of today's Army is significantly lower than it has been in the past, substantially decreasing SF's recruiting pool. Changing attitudes and a lack of motivation among some of today's soldiers has further exacerbated the difficulty of SF recruitment. Furthermore, today's Army does not train soldiers in fundamental tasks as vigorously as it once did."[44]

This shortage is compounding the problem for SOF organizations that see the need to develop a more adaptive soldier for the future. SOF organizations realize that there is a "continuing and expanding role for regional orientation; a greater level of interagency work; and the increasing importance of diplomacy-related functions, operating continuously in the turbulence of the multinational and interagency environment … create a greater need for flexibility and problem solving."[45] It is clear that the future is calling for a more intelligent and adaptive soldier in SOF units and this is likely to have a significant impact on the future of the selection and training process.

Notwithstanding the significant advances made to SOF selection over the years, historically, the process has and continues to be based on physical fitness with the belief that mission-essential skills can be given to the soldier as long as he can be trained. From an American perspective, "Trainability is defined as the candidate's aptitude for learning, and SFAS employs land-navigation exercises as the primary means for determining that aptitude."[46] This philosophic outlook has been supported by research, which "suggests that the strongest predictors of performance in the SFAS are the physical measures (including the APFT and pull-ups) and the Measures of Army experience (including Ranger qualification, combat-arms-branch type, and airborne qualification)."[47] The research goes on to reveal that, "Subject Matter Experts ratings indicate that the physical fitness attributes are the most highly assessed attributes in SFAS, and that there are fewer opportunities to measure the cognitive and personality attributes."[48]

This heavy reliance on assessing physical performance is the result of historical development and the reluctance of the SOF community to drop the physical standards that are currently in place and which are believed to be doing the job. In an effort to get as many people as possible through the process without dropping the physical standard SOF units are starting to make changes to the way they treat candidates during the selection process. In 2000, the 1st Special Warfare Training Group completed a program for the SFAS, which represents a significant change to the methodology. The new selection course emphasizes teaching, coaching, training, and mentoring as important aspects of the process. The British are also moving to this type of program. "Today, the solicitude is probably genuine and the volunteer, far from being seduced into abandoning the march, will be reminded: only another ten miles. You've come more then half way. Stick with it."[49] However, this new approach is being done at the expense of some of the sensory-deprivation training, which has been viewed as a critical aspect of the process.

Whether these changes will be sufficient to solve the recruiting and selection issues currently being faced by SOF units is difficult to say. If the future is calling for a more intelligent and adaptive soldier modifying the process by emphasizing teaching, coaching, and mentoring are not likely to help in the long run. As warfare becomes more complex and technical the competition for quality people will become more intense.

Under these circumstances, SOF will have to make some tough decisions, will they release an intelligent and adaptive soldier who has everything necessary to be an SOF soldier, but lacks fitness, or do they keep him and get him up to shape. Of course, for those who have successfully gone through the process, such a suggestion is blasphemous. The argument of current members is that if a candidate does not have the parts to come to the table with the fitness they do not have the necessary qualities to be an SOF soldier in the first place. Certainly, this has been the standard in the past. However, times have changed, and the future of SOF depends on its ability to adapt and think outside the box. Regardless, the road ahead is, as it has always been, a difficult one and for anyone engaged in selecting the SOF operators of the future it is nowhere they have not been before.

## NOTES

1. The other two are: Humans are more important than hardware and quality is more important than quantity. U.S. Joint Special Operations University pamphlet, n.d.

2. Colonel Bill Kidd, *Ranger Training Brigade* (U.S. Army Infantry Center: Infantry Senior Leader Newsletter, February 2003), 8–9.

3. Charles M. Simpson III, *Inside the Green Berets: The First Thirty Years* (Novato, CA: Presidio Press, 1983), 68.

4. Thomas Dietz, CO Sea Air Land (SEAL) Team 5, presentation to the Royal Military College Special Operations Symposium, 5 October 2000.

5. Simpson III, 68.

6. In so doing, it must be recognized that today's sophisticated process of SOF selection evolved over time, and continues to be a work in progress. It must also be realized that each SOF organization is unique and methods of selection can vary significantly between organizations. Despite these differences they all have common principles by which they operate and they all attempt to find a specific type of soldier with the right attributes and qualifications to be a successful member of the SOF fraternity.

7. Patrick K. O'Donnell, *Operatives, Spies, and Saboteurs: The Unknown Story of the Men and Women of World War II's OSS* (London: Free Press, 2004), xv–xvi. Note: Patrick K. O'Donnell, in his book, provides a quick overview of the birth of the Office of Strategic Services (OSS). He states, "While under the tutelage of the British, OSS developed many of its own independent concepts practically overnight, emphasizing an integrated 'combined arms' of shadow-war techniques. Wild Bill Donovan's vision held that 'persuasion, penetration and intimidation' ... are the modern counterparts of sapping and mining in the siege warfare of former days." Propaganda represented the "arrow of initial penetration," followed up by espionage. Sabotage and guerrilla operations would then soften up an area before conventional forces invaded. The integration of all shadow-war techniques was a groundbreaking approach to covert warfare. The British secret services were not integrated, but operated in separate divisions. A central element of the shadow war was special operations, a new concept that OSS would develop during the war. At the end of March 1941, Donovan urged the president to permit him to develop Special Operations Forces that would take the war to the Germans in an unexpected, irregular way. Teams of operatives would penetrate behind enemy lines to sow mayhem in rear areas. Donovan considered the Germans "big league professionals" of warfare, and America the "bush

league club." He explained to the president that the only way to get America up to speed quickly against Germany was to "play a bush league game, stealing the ball and killing the umpire."

8.   Denis Rigden (introduction), *How to Be a Spy: The World War II SOE Training Manual* (Toronto: The Dundurn Group, 2004), 3. Rigden states, "The Special Operations Executive (SOE) was created in July 1940 in the deepest secrecy from the fusion of three other unpublicized organizations: Section D of the Secret Intelligence Service (SIS or MI6); a branch of the Foreign office EH or CS; and a research group in the War Office initially called GS(R), later MI(R)2 these initials standing for General Staff (Research) and Military Intelligence (Research) respectively. All these small and poorly funded parents of SOE had existed only since shortly before the war. Section D — some commentators say that the D stood for 'Destruction,' while others believe it was an arbitrarily chosen initial — had begun devising various schemes for sabotage and subversion in Europe in the event of hostilities against Hitler's Germany. EH had studied how anti-Nazi propaganda campaigns might be conducted, and MI(R) had begun a broad study of irregular warfare (an assignment overlapping that of Section D)." Rigden explains that the basic concept of the coordination of irregular warfare resulted because "when Resistance fighters undertook operations independently, it usually achieved little or nothing of military value and often resulted in the enemy taking savage revenge on the local civilian population. Trained to be aware of the dangers of rash guerilla action, SOE agents strove to ensure that all irregular warfare served the strategic aims of the Allied leaders."

9.   Richard Dunlop, *Donovan America's Master Spy* (Chicago: Rand McNally & Company, 1982), 382–383. Richard Dunlop, states: "Once he had his training camps functioning, Donovan turned his attention to improving the selection of personnel for OSS." Harry Murray, John Gardner, and James Hamilton, the prominent San Francisco psychiatrist, were asked to establish a psychological testing program. "The old man looked at me with his blue eyes and said, 'I want it done in a month,'" Hamilton recalled. "'You will get the best people from the army and from civilian life. You'll get an estate in the country, and I want it done in a month.'" At the OSS "assessment school," psychological tests screened individuals who might have Axis sympathies, could not withstand frustrations, could not hold their liquor, or had other characteristics that would limit their effectiveness. Van Halsey, who assessed OSS personnel for overseas duty, found he could learn what he needed to know from the answers men and women gave to these questions: What experience made you feel like sinking through the floor? What things do you dislike seeing people do? What would you like to do if you had unlimited means? What would you teach your children? What would push you into a nervous breakdown? What moods and feelings are most disturbing to you and how often do you have

them? As the OSS grew, the psychological testing program became more and more sophisticated. After the war, it was studied by the psychology profession for its groundbreaking contributions to the knowledge of behaviour in given situations. The OSS had made considerable progress since the early days of the COI, when a recruiter once asked a friend, "Have you met any well-adjusted psychotics lately?" 382–383.

10. Sam Young, "A Short History of SF Assessment and Selection," *Special Warfare: The Professional Bulletin of the John F. Kennedy Special Warfare Center and School* (May 1996), 23.

11. *Ibid.*, 24.

12. *Ibid.*, 23.

13. *Ibid.*, 23–24. Young provides an excellent overview of the selection development process in his article. He states, "The team knew only that the common-task missions included conducting sabotage, organizing resistance groups, and developing propaganda campaigns. Beyond that, no one could assist the team in identifying personality traits consistent with mission success. Once the traits had been defined, the team also had to develop the most effective method of assessing those traits in candidates."

14. Scott Highhouse, "Assessing the Candidate as a Whole: A Historical and Critical Analysis of Individual Psychological Assessment for Personnel Decision Making," *Personnel Psychology*, Vol. 55 (2002), 371.

15. *Ibid.*, 371.

16. *Ibid.*, 371.

17. Assessment centre defined: *www.ipmaac.org/files/ac101.pdf+++OSS+situational+testing&hl=en&ie=UTF-8*, accessed 15 January 2004.

18. Introduction to Assessment Center Exercise Examinations, *www.passprep.com/overview/introduction.htm*, accessed 3 February 2004.

19. Sam Young, 24. It is important to note that the psychiatrists provided only an assessment of an individual with a recommendation based on a candidate's overall performance during his/her stay at the assessment centre. A board was established to review the findings and render the final verdict on who was to be accepted.

20. Examples of the need for champions abound in SOF history. The Commandos came into being only because of the personal interest of

Churchill, who was looking for a way to get back at the Germans and proposed the idea of a force of "leopards" that could strike at the enemy and quickly withdraw. He wrote to the chiefs of staff that "enterprises must be prepared with specially trained troops of the hunter class, who can develop a reign of terror first of all on the 'butcher and bolt principle' and I look to the Chiefs of Staff to propose me measures for a vigorous, enterprising and ceaseless offensive against the whole German occupied coastline." Messenger says, "His ideas were considered by the Chiefs of Staff at a meeting on 6 June. In particular, they were directed to draw up plans for organizing 'striking' companies, transporting and landing tanks on the beach, setting up a comprehensive system of espionage and intelligence along enemy held coastlines, and the creation of a 5,000 man 'barrage' force." Charles Messenger, *The Commandos 1940–1946* (London: William Kimber, 1985), 25–26. As Parker explains, "the British army agreed at last to the formation of 'guerrilla forces.'" See John Parker, *Commandos: The Inside Story of Britain's Most Elite Fighting Force* (London: Headline Book Publishing, 2000). In the case of the Special Air Service (SAS), Eric Morris noted, "Auchinleck gave Stirling permission to recruit a dozen officers and 60 soldiers from the remnants of *Layforce* and train them for an imminent operation; he intended to launch a major offensive in November, and Stirling's unit was to parachute behind enemy lines and knock out enemy aircraft on the eve of the battle. Dudley Clarke had created an organization called the Special Air Service Brigade. It did not in reality exist, but was intended to confuse the enemy into believing in such a force and into wasting their time and resources seeking its purpose. The credibility of such a deception would be enhanced if there were actually 'men on the ground'! Stirling's unit became 'L' Detachment of the Special Air Service Brigade, and so a regiment and a legend was born. Auchinleck accepted the last paragraph in Stirling's memo without hesitation. L Detachment came directly under his command and answered directly to his authority; there was to be no repetition of the rule by committee and misuse of specially trained personnel. David Stirling was promoted to Captain and put in command of the detachment. Their training base was established out at Kabrit, a small village on the edge of the Great Bitter Lake and about 100 miles from Cairo. Stirling might enjoy the patronage of the C-in-C, but this did not make life any easier for him. Stores and supplies were exceedingly difficult to come by, and the first recruits had to rely on initiative and ingenuity as much as anything in the early days." See Eric Morris, *Guerillas in Uniform* (London: Hutchinson, 1989); and *Churchill's Private Armies* (London: Hutchinson, 1986). The same problem also plagued the Americans. The modern American Rangers were formed on 1 June 1942, only when General George C. Marshall, chief of staff, directed the creation of an American commando organization. Marshall wanted a cadre of personnel with battle experience that could be shared throughout the U.S. Army. To this end he ordered the activation of the 1st Ranger Battalion on 19 June 1942, at Carrickfergus, Northern Ireland.

21. Sam Young, 24. According to Lieutenant-Colonel Robert W. Marrs, former commander of the 1st Battalion, 1st Special Warfare Training group, "the decision to implement Special Forces Assessment and Selection (SFAS) was monetary in nature."

22. *Ibid.*, 3. What is interesting about the date is that on 23 January 1987 the Joint Chiefs of Staff announced the formation of SOCON.

23. *Ibid.*, 3. According to research carried out by the Army Research Institute (ARI) the success rate after selection is about 85 percent.

24. Dr. Kenn Finlayson and Dr. C.H. Briscoe, "Case Studies in the Selection and Assessment: The First Special Service Force, Merrill's Marauders and the OSS," *Special Warfare* (Fall 2000), 29.

25. Neal Schmitt, and Raymond A. Noe, "Chapter 3: Personnel Selection and Equal Employment Opportunity," *International Review of the Industrial and Organizational Psychology*, C.L. Cooper and I. Robertson eds. (1986), 71.

26. Glossary of terms: *www.neiu.edu/~dbehrlic/hrd408/glossary.htm*, accessed 12 December 2003.

27. Teresa L. Russell, Michelle R. Rohrback, Marguerite T. Nee, Jennifer L. Crafts, Norman G. Peterson, and Fred A. Mael, *Development of a Roadmap for Special Forces Selection: Forces Selection and Classification Research* (United States: Army Research Institute for the Behavioural and Social Sciences, Technical Report 1033, October 1995), 4–5.

28. *Ibid.*, 4.

29. *Ibid.*, 11.

30. Michelle M. Zazanis, Robert N. Kilcullen, Michael G. Sanders, and Doe Ann Crocker, "Special Forces Selection and Training: Meeting the Needs of the Force in 2020," *Special Warfare* (Summer 1999), 27.

31. *Ibid.*, 27.

32. Adrian Weale, *Secret Warfare: Special Operations Forces from the Great Game to the SAS* (London: Coronet Books, 1997), 195. Weale quoted the passage from D.M. Horner, *SAS: Phantoms of the Jungle* (Battery Press, 1989), 259.

33. *Ibid.*, 195. Other attributes include being a team player, judgment, physical fitness, and honesty. It is within the sub-categories of attributes that one

will find the most important and these are referred to as critical attributes. The weight given to each of these attributes varies depending on the unit and what they are looking for in a candidate. However, any failure in a attribute designated critical results in immediate RTU (return to unit).

34. C.L. Cooper and I. Robertson, eds., *Review of the Industrial and Organizational Psychology 1986* (John Wiley & Sons Ltd., 1986), 53. According to the paper, "Peer assessment is a procedure whereby applicants evaluate each other, and these evaluations are used for personnel selection. According to Kane and Lawler (1978), three techniques are commonly used. One is peer nomination — each person nominates a specified number of group members as being highest on a particular dimension of relevant job performance. The second technique is peer ratings, which involve having each group member rate the others on a set of performance dimensions using one of several kinds of rating scales. The third technique is peer ranking — having each member rank all others from best to worst on one or more performance dimensions. Of the three methods, peer ratings are used most frequently and peer rankings have been used least frequently. Why are peer assessments predictive? It seems that in dealing with supervisors, subordinates may attempt to conduct themselves in a way that enhances their image. Accordingly the supervisor's assessment of the subordinate is tainted by the somewhat misleading picture of the subordinate, which may contribute to the lower validities of supervisor evaluations. However, peers seem to be more candid with each other, and may reveal themselves in ways which are identified by their associates in assessment."

35. Zazanis, Kilcullen, Sanders, and Crocker, 22. The APFT is a three-event physical performance test (which include sit-ups, push-ups, and a two-mile run) used to assess endurance. The intent of the APFT in the Physical Fitness Program is to provide a baseline assessment regardless of MOS or duty. Scoring standards are based on gender and age, which are calculated to provide a minimum standard needed to pass. Performance standards are calculated by percentile, with the sixtieth percentile being the minimum, required score. The U.S. Army Center for Health Promotion and Preventive Medicine, *www.hooah4health.com/4You/apft.htm*, accessed 17 July 2004.

36. Martha L. Teplitzky, *Physical Performance Predictors of Success in Special Forces Assessment and Selection* (Washington, DC: United States Army Research Institute, November 1991), 1.

37. Tony Geraghty, *Who Dares Wins: The Special Air Service — 1950 to the Gulf War* ( London: Time Warner Paperbacks, 1993), 503.

38. *Ibid.*, 509.

39. Teplitzky, 1.

40. This is one area where SOF does not like to see predictive testing. They want to see the candidate go the full distance and they want to make sure they are still effective at the end of the process.

41. Tom Clancy and Carl Stiner, *Shadow Warriors: Inside the Special Forces* (New York: Penguin Putnam, 2002), 132.

42. In some cases such as with the critical performance requirement of honesty, if the candidate fails, meaning they have shown they cannot be trusted they are unlikely to get a second chance and will be quickly RTU. Contrary to popular belief SOF soldiers are not the "Rambo"-type of lone soldier seen in the movies. They are and must be well adapted to working as a member of the team. Regardless of how good a soldier they are or how good an SOF soldier, they could be they will not move far into the selection process if they cannot work with a team. In fact, an inability to work as a member of a team is likely to lead to a candidate's removal if it is identified and confirmed.

43. Geraghty, 509. Despite adequate warning of the difficulties they will face, many candidates arrive for testing at the assessment centre unprepared. In the on-line literature produced by the American SF it states, "You will be trained in military subjects used in the assessment. The course is individual cross country land navigation based covering distances from 18 kilometres up to or about 50 kilometres. The distance and weight carried increases during the course, but being prepared mentally and physically for the events cannot be over emphasized." In the face of this caution, in fiscal year (FY) 1991, 2,236 candidates reported to Camp Mackall for initial SF testing, yet, of that number only 1,863 (83 percent) were available for the first event. Amazingly, a full 10 percent of the candidates reporting for the course were dismissed outright for failing the APFT. Teplitzky, 1.

44. Young, 3

45. *Ibid.*, 3.

46. Teplitzky, 1–4.

47. Zazanis, Kilcullen, Sanders, and Crocker, 21–23.

48. *Ibid.*, 21–23.

49. Geraghty, 508.

# 3

## Understanding Excellence:
### *Training Special Operations Forces*

#### Tony Balasevicius

Special Operation Forces (SOF) have played an increasingly important role in military operations throughout the world as part of the
war on terrorism, which was initiated in earnest in the aftermath of the
11 September 2001 terrorist attack against the United States. As a case
in point, they proved adaptable to changing circumstances in
Afghanistan. With an investment of only 300 soldiers on the ground,
SOF teams were able to successfully rally rival and unorganized anti-
Taliban opposition groups into a Northern Alliance, which eventually
defeated the Taliban forces. In this instance, the contribution of SOF
proved extremely effective. Kandahar fell only 49 days after these forces
became directly involved in operations.[1]

This efficiency, specifically the ability to conduct economy of force
operations against an asymmetric enemy is propelling SOF into the
forefront of current military activities. This is particularly evident in the
United States where the "White House has given US SOF forces greater
responsibility for the planning and directing of worldwide counterterrorism operations."[2] This trend is not surprising to those who understand the nature of these organizations and the quality of soldiers they
possess. SOF warriors operate comfortably in ambiguous situations and
possess the necessary skills to successfully complete complex missions.

These attributes, combined with outstanding individual initiative, have allowed SOF to transform specialist-training competencies into relevant capabilities that have thus far proven sufficiently adaptive to meet the changing threats and challenges of the twenty-first century.

In order to achieve their high levels of operational proficiency, SOF soldiers must undergo a significant period of training where they are given a variety of highly advanced skill sets. Over time, this training has evolved into a sophisticated program comprising a number of different stages with each phase building on the training outcomes of the previous. The basic components of SOF training are relatively straightforward and include individual skills, advanced skills, collective training, infiltration techniques, and language training. Within this context, training outcomes are designed to produce highly skilled and adaptive soldiers that have a great deal of confidence in their own ability and absolute trust in the skills of their team members.[3] This chapter will look at the evolution of modern SOF training and highlight the operational requirements that have made specific training a necessary part of many of today's SOF programs.

The basic philosophies that govern SOF training are the same as those that guide conventional military forces. In this respect, training is designed to achieve a number of outcomes; these include imparting within each soldier a common understanding of an organization's tactics, techniques, and procedures (TTPs) and allowing soldiers to practise these TTPs on a regular basis. More important, training allows an organization to instill in its soldiers a common set of ethos and values, which, it is hoped, will help create an atmosphere of mutual understanding, trust, cohesion, and operational excellence.[4] That being said, SOF training differs significantly, in that it is more intense and outcomes are focused on producing soldiers who are independent and versatile, yet able to comfortably work well within the context of a team. In fact, this philosophy is a key aspect of SOF training and has its roots in the Second World War origins of the first SOF units.

The first modern SOF capability to be developed was the Direct Action unit, that owes its genesis to the British Commandos. Direct Action units were conceived as "mobile and hard-hitting light troops that could raid or operate for a limited period behind an enemy's lines."[5] During the Second World War some 30 Commandos (as the tactical units were called) were formed and all were trained and equipped to conduct offensive operations against German defences along the occupied coasts of Europe. Military leaders envisioned that these operations would be classic DA missions consisting of "short-duration strikes and other offensive actions to seize, destroy, capture, recover, or inflict damage on designated personnel or materiel."[6] As such, the training program for these units emphasized the development of the individual soldier and although the skill sets they provided the trainee were little more then advanced combat techniques they were acquired under extremely demanding and realistic conditions.[7]

The intensity of Commando training produced an excellent combat ready soldier while quickly weeding out weaker candidates. In this regard, British experience in the area was so influential among the Allies that the Americans decided to have the first group of their Rangers attend the British Commando course at Achnacarry Castle, Scotland.[8] The study of the Ranger experience during their commando training is of interest mainly because their experience provides a good perspective of the training philosophy developed for Direct Action units and this is particularly relevant given the fact that the Rangers are still very much an active part of America's SOF capability.[9]

By the time the Rangers went through the Commando Training Centre at Achnacarry the British had evolved the course into an outstanding training package.[10] The program was based on a "trilogy of training" which consisted of first, each soldier having to learn the use of all of the unit's weapons and equipment; second, battle preparations, which involved training that was as realistic as possible, and third, physical conditioning.[11]

The corner stone of the Commando's fitness program was the emphasis it placed on marching, which started out with short hikes of a few miles, and gradually increased to 16-mile speed marches. Colonel William Darby, the first commander of the Rangers, expected his men to "average better than four miles an hour over varied terrain, carrying full equipment."[12] Marches, observed Darby, "gave maximum development to lungs and legs, and most importantly, to feet."[13] He added, "In the early marches we had blisters by the bushel. Finally, though, we became hardened, and our feet were able to stand up under any kind of pounding."[14] The Physical conditioning program also included unarmed combat training and a series of obstacle courses. In addition to testing physical fitness, some of the obstacles were specifically designed to test a man's courage. One event was the death slide, where candidates were expected to climb to 40 feet and slide down at a "dizzy angle of about forty-five degrees to another tree on the far bank of a roaring river."[15]

The second part of the "trilogy" focused on developing the soldiers' combat skills. Every man was expected to meet extremely high standards in the employment of all unit weapons and equipment from the use of radios and the operation of vehicles to mastering small arms and section weapons such as machine guns and bazookas. "The training in weapons," stressed Darby, "was more comprehensive than that received by the average infantry soldier at the time."[16] But the mastery of weapons was only one part of the combat skills these early SOF soldiers needed to possess. In addition, skills such as orienteering, stalking, silent killing, basic survival skills, scouting, patrolling, street fighting, disabling fortifications, and knocking out pillboxes using demolitions, were also taught to the soldiers. To do this in as realistic a manner as possible the British incorporated, into their training plan, the third part of the "trilogy" which was called battle preparedness.[17]

Battle preparedness was designed to indoctrinate the soldiers to battle conditions. The British achieved this through a variety of courses, which emphasized the importance of aggressiveness and teamwork. According to Darby, one such lesson was called the "me-and-my-pal" course. The purpose of the training was to stress the importance of two men working together as a team:

> One man would always cover his buddy and "as the latter approached a low building the man being covered by his pal would knock out a window and while hugging the building toss in a grenade. Then under his buddy's cover, he would enter and make sure the room was clear. Quickly, thereafter, he would motion for his companion to join him. Throughout the course over stone fences, under barbed-wire entanglements, across streams, up hills, the constant requirement was for one man to cover the other. Targets would spring up unexpectedly, causing one to have to shoot over his pal's head. Dangerous as this was, it stressed the confidence that a soldier must have in his friends and the type of cooperation necessary in the Rangers."[18]

Another important part of this phase of training was the concept of the three-day endurance exercise, with each event ending with a mock battle. The Commandos believed that most soldiers had little difficulty going through physical events on the first day. A good soldier could hang on for the second day, but only the best could take the abuse for three days and still fight.[19] Once these basic fighting skills were ingrained into the Rangers they moved on to their next phase of training, infiltration.

As the primary role of the Commandos was that of coastal raiders, emphasis during this phase was placed on amphibious and cliff assaults where companies "moved across the loch in canvas boats and then scrambled ashore under sniper fire."[20] The first Ranger battalion completed its training and was fed into battle on 8 November 1942, during Operation Torch, the Anglo-American invasion of French North Africa. During the operation it quickly became evident that the training the Rangers had received at Achnacarry Castle had hit the mark. During their debut in battle they quickly secured their objectives and in the proceeding months set a standard of battlefield excellence that would secure their place in history as a first class fighting unit.

The Commando Training Centre at Achnacarry Castle and the program it developed achieved a number of things for SOF training. It set the benchmark for the individual combat skills required by the SOF soldier. Specifically, these skills included "physical fitness, weapons handling (including both friendly and enemy weapons), demolitions, orienteering, close quarter combat, silent killing, signalling, basic survival skills, amphibious and cliff assault, and the operation of vehicles."[21] Not surprisingly, a number of other SOF training traditions began with the Commandos and these reappear in various forms within SOF training programs to this day. Long days of training under realistic conditions, officers and men working together on the same course, the maintenance of high standards, the "buddy system," and common instruction on all the unit's weapons and equipment are but a few. In fact, the Commando training plan of 1942 was so good that the concept of individual training as the foundation on which to develop more advanced skills is a key part of today's SOF training philosophy.

By 1942, however, the need for large-scale DA missions was diminishing. Units such as the Commandos and the Rangers were originally raised as highly trained raiders, but over the course of the war their role continued to narrow so that by the time of Operation Torch, they had become little more then light infantry forces expert in amphibious assault.[22] Propitiously, even before large-scale DA missions had begun to wane as an SOF capability, special operations began to evolve towards employing small teams that were trained to carry out a broader range of tasks over a much longer period.[23]

However, in order to deploy for extended periods small teams needed to be self-contained. This meant that they required very specific skills, which by necessity had to be distributed among all members. Over time these specialized skills became critical to the success of the SOF mission and came to dominate the organization of the teams. The Long Range Desert Group (LRDG), which had a mission to deploy deep behind enemy lines to report on enemy movements and activities in the African desert, is a good example of this evolution.

The LRDG organized their 15-man patrols around four specialties which meant each patrol required a signalman, a navigator, a mechanic, and a medical orderly. The remaining team members became drivers and gunners who could also be cross-trained in one of the four skills to provide some redundancy within each patrol.[24] "Men in L.R.D.G. were specialists in something," explained Captain Kennedy Shaw, an officer with the group. He added, "of all these experts the signalmen were probably the most important, though the navigators ran them close."[25]

Shaw believed that the LRDG was primarily a reconnaissance unit so the ability to maintain communications with its operational headquarters was essential. "Without them a patrol, three or four hundred miles away from its base, could neither send back vital information nor receive fresh orders. If signals failed the best thing to do was to come home."[26] According to historian Eric Morris, "these operators were a vital part of the team and it was their task to ensure that when the time came to signal coded data to Headquarters, they and their sets were on top line."[27] This meant that the team's signallers had to learn how to operate the communications equipment, carry out basic communication procedures and techniques. More important, they had to learn how to repair and maintain their equipment while they were away from home base.

The importance of good navigation skills in the desert becomes evident "when you consider that on a journey of 500 miles a two-degree error would miss the objective by 17 miles, and for a patrol behind enemy lines, or one searching for a supply dump and much needed replenishment, that could spell disaster."[28] As there were few maps of Africa available to the unit, the LRDG had to navigate by using compass and astro-fix observations. As a result, members of the unit were given extensive training on how to navigate by making a sun compass, which is little more then a circle fixed to a horizontal plane divided into 360 degrees. Soldiers were taught, "That by rotating the circle, which is fixed to the dash board of the truck, throughout the day to correspond to the sun's movement through the sky, the shadow is made to indicate the true bearing on which the truck is travelling."[29]

Clearly, the LRDG patrols were totally dependent upon their vehicles. Therefore, SOF operators had to be trained to maintain and fix the vehicle during the long periods away from camp. As such, soldiers had to be trained in mechanics, specifically the ability to maintain, fix, and make modifications to various parts of the vehicles, as well as understanding the procedures for servicing and troubleshooting when necessary. They also had to understand maintenance procedures for everything from engine cooling, lubrication, and exhaust systems, to transmissions, steering and suspension systems, and the engine itself. However, their key asset was their ability to improvise with a limited amount of available spare parts.[30]

Despite the impressive level of skills developed by many of these soldiers the most important capability imbedded within the teams was the patrol's medic. Soldiers that carry the medical speciality had to have sufficient knowledge to be capable of providing basic primary care for their team throughout the mission. More important, they had to be capable of sustaining a combat casualty for a short period. In this respect, SOF medics must be trained to function as independent health care providers while the team is deployed. Tony Geraghty, an author and noted authority on the Special Air Service (SAS),[31] reinforced the importance of this specialist skill to the functioning of the SOF team. "The need for a medical specialist well versed in emergency first-aid and basic surgery," he observed, "does not require a qualified doctor to satisfy it. If the situation is critical, a doctor will be flown or parachuted to the scene and the casualty will be evacuated. A good 'bush doctor' [medic] will know whether such assistance is imperative. He will also weigh against that need the risk that the turbulence and noise inherent in a casualty evacuation may 'blow' the security of a secret operation ..."[32] Geraghty added, "The patrol medic is also valuable in dispensing simple medical care to civilians and their farm stock in a primitive environment as part of ... policy to gain the co-operation of the indigenous population ..."[33]

Within conventional military organizations, this level of knowledge can only be found in specialized sections or units. Moreover, because these capabilities are often in short supply they are temporarily allocated to sub-units as required and based on priorities and mission needs. As SOF teams cannot fall back on this type of limited support, particularly once they are deployed, they have to bring the most essential of these skills with them and this is what specialized SOF training is designed to achieve.

The SOF operator must also be able to live for long periods of time in remote, harsh environments. The ability to operate behind enemy lines for extended periods requires soldiers that understand the realities of the environment they are working in. For western military forces based in temperate climatic zones this can sometimes be a challenge. Captain Shaw, put the situation the British had to face in North Africa during the Second World War into perspective:

> There can be no doubt whatever that much of the early and continued success of L.R.D.G. was due to the speed and thoroughness with which the New Zealanders learned desert work and life. For it is not enough to have learned how to operate, in the military sense, in the desert, though that may be half of the battle. Naturally the driver must be able to drive in conditions entirely new to him, the signalman to keep in touch, the navigator to find his way, the gunner to have his sand-filled Vickers ready for instant use. But there is more to it than that. To exist at all in the Qattara Depression or in the Sand Sea in June or in the Gebel Akhdar in February is in itself a science which practice develops into an art. The problem is to make yourself so much master over the appalling difficulties of Nature — heat, thirst, cold, rain, fatigue — that, overcoming these, you yet have physical energy and mental resilience to deal with the greater object, the winning of the war, as the task presents itself from day to day.[34]

The capacity to master the difficulties of nature can be an arduous task. As a result, most SOF forces put a great deal of emphasis on teaching specific environmental skills to their soldiers. They do this by integrating environmental acclimatization into their normal training program, as was the case with the LRDG or by moving all, or some, of the training into specific geographic/environmental areas. For example, in today's SAS training is still heavily influenced by the unit's experience in the jungle during the Malayan campaign in the 1950s.

The SAS was created in 1941 under the command of David Stirling for the purposes of carrying out small-scale DA missions behind German lines in North Africa.[35] The majority of the original recruits for this force were selected from soldiers of 8 Commando, where Stirling had been an officer. Because the unit's principle task was to be DA missions the commando skills many of them possessed provided a good foundation for their further training. In fact, the unit's initial training added to and improved on many of these skills but was focused to meet the specific requirements they thought would be needed to operate in the "desert."[36]

Despite some early setbacks the concept of a smaller unit carrying out small-scale DA missions worked extremely well. With the defeat of the Germans in 1945, the SAS, like many other SOF units that were raised during the war, was removed from the order of battle, albeit it was retained as a territorial unit. However, the SAS was brought back to life in the 1950s as a result of a specific capability gap in the regular British Army. The British were trying to deal with a guerrilla war in Malaya, and were looking for a way to counter the insurgents that were operating deep inside the Malaysian jungle.[37] The SAS were seen as being able to fill this void.

During its Malaysian operations the SAS had to endure significant hardships in the jungle and this experience had a lasting effect on the regiment. Veterans of the campaign believed that there was no harsher environment in which to operate than in the jungle and reasoned that anyone who could operate in that environment could operate anywhere in the world. For this reason, SAS candidates are still sent to the British Jungle School for six weeks of their training program. During this phase of their training they are taught how to live, move, navigate, use demolitions, and fight in the jungle environment.[38]

Other techniques that are taught during this environmental phase include the construction of tools and survival equipment, preparation of various types of game for food, shelter construction, and starting a fire, as well as identification of poisonous and edible plants and animals.[39] Once the basic survival skills are provided to the soldier he tends to gain much greater confidence in himself and in his ability to master his own destiny regardless of where he may be operating.

Nonetheless, self-sufficiency and self-reliance is only one important asset. In order to be operationally effective, SOF soldiers must also be able to work extremely well as a member of a team. The LRDG understood this requirement well. As members of the unit completed their specialized/environmental training, they were formed into patrols and immediately started the next phase of training. While one purpose of this subsequent stage was to confirm newly acquired individual skills, the main aim was to mould soldiers so that they could work in a collective setting as a member of a team.

Collective training, as it is commonly known today, is a mechanism by which a commander takes a full complement of qualified soldiers and with time, resources, and applied doctrine and standards, produces a cohesive combat-capable tactical grouping.[40] This phase of training is structured to be progressive in nature and can include a number of levels depending on the size of the teams to be employed. Within each level there are three stages that must be completed: preliminary, practice, and confirmation. The confirmation stage of training is the final step at each level of the collective training experience and is generally carried out in the form of a military exercise that is of sufficient scope and duration to adequately test teams in all aspects of the missions and tasks that they could be assigned.[41]

Confirmation training for the LRDG was a key part of their collective training program and involved each patrol traveling into the desert where they set up caches that contained petrol, water, and other supplies along designated ingress and egress routes. This allowed patrols to start working together while they carried out low-risk operational missions. In fact, confirmation training went extremely well for the unit and within a relatively short period the patrols were ready for missions.[42]

In the end, the many innovative training approaches of the LRDG added a number of new dimensions to SOF organization and training. Namely, if small teams wanted to remain deployed for extended periods free of national support, each soldier needed to become far more independent and much more highly specialized than the well-trained, general purpose soldiers that existed in the Commandos.[43] More specifically, the LRDG introduced the concept of a specialized training phase where each SOF team member received a different skill set above the individual combat skills common to all team members. They also introduced the idea of environmental training and a collective and integrated confirmation phase that is now common practice within many SOF programs. In fact, the training regime and organization established by the LRDG to meet their requirements are now fundamental to many of today's SOF units. In addition, subsequent operations carried out by the LRDG validated the concept of employing small patrols behind enemy lines for extended periods. They demonstrated that such operations could succeed if small very skilled groups carried out sound planning, had an adaptable organization, the right training and equipment, proper communications, and the ability to move in and out of their area of operations.

SOF's ability to infiltrate in and out of their area of operations has been an important capability from their inception and remains a key component of their training process. In the case of the British

Commandos and American Rangers, insertion capabilities focused on amphibious operations and were carried out at the end of their training program.[44] Due in part to the necessity to conduct large-scale DA operations these units generally focused on only one primary method of infiltration, which was limited to those methods capable of deploying and sustaining a large number of troops. These capabilities include airborne (static line), maritime (amphibious) and airmobile techniques. Smaller SOF teams, such as the SAS, tend to use smaller teams and therefore, have the option to use a greater variety of infiltration methods, which provides them with far more flexibility and a better opportunity to enter an area of operation undetected.

The philosophy of training SOF team members in a number of infiltration methods has its roots in creation of the SAS during the Second World War. Its founder David Stirling hypothesized that by hitting multiple targets at the same time, fewer troops and less equipment would be needed, as they could use the resulting surprise to exploit the situation. Stirling realized that there were a number of challenges to this concept, and that the key to success in mounting such operations would be based on surprise, mobility, and the ability to inflict significant damage to the enemy with so much speed, shock, and violence that his force could withdraw before the enemy could react.[45] He believed that by using multiple insertion techniques the necessary surprise and mobility could be achieved. Ultimately, Stirling was able to convince the chain of command of the value of his idea and the SAS was born.[46] In fact, during the course of the war the SAS used an assortment of airborne, maritime, and over land vehicles as their primary insertion techniques.

Over time, common infiltration capabilities have grown to include techniques based on these three categories. They include the use of small boats, underwater vehicles, parachuting, paragliding, walking, and the use of land vehicles.[47] Having the ability to enter an area of operations using a myriad of options provides SOF units with greater flexibility. This in turn gives them a better chance to achieve surprise. However, each additional capability adds significantly to the overall training requirement. Not only is there a bill for the initial qualification training, but there can also be a considerable cost for a continuation training program, and in some cases, the infrastructure that is necessary to support the capability. This burden can be seen when one considers an insertion capability such as parachuting.

A three week course is needed to complete a basic static line jump course and this must be done before the soldiers can move on to more advanced stages where they are taught freefall techniques. After this training is completed a jump is required every three months in order for the soldier to remain current. If the soldier loses currency they must undergo what is commonly referred to as refresher training, which must be carried out prior to jumping. To maintain the capability the unit needs various specialists to maintain both a safe capability and to plan and coordinate specific insertion operations. More important, manning these positions with SOF soldiers takes them out of the teams.

To overcome this problem SOF units tend to focus on providing soldiers with low skill insertion techniques such as walking or the use of small boats, in shallow inland water operations, during the various phases of the initial training process, while providing more advanced skills once the soldier is in the unit. In order to accommodate the ever-growing list of additional infiltration and environmental skill sets, SOF organizations have begun to designate sub-units as environmental and infiltration centres of specialization. For example, today's SAS has created a system of specialized troops within each of its squadrons. Currently, each squadron is "organised into an Air Troop specialising in parachuting insertions, a Mountain Troop, a Boat Troop and a Mobility Troop."[48]

Mobility Troop focuses on the operation of specialized vehicles. To achieve this, members must go through weeks of training where they learn the mechanical aspects of maintaining and fixing the vehicles, as well as how to drive them in cross-country conditions. Interestingly, Mobility Troop traditionally functions in the desert and is still trained to use sun compass, theodolite, and astro-navigation. Boat Troop concentrates on all types of water insertion. Soldiers posted to the troop learn how to conduct amphibious operations using small boats, canoes or in some cases even submarines.

Air-insertion Troop is given training in advance free-fall practises such as HAHO (High Altitude High Opening). This troop normally operates in the path-finding role, going in ahead of the main force to secure and mark a drop zone or landing area when necessary.[49] Mountain Troop is responsible for acquiring knowledge in all aspects of mountaineering and skiing and their training also includes rock-climbing and ice and snow work.[50] Mission requirements will determine which troop will be deployed or will take the leading role in an operation.

Another key component of the SOF soldier's capabilities, particularly when the mission requires teams to deal with the local population, is language and cultural training. The importance of language and cultural training for SOF soldiers cannot be overstated, as the benefits of speaking the native tongue were clearly evident when the Allies deployed teams into the German-occupied territories during the Second World War to carry out covert activities.[51] The British Special Operations Executive (SOE) and American Office of Strategic Services (OSS) were specifically setup to coordinate covert activities in occupied Europe. These activities included everything from radio broadcasts into occupied territories to the insertion of highly trained teams to support resistance movements by providing advice, arms, or other aid. In fact, many of the SOE and OSS agents were Allied foreign nationals recruited specifically for their language ability and cultural knowledge of the local area.[52]

The importance of language ability and cultural knowledge was reinforced for the British in Malaya where they were trying to win the hearts and minds of the locals. They needed to establish contact, and thus an understanding the local language became critical. To meet the needs of a counter-insurgency campaign some SAS soldiers "were starting to learn the Malay language or at least a sort of 'lingua franca,' which allowed them to conduct basic conversations with the aborigines who lived and worked in many of the areas of interest. Strangely, the importance of this skill was not recognized by the newly formed unit until a very late stage of the conflict and then formal language training began."[53] With the move of many western SOF forces into unconventional warfare (UW) operations, which are designed to organize, train, equip, advise, and assist indigenous and surrogate forces in military and paramilitary operations and where interaction with the local populations is critical to the success of the mission, language, and cultural training is becoming increasingly important in the SOF skill set.

In theory, each SOF soldier is provided with extensive cultural training and a working knowledge of the principal language in his unit's designated area of focus, so that when they enter a country, they understand the customs of the local population and do not alienate the people they want to help.[54] The reality is often quite different. Unless the soldier has been selected, based in part on his language skills, the amount of training that is necessary to gain an effective skill level is significant. More important, most SOF units are small and can only focus on language skills in select areas, and if they are not deployed to that area most of their language training is wasted. As a result, despite significant efforts, proficiency in second language skills among SOF solders is at best inconsistent.

Notwithstanding this, language training does receive a high priority within most SOF forces and is carried out in one of two ways, at the end of the initial training process in a one, nine, or 10-month course or as a series of three to four month blocks that are given at various times throughout the process. Language training, along with all the other training given to SOF soldiers continues once he is posted to his operational unit. In order to put all these skill sets into the context of a modern SOF training program we will examine the sequence and training objectives of the U.S. Special Forces (SF).

Modern American SF specializes in UW. Intriguingly, this SOF mission had its origins outside the conventional military establishment during the Second World War. It started when the OSS developed the concept of the Operational Groups (OG). The OG could either work independently or in cooperation with partisan groups and carried out a number of tasks such as ambushing enemy columns, disrupting lines of communications, blowing up railroad lines and bridges, as well as helping to provide supplies to the various resistance factions.[55]

At the end of the war the OSS was disbanded and most of its operational intelligence activities were handed over to the newly created Central Intelligence Agency (CIA). Initially, the U.S. military did not see a need to develop an unconventional warfare capability; however, to meet the growing Soviet threat in Europe, the 10th Special Forces Group (Airborne) was activated in 1952 for the purpose of conducting UW behind Soviet Army lines in the event of a Russian invasion of Europe.[56]

The organization of the 1952 SF Operational Detachment was similar to the OG that had deployed to France.[57] It was authorized a strength of 15 men, which included a detachment commander, an executive officer and 13 enlisted personnel. Theoretically, the FA team was capable of organizing, supporting, and directing a regimental-sized guerrilla organization. The functional specialties within the team included medical, demolitions, communications, weapons, as well as operations and intelligence.[58]

This organization was heavily influenced by people such as Colonel Aaron Bank, "who was a member of the Special Operations Branch of the OSS, and was involved in and exposed to the OSS/SOE field activities in the European, Mediterranean, and China-Burma-India theatres of operation."[59] Over the years the structure of the SF has remained basically the same but their training program has been refined significantly. In the late 1980s the SF introduced a number of major changes to the way their selection and training process was conducted.[60] This process is now commonly referred to as the Special Forces Qualification Course (SFQC) and is broken down into five phases: Individual skills, military occupation specification (MOS) qualification, collective training, language training, and out-processing.[61]

The Special Forces Assessment and Selection (SFAS) program is designed to select soldiers for attendance on the Special Forces Qualification Course (SFQC). Selection allows the SOF an opportunity to assess various attributes that are considered essential to the SOF soldier. This process can take up to 30 days and includes both training and assessment in key military subjects that will be needed to carry out the assessment process. The focus of this phase is on navigating though various points between 18 to 50 kilometres carrying increasing amounts of weight as the assessment phase progresses. Successful candidates are allowed to continue to the next phase, commonly referred to as the "individual skills" phase. The course content given during this phase is similar, in many respects, to the skills taught to the British Commandos in 1942 and to the Rangers today.[62]

The individual skills phase is approximately 13 weeks and candidates start with land navigation (cross-country), marksmanship training, and military operations in urbanized terrain.[63] They then move on to more advanced subjects such as small unit tactics, mission planning, live fire exercises, and a number of patrol exercises.[64] General Carl Stiner, former commander of SOFCOM, captured the essence of this training:

> Everyone in an A-Detachment was trained in the following: each soldier had to be an expert marksman on his individual weapon (a pistol) and his M-16 rifle, and be familiar with weapons, such as AK-47s ... He had to be able to shoot them with reasonable accuracy, and to take them apart and maintain them. In the case of larger weapons such as mortars and machine guns, he had to be able to emplace and employ them properly ... Each soldier was trained in explosives.... [and] was capable of operating any kind of communications gear they might be using. Each soldier received advanced first-aid training [and] learned how to ... set up a field for landing airplanes and bring them in, and how to set up parachute drop zones.[65]

Once soldiers have completed the individual skills phase they move on to what is referred to as their functional specialties. This stage of training can last between 26 and 59 weeks and may include activities such as language training depending on the length of a candidate's specialized training. According to unclassified sources, soldiers are also trained in different functional specialties that include:

- Detachment Commander — training emphasizes the leadership skills necessary to "direct and employ other members of his detachment."[66]
- Weapons Sergeant — covers "tactics, anti-armor weapons utilization, functioning of all types of U.S. and foreign light weapons, indirect fire operations, man portable air defense weapons, weapons emplacement, and integrated combined arms fire control planning."[67]
- Engineer Sergeant — trains in "construction skills, field fortifications, and use of explosive demolitions.
- Medical Sergeant — receives training in "advanced medical procedures to include trauma management and surgical procedures."[68]
- Communications Sergeant — training includes the installation and operation of SF high frequency and burst communications equipment, antenna theory, radio wave propagation, as well as communication operations procedures and techniques.[69]

According to the Americans, the decision regarding who goes into which specialty is based on a number of factors including the individual's background, aptitude, desire, and the specific needs of the organization.[70]

SFQC (Phase V): Language Training may be up to 24 weeks in duration or may be exempted if the soldier already possesses an appropriate SF language profile.[71]

Once all this specialty training is completed SF candidates are brought back for collective training and a final confirmation phase, which lasts about 38 days. During this time soldiers are given additional common skills training, but these focus specifically on the SF's primary mission focus, unconventional warfare techniques.[72]

The final exercise in this phase is called Robin Sage and is conducted to amalgamate all the instruction and training together. During the exercise candidates are formed into simulated detachments and deployed to a fictional country where they must organize locals into guerrilla organizations. Finally, SFQC (Phase V) arrives and lasts about a week. This phase is little more than an out-processing routine for the solder. It involves his move to his initial posting within the SOF community, where he will be expected to put his training to good use at a key member of the SOF team.

The training qualifications today's SOF soldiers bring to their teams have evolved directly from the missions they were originally formed to carry out and the conditions under which they were expected to operate. These factors have had an important impact on the methods SOF units organize and train their soldiers. Despite its complexity and length the basic components of this training process remain rather simple. What differs between various SOF units is the emphasis on what speciality training occurs and what each phase of the training will emphasize.

In this regard, there is no right or wrong combination as good training plans are a combination of art and science. That being said, all soldiers are initially provided with some type of baseline training that is similar to what the British Commandos received during the Second World War. From this baseline training SOF unit's advance to more specialized training where, like in the case of the American SF and the LRDG, they receive specialized skills needed to keep the team functioning while deployed and to carry out their missions. They then go on to conduct some type of confirmation training. Furthermore, soldiers who are expected to operate in harsh theatres of operation for extended periods of time will receive environmental training and training in survival techniques. At some point they will also receive training in specialized advance infiltration, which may be done during initial training or at a later time. All this training gives SOF organizations a great deal of flexibility, which is why they are called upon to do so many things.

Although SOF organizations are very flexible, they do have their limitations. It must be remembered that the flexibility of the SOF team is derived from the scope of capabilities given to the individual soldiers and by the fact that they can do a number of these tasks very well. In this respect there is a limit to how many skills can be given to each soldier and still maintain a high standard.

Whatever the future holds for the SOF it successes will continue to be based on their soldiers' ability to get the job done. This can only be accomplished with excellent training. However, it must also be remembered that training, regardless of how good it is, will only be effective if it is being given to the right people. Equally important, these people must be led by the right leaders.

## NOTES

1. John T. Carney and Benjamin F. Schemmer, *No Room for Error: The Covert Operations of America's Special Tactics Units From Iran to Afghanistan* (New York: Ballantine Books, 2002), 23.

2. Andrew Feickert, *US Special Operations Forces (SOF): Background and Issues for Congress*, *www.au.af.mil/au/awc/awcgate/crs/rs21048.pdf+Afghanistan+ SOF+&hl=en*, accessed 15 March 2004. According to the report "U.S. SOF units total roughly 47,000 active and reserve personnel in the Army, Navy, and Air Force, or about two percent of all U.S. active and reserve forces." *Ibid.*, 1.

3. Robert N. Kilcullen, Fred A. Mael, Gerald F. Goodwin, and Michelle M. Zazanis, *Predicting Special Forces Field Performance* (United States Army Research Institute, May 1988), 3.

4. Canada, Land Force, *Training Canada's Army (English) The Aim and Purpose of Training*, B-Gl-300-008/Fp-001 Department of National Defence, Chapter 1, 1.

5. Wikipedia Encyclopedia online, British Commandos, *http://en.wikipedia.org/ wiki/British_Commandos#Formation*, accessed 15 February 2004.

6. Joint Pub 3-05, II–11.

7. Peter Young, *The First Commando Raids: History of the Second World War Series* (BCE Publishing Ltd., First Edition 1966), 1–4.

8. David Bohrer, *America's Special Forces: Seals, Green Berets, Rangers, USAF Special Ops, Marine Force Recon* (St. Paul: MBI Publishing Company, 2002), 45.

9. In fact, since the inception of the large-scale direct action (DA) units during the early stages of the Second World War, this capability has moved away from the purview of SOF into the domain of conventional forces. Unfortunately, military institutions created these units with the mistaken idea that they can provide an SOF capability that can also be used for other, conventional tasks. This lack of understanding of SOF in general and of the large-scale DA capability in particular often leads to misemployment because military commanders do not understand the limitations of these forces. The concern of misemployment is extremely relevant today as SOF is in high demand and the temptation to provide a quick fix with a hybrid capability such as the Rangers is a tempting option. Rangers are highly trained light infantry that have developed a very specialized mission

capability that fits within the context of the U.S. Army's total spectrum dominance very well. When used within this limited context such a capability can produce outstanding results. However, with few exceptions, the opportunities to employ these large DA forces in appropriate operations are limited. See Michael J. King, *Rangers: Selected Combat Operations in World War II* (Fort Leavenworth, KS: Combat Studies Institute, U.S. Army Command and General Staff College June 1985), Introduction.

10. Rangers: *World War Two Ranger Battalions, www.geocities.com/Pentagon/ Quarters/1695/Text/rangers.html*, accessed 17 March 2004.

11. William O. Darby with William H. Baumer, *Darby's Rangers: We Lead the Way* (New York: Random House, 1980), 31.

12. *Ibid.*, 37.

13. *Ibid.*, 37.

14. *Ibid.*, 37.

15. *Ibid.*, 39.

16. *Ibid.*, 38.

17. *Ibid.*, 38–39.

18. *Ibid.*, 40.

19. Bohrer, 45. Bohrer states that the training was so rigorous "Of the 600 volunteers Darby brought with him, 500 survived the commando training to form the battalion." *Ibid.*, 45. According to the *History of the US Army Rangers* "Rangers Lead the Way," *www.grunts.net/army/rangers.html*, accessed 8 March 2002, "the 1st Ranger Battalion was shipped to the British Army's Commando Training Center in Scotland. For several weeks, the American Rangers were tested to their limits by the Commando Center trainers. When it was over, 85% of those who started the course, graduated."

20. Darby, 44. Emphasis was then placed on larger group and amphibious training at company and unit level. The focus was on amphibious operations and assaults where companies were expected to "moved across the loch in canvas boats and then scrambled ashore under sniper fire." During this phase they also learned techniques of maritime navigation. Unfortunately, the Rangers had only gained limited combat experience before the U.S. Army was committed to combat in North Africa.

21. King, *Rangers: Selected Combat Operations in World War II*, introduction.

22. Adrian Weale, *Secret Warfare: Special Operations Forces from the Great Game to the SAS* (London: Hodder Headline PLC, 1998), 76.

23. Alan Hoe and Eric Morris. *Re-Enter the SAS: The Special Air Service and the Malayan Emergency* (London: Leo Cooper, 1994), 3–5.

24. Kennedy Shaw, "Britain's Private Armies: Western Desert, August 1940/December 1941," *History of the Second World War*, 1966, 776. "Though the first patrols were larger the eventual strength was one officer and about 15 men in five vehicles. Of the men four were specialists — a signalman, a navigator, a fitter (mechanic/tech expert), and a medical orderly. The others were drivers and gunners. Without effective signals a patrol was useless for it could neither receive orders nor send back information. It is an illustration of this problem of communications to give the distance in miles from Group HQ."

25. *Ibid.*, 776.

26. Shaw also points out, "There can be no doubt whatever that much of the early and continued success of L.R.D.G. was due to the speed and thoroughness with which the New Zealanders learned desert work and life. For it is not enough to have learned how to operate, in the military sense, in the desert, though that may be half of the battle. Naturally the driver must be able to drive in conditions entirely new to him, the signalman to keep in touch, the navigator to find his way, the gunner to have his sand-filled Vickers ready" Kennedy Shaw, *The Long-Range Desert Group* (Novato, CA: Presidio Press, 1989), 18.

27. Eric Morris, *Guerrillas in Uniform: Churchill's Private Armies in the Middle East and the War Against Japan 1940–1945* (London: Hutchinson, 1989), 71–75.

28. *Ibid.*, 776–777. According to Shaw, "The absence of landmarks compels the deep-sea mariner to rely on sun, stars, compass, and log to show him where he is; and in the desert almost equally devoid of recognizable features (and if these existed they were often unmapped), the sand sailor must use the same means. The method used by the LRDG was that of a sun compass and speedometer traverse by day, checked by positions determined by star sights at night."

29. *Ibid.*, 776–777.

30. *Ibid.*, 13 –14.

31. The Special Air Service (SAS) was created in mid-July 1941, by David Stirling to carry out small-scale DA missions behind German lines in North Africa. Although the SAS, like many other British SOF units raised during the war, was removed from the order of battle in 1945, it was resurrected in the 1950s when the British were dealing with a guerrilla war in Malaya, and were looking for a way to counter the insurgents that were operating deep inside the Malaysian jungle. Major Mike Calvert DSO, a former commander of the wartime SAS Brigade, was asked to provide recommendations on how to deal with the situation and suggested the creation of an SOF unit similar to the SAS. The proposal was accepted and the new unit was activated initially as the Malayan Scouts (SAS). Tony Geraghty, *Who Dares Wins: The Special Air Service — 1950 to the Gulf War* (London: Time Warner Paperbacks, 1993), 331–334.

32. Geraghty, 516–553.

33. *Ibid.*, 516–553.

34. Shaw, 18–19.

35. Weale, 96. Also see Philip Warner. *The Secret Forces of World War II* (London: Granada, 1985), 18. According to Philip Warner, "The LRDG was very well established by November 1941 but, because its primary function was unobtrusive reconnaissance, it was something of a contrast to the SAS, which could hardly fail to draw attention to itself. Nevertheless, after the disaster of 17/18 November, the LRDG had been at hand to collect up and carry away all that remained of the SAS force, and when asked if it would be prepared to do the same in future raids readily agreed. Even more to the point, the LRDG agreed to make its resources available for Stirling's men to reach their targets. So, a fruitful cooperation between the SAS and the LRDG was born. LRDG trucks, incidentally, were camouflaged by being painted pink, a colour, which made them almost invisible from the air. The properties of pink as a camouflage colour had been discovered by accident: a lone aircraft some years before had been coloured pink, under the impression that this would make it easily visible. However, when it came down in the desert it was not found for several years, and then only by chance." *Ibid.*, 18.

36. Weale, 155. To this end, "emphasis was placed on, survival training, weapons refresher, desert navigation, weapon handing and demolitions and infiltration techniques."

37. Hoe and Morris, 101. One of the key aspects of the SAS turnaround in Malaya was an operational pause for retraining, which occurred under a new commander. The SAS underwent six weeks rest and strenuous

CASTING LIGHT ON THE SHADOWS

retraining in Singapore. This break allowed the regiment time to regroup and focus itself on improving operational efficiency, while giving officers and soldiers the opportunity to get to better know each other. This period of intense training and the subsequent deployments had an immediate impact and produce superior patrolling techniques and improved navigation considerably. The unit also started to emphasize basic skills such as track concealment and physical tracking. Another interesting development that occurred during this period, was the use of self-criticism, which still goes on in the SAS today. According to Alan Hoe and Eric Morris, quite simply, "The principle of this system is simple. Any mistakes made were picked apart in the most minute detail at sessions during which every man, regardless of rank and seniority, was encouraged to give voice. Successes were rarely analyzed. It was those occasions when something went wrong where lessons were to be learned ... It was and is a most valuable tenet and in this case it was an important part of the process of adding muscle and sinew to the skeletal bones."

38. Geraghty, 516.

39. In some cases these skills may be given or enhanced as part of Escape and Evasion package that is carried out near the end of the training process. For the American SOF this training is known as the Survival Evasion Resistance and Escape (SERE). SERE is a formal course of approximately 19 days carried out at Camp MacKall, NC. The aim of training is to teach soldiers survival, evasion, resistance, and escape, and personnel are taught the basics of how to survive if they become separated from their unit; to evade a hostile force and make their way back to friendly forces; and to avoid capture. In the event that soldiers are captured, SERE training prepares them to resist the enemy's attempts at exploitation, and to escape from captivity if necessary. For the SAS, this training is focused when the candidates move on to the Escape and Evasion and Tactical Questioning (TQ) phase at the end of their training. During this phase candidates learn how to live off the land by catching their own food. Classroom lectures include talks from former prisoners of war who discuss their experiences and how they were able to live through the ordeal. Escaping from the enemy is also taught. The course ends with a final exercise usually lasting for about three days. See Special Air Service, *www.specwarnet.com/europe/sas.htm*, accessed 2 February 2004.

40. Land Force, *Training Canada's Army (English)*, 1–4.

41. *Ibid.*, 1–4.

42. Long Range Desert Group preservation society, *www.lrdg.org/Trevor*, accessed 15 February 2004. Her Majesty's Stationery, "During Sept (1940)

80

the new unit went out on it's first long patrol. The crossings of the sand sea were further explored; several Italian landing grounds between Jalo and Kufra were visited and damaged; the exits from Kufra and Uweinat were reconnoitred, and some prisoners and transports were taken. Contact was also made with the French past at Tekro. Meanwhile quantities of petrol, food and water were dumped at points beyond the Libyan frontier for future use, and with the help of the Air Force a number of sites for landing grounds were chosen. These successes confirmed General Wavell's opinion that the Patrol was making an important addition to the anxieties and difficulties of the enemy, and the War Office agreed with his proposal that the unit should be doubled and become the Long Range Desert Group."

43. These specialized skills included communications, medical, navigation, and mechanical qualifications. Today, however, all SOF soldiers are expected to be able to navigate. In fact, this is a skill that must be acquired to pass the selection process.

44. Darby, 44.

45. "History of the Second World War," Volume 1, *http://hem.passagen.se/inla-jn/info/usual/history.htm*, accessed 17 February 2003. "Stirling believed that the unit needed flexibility in its infiltration methods, and was able to acquire a number of parachutes for that purpose. After some initial training problems the unit was qualified but rarely use the capability operationally."

46. Hoe and Morris, 3–5.

47. The advantage of vehicles is that they provide the SOF with tactical mobility in the area of operations. This is highly desirable in areas where distance can be a factor such as in the desert.

48. According to Geraghty, "The troop to which the SAS is assigned is part of a larger unit known as a squadron, of which 22 SAS, the regular regiment, has four. Each squadron consists of four troops plus a squadron commander (a major), a second-in-command, a sergeant major, quartermaster and clerks — total seventy-two men and six officers. Theoretically, the novice is not basically proficient until he has exercised with the whole squadron, though fighting actions involving an entire SAS squadron are rare. At any one time, parts of the squadron may be dispersed all over the world in small 'team jobs', either training friendly forces or on highly secret operations, often concerned with counterterrorism in friendly states. But one complete squadron of 22 SAS is always on instant stand-by at Hereford, gear packed and a codeword, signalling an alert, memorised. Readiness is routinely tested, and men are extracted from their beds or their favourite pubs at unsocial hours."

49. Hoe and Morris, 114. Parachuting started in the desert but was quickly abandoned. However, it developed into an important capability in Malaya where jumping into trees "became a recognized form of entry for the SAS and was used on a number of occasions. As time went on it was concluded that in fact it was safer deliberately to drop into good primary jungle than onto DZs, which may have rocky river beds and bamboo in close proximity. The system which eventually evolved from the trials, though it was many months later, was the use of a webbing strap, some two hundred feet in length, which was threaded through a 'bikini' bottom and a steel suspension ring. The principle was that the free end could be attached either to the webbing of the parachute harness or a handy branch if such was in reach. From that point the parachutist was able to make a steady controlled descent to the ground." They go on to say, "During this period of late 1951 another similarity to the early desert days occurred in that it was an officer within the SAS rather than the commander who began to take an interest in parachuting as a means of entry into deep jungle. It is generally acknowledged that Major Freddie Templer (a cousin to General Templer) started the business along with Alistair MacGregor. Very much a hit and miss affair, the subject of dropping into trees was treated initially as being a possible misfortune which may befall a parachutist rather than a deliberate tactic and some strange 'tree lowering' harnesses were concocted by utilizing the skills of a local furniture maker! MacGregor recalls that, though he was parachute-trained, all he could remember was a vague instruction that one should keep one's feet and knees together prior to landing. Nonetheless, between them the pair made some thirty descents over a period of a week. A little later the interest was sufficient for a more formal trial to be conducted in the Betong Gap area of Selangor; to the team was added Johnny Cooper (one of Stirling's original 'L' Detachment), Sergeant 'Crash' Hannaway and Peter Walls of 'C' Squadron. The trials were not without mishap but at least a crude method of getting down from a tree-suspended parachute evolved."

50. Special Air Service, *www.specwarnet.com/europe/sas.htm*, accessed 5 June 2004. Also see Geraghty, 521–524.

51. William Mackenzie, *The Secret History of the SOE: The Special Operations Executive 1940–1945* (London: St. Ermin's Press, 2000), 228–230.

52. General Donovan, head of the Office of Strategic Services (OSS), believed that the ethnic makeup of the United States could provide American soldiers with language skills "who, if organized in small groups and trained with commando capabilities, could be parachuted into enemy occupied territory to harass the enemy and to encourage and support local resistance organizations."

53. Hoe and Morris, 101–102.

54. Tom Clancy and John Gresham, *Special Forces: A Guided Tour of the U.S. Army Special Forces* (New York: Berkley Books, 2001), 89.

55. Ian Southerland, "The OSS Operations Groups: Origin of Army Special Forces," *Special Warfare: The Professional Bulletin of the John F. Kennedy Special Warfare Center and School*, Vol. 15, No. 2 (June 2002), 10. General Donovan, head of the OSS, believed that the ethnic makeup of the United States could provide American soldiers with language skills "who, if organized in small groups and trained with commando capabilities, could be parachuted into enemy occupied territory to harass the enemy and to encourage and support local resistance organizations."

56. Sam Young, "A Short History of SF Assessment and Selection," *Special Warfare* (May 1996), 23.

57. *History of the 10th Special Forces Group (Airborne)*, *www.soc.mil/SF/history.pdf*, accessed 10 January 2003, 1.

58. Southerland, 10–11. "The field radio repairman was added to the FA Team organization because of the problems the OSS operational teams had experienced with their communications equipment in the field. In southern France, the next echelon in the OG organization functioned in a similar manner to that envisioned for the FB Team, Special Forces Operational Detachment District B."

59. *Ibid.*, 11.

60. Susan L. Marquis. *Unconventional Warfare: Rebuilding U.S. Special Operations Forces* (Washington, DC: Brookings Institution Press), 20.

61. American Special Forces training is broken down into the following phases: Phase I — Special Forces Assessment and Selection, Phase II — Small Unit Tactics, Phase III — Military Occupational Specialty (MOS) Specific Training, Phase IV — Culmination Exercise (Robin Sage), Phase V — Language Training, and Phase VI — Survival, Evasion, Resistance and Escape (SERE). It should be noted that the Americans have recently made some significant changes to their program. It appears that they have broken up the language training, which used to be a block course near the end of training and is now covered throughout the training process.

62. Today's American Army Rangers carry on many of the traditions of their commando roots. They still believe that to be effective, training must be physically and mentally challenging. A key element of Ranger training is

realism and they believe that soldiers must be put into training situations where they require the same focus they will need in battle. They also believe that realism and stress in training will result in faster learning and better retention of skills. (Appendix G, Field Manual No. 7–85.) Emphasis is placed on land navigation, patrolling, movement techniques, fighting positions, mine and countermine training, limited visibility operations, and operation security. Live fire is also an integral part of current Ranger training with specific attention being placed on basic soldier's skills that include physical conditioning, weapons training, and battle preparedness. Unlike most SOF organizations, soldiers wanting to join the Rangers do not go through an initial course before moving into the unit. They will do this later; if they want to become a leader in the Ranger regiment they must attend the Ranger course, which is 56 days long and very similar in concept to the original Commando course. It is a very physically demanding course that teaches troop-leading procedures, operation orders, and small unit patrol actions. Soldiers must meet the following physical fitness standards: (1) Score 80 points for each U.S. Army physical readiness test (APRT) event and do six chin-ups. (2) Pass the Ranger swimming test. (3) Complete an eight-kilometre run in 40 minutes. (4) Complete a 12-kilometre road march in three hours (with rucksack, helmet, and weapon). (5) Meet the U.S. Army height and weight standards. If they are selected they will then attend a three-week Ranger indoctrination program. This too is physically demanding and is designed to indoctrinate and teach basic skills and techniques used by the Ranger units. The program identifies and eliminates applicants who do not show dedication, motivation, physical fitness, and emotional stability. A similar program is given to officers and NCOs who want to join the unit. Bohrer, 53–57.

63. Department of Defense, *Special Forces Assessment and Selection: Overview of SFAS and "Q" Course*, *www.goarmy.com/job/branch/sorc/sf/sfas.htm*, accessed 14 December 2003.

64. *Ibid.*

65. Tom Clancy and Carl Stiner, *Shadow Warriors: Inside the Special Forces* (New York: Penguin Putnam, 2002), 132–134.

66. Department of Defense, *Special Forces Assessment and Selection: Overview of SFAS and "Q" Course*, *www.goarmy.com/job/branch/sorc/sf/sfas.htm*, accessed 14 December 2003. The site states that, "1-4 Company A, 4th Bn, conducts the 18A Officer Course, which lasts 65 days". It trains and qualifies officers in the basic skills and knowledge required to perform duties as an SFODA commander. This training consists of general subjects, special operations, Special Forces planning (using the military decision-making process), engineer and weapons training, communications and medical

training, special reconnaissance, direct action, unconventional warfare, foreign internal defence, and counter-insurgency operations. Also see *www.globalsecurity.org/military/agency/army/jfksws-training.htm.*

67. *Ibid.*

68. *Ibid.*, 133–134. Company D, 4th Bn, conducts the 18D Special Forces Medical Sergeants Course. The course lasts 322 days. The company is responsible for all medical training at the USAJFKSWCS. The Special Forces Medical Sergeants Course consists of the 24-week Special Operations Combat Medic (SOCM) Course and an additional 22-week training cycle that completes the 18D's medical training. The 24-week Special Operations Combat Medic (SOCM) course is also taught to enlisted Army personnel from the Ranger Regiment, Special Operations Aviation Regiment (SOAR) and Special Operations Support Battalion (SOSB). U.S. Navy (USN) Sea Air Land (SEAL) forces and USN personnel supporting U.S. Marine Corps Recon units as well as Air Force Special Operations Command (AFSOC) ParaRescue personnel also attend the SOCM course. Although 19 of the 24 weeks of SOCM training is focused on anatomy and physiology and paramedic training, the remaining five weeks cover such militarily unique subjects as sick call medicine and environmental medicine. A four-day field training exercise in a simulated combat environment culminates the SOCM course. During the SOCM course students receive American Heart Association certification in Basic and Advanced Cardiac Life Support (ACLS) as well as certification by the National Registry of Emergency Medical Technicians at the EMT-Basic and Paramedic levels. Upon graduation a SOCM is capable of providing basic primary care for his Special Operations team for up to seven days and is capable of sustaining a combat casualty for up to 72 hours after injury as required. Special Operations Combat Medic students receive clinical training in both emergency pre-hospital and hospital settings. This training is conducted during a four-week deployment to one of two major metropolitan areas: New York City or Tampa, FL. U.S. Army Special Forces students attend the 46-week Special Forces Medical Sergeants (SFMS) course. Students in this course must successfully complete the 24-week SOCM curriculum before continuing on for an additional 22 weeks of specialized training in medical, surgical, dental, veterinary, laboratory, pharmaceutical, and preventive medicine subjects. Upon completion of this course students are trained to function as independent health care providers. In addition to the four weeks of clinical training provided during the SOCM portion of their training, SFMS students receive another four weeks of clinical experience at selected health care facilities throughout the United States. The focus of this training is on honing student skills as independent, general practice, health care providers. See *www.globalsecurity.org/military/agency/army/jfksws-training.htm.*

69. *Special Forces Assessment and Selection*, 1–4.

70. *Ibid.*, 1–4.

71. *Ibid.*, 1–4. Also see *www.globalsecurity.org/military/agency/army/jfksws-training.htm*. The languages are divided into four categories: Category 1: Spanish, French, and Portuguese (18 weeks, three days), Category 2: German, Indonesian (18 weeks, three days), Category 3: Czech, Persian-Farsi, Polish, Russian, Serbo-Croatian, Tagalog, Thai, and Turkish (24 weeks, two days), and Category 4: Arabic, Korean, and Japanese (24 weeks, two days).

72. *Ibid.*, 1–4.

# 4

## Thinking Outside the Box:
### *Understanding SOF Leadership*

Tony Balasevicius

Experts in the field of leadership believe that for military organizations to be successful in the new environment of the twenty-first century they will need to develop leaders who can analyze and deal with complex problems in the new multifaceted political, military, and social environment that has been emerging during the past 10 years. More importantly, they feel that to be effective, military leaders must be able to quickly align their operational activities with other governmental and non-governmental agencies.[1] These skills apply to all levels of command but have special significance at the junior level where leadership is at its most inexperienced and where leaders are often at the forefront of conflict with little or no time to rationalize the decisions they must make. According to Colonel Bernd Horn, a prolific writer on the subject of leadership and future war:

> The future battlespace will be volatile, uncertain, constantly changing, and ambiguous. There will be an increased emphasis on information operations and small, agile, dispersed, situationally aware units operating in a non-linear environment supported by instantaneously delivered precision-effects weaponry.... Conflict will become increasingly complex

because of the asymmetric nature of the threat, [and] the use of urban terrain.... Furthermore, operations will be multi-dimensional, requiring not only the close integration of all three environments, but also that of governmental and non-governmental agencies to achieve desired outcomes.... To function in this daunting environment will require a reorientation of how we think and operate on the battlefield.[2]

Although this evolving environment may represent a "new" development for conventional military forces, in many respects, Special Operations Forces (SOF) have always had to operate in a complex asymmetric and multi-dimensional battlespace.[3] In order to succeed in these circumstances, SOF has placed a great deal of trust in well-trained, intelligent, and resourceful junior leaders. These leaders are expected to operate on their own for extended periods of time, often in austere and hostile environments where they must exert control over all aspects of the political, administrative, and operational activities within their assigned area of operations.[4]

The scope of SOF duties is such that they demand leaders that can be relied upon to carry out their mission with little or no supervision or direction. People selected for such positions must have high levels of cognitive, physical, and technical abilities, and they must possess a flexible and adaptive leadership style that can maximize the capabilities of the soldiers and resources under their command. From the start, during the early stages of the Second World War, SOF has had the good fortune to attract just such leaders.

The early leaders were extremely fit, possessed high levels of cognitive ability, and had a very charismatic style of leadership. Moreover, they were visionary men, not encumbered by traditional conservative ideas. They were able to think outside the box and often developed practical solutions to the operational problems they faced. Out of necessity they inculcated future generations of SOF leaders with many of these same traits and in the process developed a unique and far more flexible style of leadership than that found in conventional military units. Over the years this supple and adaptive leadership style has come to dominate SOF command philosophy creating a relaxed but extremely innovative culture.

The basis of this innovative and adaptive culture has evolved from a number of factors, which include a general lack of formal military experience on the part of many of the early officers arriving at the newly created SOF units, and the high level of technical skill and experience possessed by the soldiers. This combination had the effect of making soldiers more independent and, as a result, they tended to accept far more responsibility for their actions than conventional soldiers. This notion of the "independent soldier" developed from the early operational concept of the British Commandos, which were initially designed to produce soldiers capable of fighting unconventionally, but when necessary they could be quickly be brought together to form ad hoc units for specific missions.[5]

The characteristic of "independence" has remained fundamental to SOF. It became evident that the type of soldier best suited to carry out SOF operations was an independent-minded person possessing initiative and intelligence, who was highly motivated. It was also quickly realized that such men needed to be treated differently and that they did not have to be subjected to the parade square discipline found in the conventional military units to produce effective results. In fact, over time, SOF organizations began to see the benefits gained from treating highly skilled soldiers as partners in the planning and conduct of missions and this was to have an important impact on the development of their leadership philosophy.[6]

To properly understand SOF leadership, it is critical to comprehend how it has evolved to meet the specific requirements of SOF forces. However, before undertaking such a study, a general definition of leadership must be determined and an examination of the leadership model common to conventional military units must first be provided as a baseline of analysis. Once this is understood an examination of the evolution of SOF leadership can then be undertaken. In this respect, this chapter will examine SOF leadership philosophy and its evolution from the conventional military models.

Leadership and the people who successfully practise it have always fascinated the common person, but despite the enormous amounts of research into the subject, leadership is still a concept not well understood. Over the last 30 years many people have defined leadership many different ways.[7] Unfortunately, most definitions are wrapped around personal experience and individual perspectives that may or may not be linked to the direct practice of leadership. According to Gary Yukl, a leading researcher on the subject, "Leadership has been defined in terms of traits, behaviour, influence, interaction patterns, role relationships, and occupation of an administrative position."[8] Yukl goes on to suggest that most definitions of leadership reflect to some extent the assumption that it involves a process whereby one person exerts intentional influence over other people to guide, structure, and facilitate activities and relationships in the group or organization.[9]

This definition has merit as the concept of effective leadership from the perspective of the conventional military establishment. Many military manuals on the subject define leadership as "the art of influencing human behaviour so as to accomplish the mission in a manner desired by the leader."[10] The American Army's doctrine on leadership also follows this theme and states; "Leadership is influencing people — by providing purpose, direction, and motivation — while operating to accomplish the mission and improving the organization."[11] Within this framework the expectation of good leadership is seen as someone that can give clear direction, show consideration for the follower, exhibit professionalism and set a good example.[12] However, the practical applications of this type of military leadership must be placed in context.

Although modern militaries are becoming increasingly complex and will continue to demand more highly sophisticated and intelligent soldiers, the skill sets of military followers, who must do most of the close combat, will by necessity remain basic in its nature. This is because military training during periods of major conflict is focused on training a nation's reserves and this training is designed to produce soldiers as quickly as possible. Within this perspective, the combat soldier's skills are generally limited to those absolutely necessary in the performance of basic battlefield tasks.[13] As a result, specialization of tasks within the basic combat grouping of a section (10 men) or platoon (35 men) is limited and interaction between the leader and follower is for the most part restricted to giving and following orders.

This narrow interaction process is achieved by ensuring followers quickly adapt to established group and institutional norms and is accomplished by using the transactional leadership model.[14] Bernard M. Bass, a noted authority in leadership theory, believes transactional leadership "depends on the contingent reinforcement, either by positive contingent reward, which is the method used when a leader assigns or gets agreement on what needs to be done and promises rewards or actually rewards others in exchange for satisfactorily carrying out the assignment, or by the more negative active or passive (component) form of management by exception. In the active form the leader arranges to actively monitor deviancies from standards, mistakes, and errors in the follower's assignments and take corrective action as necessary."[15]

Bass goes on to say that the more passive form of the transactional style implies waiting passively for deviancies, mistakes, and errors to occur and then taking some type of corrective action.[16] This process emphasizes the traditional aspects of authoritative leadership and is the dominant style of command within conventional military forces at all levels in the chain of command.

The U.S. Army identifies three very distinct levels of leadership: Strategic, Organizational and Direct.[17] However, it is at the level of direct leadership that junior leaders both within SOF and conventional forces generally operate and it is at this level where the styles of leadership used by each differ significantly. According to the U.S. Army, direct military leadership is defined as, "Face-to-face, first-line leadership. It takes place in those organisations where subordinates are used to seeing their leaders all the time: Teams and squads, sections and platoons, companies, batteries, and troops — even squadrons and battalions. The direct leader's span of influence, those lives he can reach out and touch, may range from a handful to several hundred people."[18]

The major source of direct leadership within any military organization is found at the non-commissioned officer (NCO) and junior officer level. These two groups generally face more certainty and less complexity than organizational and strategic leaders because they are close enough to the action to see the situation unfolding. They are responsible for supervising the soldiers that carry out orders, so they can see how things are working. This gives them the ability to quickly assess, and if necessary, address problems in a timely manner.[19]

Furthermore, it is the junior officer and senior NCO that are primarily responsible for training the soldiers they lead and they are expected to develop the follower's skills with emphasis on obedience to orders and instructions, while instilling the notion that the completion of the mission must, and will, come first.[20] In this regard, the transactional leadership style has proven very effective in combat. It is a particularly efficient type of leadership when an army must quickly mobilize large numbers of inexperienced citizens and turn them into soldiers who can fight.

The main weakness of transactional leadership lays in the fact that it relies on the leader personally possessing the knowledge and experience necessary to carry out all tasks assigned to the group. In this respect, junior combat leaders are not necessarily trained in the art of military leadership as much as they are trained to direct and supervise specific events. For example, soldiers undergoing leadership training are taught to carry out an attack; they are given a checklist and told to follow each of the steps in the process outlined for attacks. If they can do this, they are considered to be effective leaders. Unfortunately, the emphasis on this type of leadership training is placed more on controlling soldiers through each step of the task rather then actually leading them.[21]

In effect, the leader directs his followers through each mission under very close supervision using one style of leadership based on the "I say — you do" concept that is so prevalent in the transactional model. In this type of environment the leader controls his followers based on his authority, and knowledge of the specific skills needed to complete each of the group's tasks. In this regard, the leader maintains control over the group through his level of knowledge. According to William Darryl Henderson, a former U.S. Army officer and writer, "the leader derives his influence over the follower from several bases of power. One of these bases comes from what Henderson refers to as expert power."[22]

Henderson defines expert power "as the soldier's compliance with a leader's orders because the leader is perceived as having superior knowledge and ability important to the soldier's survival within the context of a current or expected situation. In hardship situations and in combat especially, leadership expertise that allows the leader to cope successfully with the situation is a significant source of power." Henderson goes on to argue that "The proven ability to carry out a tactical plan, to arrange for and adjust artillery, to demonstrate professional expertise with weapons, to navigate well, and to provide medical care and supplies are all significant sources of power."[23] Although the transactional approach towards leadership works well in high-stress situations where the leader is practised and many of the subordinates are inexperienced, it does have drawbacks.

The main difficulty with the transactional approach is that it leaves little room, outside of a leadership position, for the follower to be a contributing and proactive member of the team. This is due to the underlying assumption that the follower lacks the highly developed skills necessary to participate in any meaningful way. As young soldiers are usually inexperienced, the ability of the conventional military leader to move away from the transactional model is difficult and institutionally is generally not encouraged. However, this style of leadership becomes problematic once a leader must deal with experienced or more highly skilled soldiers that are commonly found in long standing professional military forces and who are prevalent within SOF organizations.

SOF soldiers tend to be older, more intelligent, better trained, and more experienced then their conventional counterparts. Brigadier Michael Calvert, former wartime Special Air Service (SAS) Brigade commander and the founder of the post–Second World War SAS, summed up the difficulty of having these better quality soldiers to conventional military forces where he stated, "Volunteer units such as SAS attract officers and men who have initiative, resourcefulness, independence of spirit, and confidence in themselves. In a regular unit there are far less opportunities of making use of these assets and, in fact, in many formations they are a liability, as this individualistic attitude upsets the smooth working of a team. This is especially true in European warfare where the individual must subordinate his natural initiative so that he fits into a part of the machine."[24]

Calvert's assessment is backed up by Kennedy Shaw, a former officer in the Long-Range Desert Group (LRDG), "Brains, initiative, reliability, endurance and courage," he argued, "were probably of equal importance."[25] People with such qualities allow SOF organizations to provide soldiers with a verity of highly developed skill sets that play an essential role in the overall success of the team.[26] In fact, the idea of providing soldiers with a greater versatility of skills was a key part of the LRDG's operating philosophy.

The LRDG's concept of operating behind enemy lines for extended periods relied heavily on the ability of small groups to be self-sufficient. As the size of the patrols was relatively small, the skills needed for them to function had to be distributed among its members regardless of their rank. Over time these skills became extremely specialized and leaders were forced to rely on the qualifications of the soldiers to ensure the patrol's success. Shaw provides clarity on this unique military situation. "Men in the LRDG were specialists in something," he stated, "of all these experts the signalmen were probably the most important, though the navigators ran them close." He added, "For what was primarily a reconnaissance unit good signals were essential. Without them a patrol, three or four hundred miles away from its base, could neither send back vital information nor receive fresh orders. If signals failed the best thing to do was to come home."[27]

Under such circumstances SOF leaders were no longer able to rely solely on their ability to dominate followers with their extensive knowledge, their skill sets, or their institutional authority as they could easily do in the transactional style of leadership. In order for the teams to function, SOF needed to develop a more flexible way to command, one that would take full advantage of the highly developed skill sets possessed by the soldiers. The solution was to move the emphasis away from the leader-follower relationship towards a focus on the leader and his command of the team. This change in emphasis refocused the dynamics of leadership within the context of the group and fundamentally changed the role of the military leader. Under this new arrangement the leader was expected to involve members of the team in the decision making process and to coordinate the activities of each member's expertise towards the accomplishment of the team's mission.[28]

Although the evolution towards this team-based leadership approach within SOF occurred for very practical reasons, the background and philosophic outlook of the early SOF leaders also heavily influenced the development of this unique leadership philosophy. In most cases, these leaders had either limited military experience or were somewhat unconventional in their thinking. David Stirling, the founder and first commander of the British SAS, is an example.

Before the outbreak of war Stirling attended Ampleforth College and Cambridge University, and was an art student in Paris. He also trained to be an architect and then went on to be a cowboy in North America. Interestingly, he was training in the Canadian Rockies for a proposed climb on Mount Everest when the war started. He quickly returned to England and became a volunteer in the embryonic Commandos.[29] Stirling was typical of leaders drawn to the early SOF community. Not only were they intelligent adventurers, they were also very intellectual men with the vision and influence to effect the necessary transformation within what tended to be very conservative establishments reluctant to embrace change. Arguably, one of the most intellectual of these early leaders was Major Ralph A. Bagnold.

Bagnold became an officer in the British Army Royal Engineers in 1915, and after the First World War he studied engineering at Cambridge University, receiving an honours degree in 1921, after which he returned to active duty with the Army. Between the world wars he spent much of his free time exploring the African desert, and after his retirement he continued his research, eventually publishing his findings in 1941 under the title *The Physics of Blown Sand and Desert Dunes*. Although retired, he was recalled to active duty as a signals officer in North Africa after war erupted in Europe.[30]

Understanding the dynamics of desert war, Bagnold was concerned about the immense unprotected desert flank west and south of Cairo, and proposed the establishment of a small organization equipped with desert-worthy vehicles to travel deep behind enemy lines for extended periods. They were to observe traffic along the coastal road in northern Libya and Egypt and if the opportunity presented itself to attack remote desert outposts and airfields. The proposal was eventually accepted and the LRDG was created.[31] The type of leaders that Bagnold and other SOF commanders selected for their new commands were at first glance somewhat odd choices. In the case of the LRDG few were experienced soldiers, which appears to go against the common held perception that to be effective SOF can only be commanded by experienced military officers.

However, all of Bagnold's officers had considerable intellect and highly specialized areas of expertise. They also held extensive knowledge of the desert and an understanding of how to live and travel in that inhospitable terrain. Pat Clayton, who served under Bagnold as a captain in the LRDG, was a government surveyor in Tanganyika prior to the war. During the 1930s, he had explored much of the desert with Bagnold. Shaw was a curator at the Palestine Museum in Jerusalem and during the 1930s, he too was a desert explorer who had been associated with Bagnold's expeditions.[32]

Initially, Bagnold was the only leader in the LRDG that had knowledge in both military affairs and the complex environment in the desert. However, he was able to use his knowledge and leadership skills to bring together people with different capabilities and turn them into a cohesive entity in a relatively short period. According to Shaw, "Starting from scratch, in five weeks the LRDG had been created. I do not think that any one except Bagnold could have achieved this. Some had the necessary knowledge of the Army, others the necessary experience of the desert, none had both." The academics and adventurers that became Bagnold's patrol leaders had little concept of the traditional aspects of transactional leadership that was practised by the military and out of necessity, as much as circumstances, they brought to the SOF a very different approach to the way soldiers were commanded.[33]

This different approach to command focuses on the potential of the leader/follower relationship within the larger context of the team and is significant given the historical success of many SOF units like the LRDG. Much of this success was derived from the highly developed leadership traits that were found in these early pioneers. Understanding the specific leadership qualities exhibited by these leaders is important to gaining insight into the SOF leadership philosophy. However, to do so it is necessary to develop a construct of an effective leader within the context of the leader/follower and their relationship within the team and determine specific traits that produce success.

Interestingly, Bass believes that in order to be effective, leaders must have five basic competencies that will not only make them better equipped to meet the demands of the new environment but will also provide a foundation for the future development of these leaders to more senior appointments. These include critical evaluation and problem detection, envisioning, communication skills, impression management; and the knowledge to empower followers.[34] Interestingly, these five competencies represent many of the traits exhibited by the early and high profile SOF founders and leaders. This style of leadership is commonly referred to as the transformational model.[35]

Transformational leaders generally take a more proactive approach with followers and often produce excellent results:

> [They] do more with colleagues and followers than set up simple exchanges or agreements. They behave in ways to achieve superior results by employing one or more of the components of transformational leadership ... The components include leadership that is charismatic such that the follower seeks to identify with the leaders and emulate them. The leadership inspires the follower with challenge and persuasion providing a meaning and understanding. The leadership is intellectually stimulating, expanding the follower's use of their abilities. Finally, the leadership is individually considerate, providing the follower with support, mentoring, and coaching.[36]

In this environment the extent to which SOF leaders are able to exert real power rather than merely symbolic authority is based on the leader's qualities and ability to utilize these resources. Specifically, they must understand the dynamics of the team and tap into team members wants, motives, expectations, attitudes, and values in order to induce or compel members to behave as required.[37] The essence of the SOF leader's power in this context has less to do with style and role and more to do with their ability to satisfy the specific needs of the follower while keeping those needs within the overall goals of the group.[38] As a result, SOF leaders must develop and employ a number of leadership styles to meet these different and constantly competing requirements.

The concept of SOF advanced successfully because leaders such as Stirling and Bagnold were able to provide that flexible approach to leadership that was needed and ensured mission success. In turn, these early SOF leaders were able to provide the necessary leadership because they possessed the traits described by Bass in his transformational model. For example, they were able to envision that success in conventional military operations could be achieved with assistance from unconventional methods. They were able to think outside of the box and put forward a compelling vision of what they could achieve and how. The concept of envisioning is defined as the process of considering and understanding the art of the possible and can be "fostered in learning programs that develop the creative thinking process. These two competencies teach the leader how to vary or change their behaviours and to contemplate profound changes."[39] In order for Stirling and Bagnold to come up with their original concepts or visions they needed the ability to critically evaluate the situation by defining the problem and then producing a solution. According to Bass, evaluation and problem detection is defined as "the ability to understand the problem and come up with an effective solution."

In this respect, the importance of Bagnold's evaluation and problem detection, which led to his vision for the LRDG, is placed into proper context by Shaw. "Three years later, looking back to 1940," commented Shaw, "one saw how sound Bagnold's original conception had been. With a few minor changes the organisation had stood the test of time and battle ... and what is more, I think no one had also the vision to see just what was needed for the job."[40] In fact, the development of the SAS concept by Stirling for small-scale direct action missions was based on the same sound conceptual thinking and critical assessment used by Bagnold and advocated by Bass.

In 1941, Stirling, only a lieutenant at the time, believed that commando raids such as those conducted on German positions along the coast of Cyrenaica by Layforce (British Commandos commanded by Lieutenant-Colonel Robert Laycock)[41] were of little value since the Germans had started constructing heavy defensive positions around key costal installations. As a result, these operations were placing heavy demands on both personnel and resources, and at best delivered only a temporary inconvenience or setback to the enemy. Moreover, experience had shown that even if initial surprise could be achieved the action would always draw local reserves, which always resulted in a fighting withdrawal and heavy casualties.[42] Stirling believed that if a small force could overcome the difficulties of moving over the vast desert areas to the south it would be possible to infiltrate a force behind enemy lines and withdraw them quickly. He produced a paper entitled, "A Special Service Unit," detailing his thoughts on the potential for small teams of Special Forces to attack enemy airfields, transport and fuel parks.[43] Ultimately, Stirling was able to make a compelling argument in support of such an organization and the SAS was born.[44]

Both Stirling and Bagnold were able to use highly developed critical evaluation and problem solving techniques to create a vision. As well, each was also able to articulate that vision to superiors and incorporate the concept into existing military operations that worked extremely well. This ability to think outside the box and come up with unorthodox solutions is a key attribute required by successful leaders.[45] However, regardless of its importance, the process of creative thinking, envisioning, and the ability to articulate that vision to superiors and subordinates is only part of the leaders domain and it does not explain what made the operational SOF teams function as well as they did nor does it explain the cohesiveness that was achieved within many of those teams.

The success of SOF units like the LRDG and the SAS was also due to the training and cohesiveness of their patrols. Cohesiveness is based on group identity and comes from a number of things including mutual respect and trust among members and between leaders and subordinates. SOF soldiers develop that bond because they perceive themselves as a valued members of the team. This perception of worth is derived from the willingness of the leader to accept the follower's advice based on area of expertise, the strength of the idea, and not on rank. More implicitly, it is the ability of the SOF leader to empower followers to do their job the way they see fit based on the extensive abilities each follower possesses that provides that basis of trust. This concept of empowerment is a critical component of SOF leadership and a key part of the dynamics within the SOF team.

Empowerment is the process of giving the follower the ability to provide advice and make decisions. This enables the follower to buy into the mission and become a stakeholder with a shared interest in its successful completion. It is further enhanced when members feel they actually participate in the decision making process.[46] The concept of empowerment has always been an important element of SOF culture beginning with the establishment of the first British commandos in 1940.[47] It is this concept combined with a greater emphasis on the individual that has helped create the less formal but far more innovative working environment found within the SOF.

The less structured and more informal environment is often misunderstood by outsiders and tends to create a perception of an ill-disciplined organization. This negative view is especially prevalent with conventional military leaders that do not understand the concept of leadership and discipline within the transformational context. Unfortunately, this perception has been further reinforced by the unique working conditions SOF soldiers experience; their need to adapt to the extreme environments they must often face; and poor command decisions. Shaw elaborates on this situation. "A stranger meeting a LRDG patrol returning from a month's trip in Libya," he explains, "would have been hard put to it to decide to what race or army, let alone to what unit, they belonged. In winter the use of battle dress made for some uniformity, but LRDG in summer, with a month-old beard thick with sand, with a month's dirt (for the water ration allowed no washing), skin burnt to the colour of coffee, and clad in nothing but a pair of torn shorts and 'chapplies' (i.e., the North West Frontier [of India] pattern sandals imported by Bagnold) a man looked like a creature from some other world."[48]

A similar experience was faced by the SAS in Malaya, where relaxed dress became an issue with the chain of command. Captain John Woodhouse, a future commander of the SAS, commented "men were allowed to grow beards in the jungle, which was a sensible idea in that it did hide a white face in the undergrowth but unfortunately they were allowed to keep the beards when they came out."[49] He added, "This was contrary to all sorts of military traditions and the sight of smelly, scruffy, bearded soldiers coming out of the jungle was one which caused apoplexy in the staff and derision amongst all the other units of the army."[50] It is important to remember that the conditions under which SOF often operates are extremely harsh and the standard conventional issue of equipment has not always been suited to those particular demands. This situation results in SOF leadership allowing some leeway with things such as dress if it makes sense to do so.[51]

For all its benefits, the practical leadership style developed by SOF is not without its shortcomings. Such an approach can be dangerous in situations where leaders do not fully understand the dynamics they are facing or when soldiers are allowed to abuse the latitude they are given and attempt to set cultural norms in an effort to gain dominance within the team. The reintroduction of the SAS during the Malaya campaign clearly demonstrates what happens under such circumstances. "Despite a sound operational concept, Calvert's original capability had difficulty because many of its soldiers did not have the aptitude or the self-discipline to handle the particular demands of Special Forces soldiering."[52] Woodhouse believed that the reason for the many problems was "that the officers and men were not selected in the latter sense, they didn't go through a selection course; as far as the soldiers were concerned they were simply selected in the sense that volunteers volunteered and, as far as I know, all those who volunteered were accepted."[53]

More important, the SAS's leadership appeared unable or unwilling to deal with those soldiers who should not have been in the unit. [54] "Discipline," explained Woodhouse, "was really non-existent [in the unit]. Why Colonel Calvert didn't clamp down hard I've never entirely understood ... other officers including myself didn't take a firm line with the troops at that time."[55] Having even a small number of poor soldiers in SOF units becomes problematic and will have a disruptive affect on the entire unit. This is because the unit relies on the ability and proficiency of small teams for its operational efficiency and if these teams are not functioning properly the unit suffers. As Woodhouse points out, "It's a bit unfair to brand 'A' Squadron as being just a bunch of buccaneers. There were many good soldiers in that squadron, in fact certainly a majority and the same was true of the early officers in the troops. I would say that certainly four out of five officers would have passed into the SAS at any time in later years, so the material was quite good."[56] The situation faced by the SAS during the Malayan Emergency emphasizes a key aspect of SOF leadership, which is despite the leadership model one is using the leader is still in command, as such he will always be responsible for the discipline and the success and failure of the team's activities.

In this regard, the leader must be able to balance the requirements between the needs of very highly skilled and forceful soldiers with the demands of the mission, which can at times be a difficult process. This often complex environment tends to create significant problems for newly arrived transactional-oriented leaders who are quickly confronted with unfamiliar and often aggressive leadership situations. This is due to the fact that prior to entering the world of SOF, the leader is given respect based on his rank and this is reinforced by an institutional structure that ensures respect is maintained, whether deserved or not.

In the context of SOF, however, respect is given based on the perceived competence of the individual and what that individual can provide to the team. It is also likely that all members within the SOF team are leaders in their own right and could easily command effectively, given the opportunity. Under these circumstances the leader may be appointed, but in the eyes of the group he must still earn the right to lead. This is achieved by showing the team that he, like them, has passed through the selection and training process, and that he is capable of coordinating each of the different individuals and tasks within the team. In the end, if he can prove he can do the job he will get the respect he is seeking. Shaw provides an example of how this process of gaining respect is earned within the SOF:

> Occasionally it fell to a British officer to command a New Zealand patrol. Knowing the conventional opinion held by the New Zealanders of the average Englishman this was a task approached with some misgivings. But if you could show that your first object was to get on with the job, and that you knew as much or even a little more than they did about doing it, then the patrol, awarding perhaps the high praise that you were not such a bad sort of bastard after all, would achieve all and more than you could ask.[57]

The need for the leader to gain the respect of his team before it can begin to operate as a cohesive entity is an unknown concept within transactional leadership. And under any circumstances this process can be very intimidating for a leader to undertake. Reactions to this situation vary but can generally be broken down into one of three possible courses of action. First, if the leader is good he will naturally adapt his style to meet the requirements of the specific group and or situation he is involved in. Second, if he does not have a flexible leadership style and is unable to develop it he will likely maintain his transactional leadership approach. Although such an approach will provide the necessary leadership to maintain discipline, it is likely to undermine cohesion and limit the overall performance potential of team members. The third, and most risky outcome, which partly explains the problems faced by the SAS in Malaya, is when the leader backs off and takes a laissez-faire approach to the leadership of the group believing this is the way good teams should work and develop.[58]

In taking a laissez-faire approach, the leader allows the group to control events as he fools himself into believing this is the way it is done in the unit or this is how good teamwork is developed. The situation becomes dangerous when a leader with a laissez-faire style of leadership is paired with poor soldiers who are attempting to dominate the team.

To prevent this from happening SOF attempts to gets the type of leaders they need by putting leadership candidates through a leadership selection process and then providing them with specific training and development opportunities that will allow them to effectively lead in the SOF environment.

Before describing the leadership selection process, it is important to review the competencies leaders need to command SOF soldiers. In this respect, it cannot be forgotten that the primary task of a military leader is to lead soldiers during highly stressful operations and in this regard the transactional leadership style has withstood the test of time. Thus, the requirement for SOF leaders to use the transactional approach as part of their command philosophy will always be necessary and the conventional leadership training they receive provides a sound basis on which to develop the SOF leader. However, SOF leaders also require a more effective and multi-dimensional approach with their subordinates who are expected to play a more active and meaningful part in the accomplishment of the group's mission than their conventional counterparts.

To this end, SOF leaders must be good and adaptive military commanders who know their job and understand the people that work for them. As a starting point the early SOF leaders provide an example of the common traits that are necessary for commanding SOF soldiers. In a broad sense, these traits include those described by Bass such as critical evaluation and problem detection, envisioning, communication skills, impression management, and the capacity to empower followers. However, in addition to those, one must also include physical fitness, the ability to lead by example, the skill to maximize available resources and the ability to take criticism and advice from subordinates.[59]

During the SOF leadership selection phase candidates are tested for these traits a number of times in a process that will normally last three to five days and involve a number of stands/tests similar to those they would have encountered during the all ranks selection process. However, the stands or tasks tend to be very specific and their focus is on problem solving, planning, and the ability to delegate. To achieve this, in a military context, candidates will often be given a tactical problem and be asked to assess it and then be prepared to brief an evaluator on a number of possible options. They will then be asked to provide a recommendation on the best course of action. In fact, part of the process of modern SAS selection is to have veteran soldiers as evaluators who will critique the performance of these potential leaders. For example:

> Among officers who volunteer for SAS selection, the sickener factor, though no longer known by that name, is still apparent. For a week before the beginning of the basic course, they are taken on long and tiring marches round the hills, then brought back to the Hereford base to be given Staff tasks — for example, calculate the amount of fuel and ordnance required to move a troop to a particular objective and demolish it, and produce a plan for the operation. The officer must then present his plan to a conference of veteran SAS troopers and NCOs, who will treat it with derision. 'You must be joking!' 'Where were you trained, the Boy Scouts?' are not responses young lieutenants have been taught to expect from other ranks. For some it is a punishing emotional experience. The officer's reaction to such criticisms will be carefully noted.[60]

The reactions to the criticisms are carefully noted because this type of test can determine whether the leader, in this case an officer, is willing to accept criticism from soldiers, which he deems below his rank level. If he is unable to tolerate this type of criticism from subordinates he is unlikely to be able or willing to adapt to the specific needs of the SOF where soldiers expect to be given the opportunity for a fair hearing. It is important to understand that during the selection stage evaluators are only looking for the potential of the candidate to transition to a more transformational style, as it is understood that most candidates have been trained in the transactional model and will initially rely heavily on this training. Once a leadership candidate passes the selection phase they start training.

The leadership style expected of SOF leaders is inculcated into them throughout most of their training. For example, officer candidates in the U.S. Special Forces are expected to successfully complete the detachment officer course, which is a separate phase of training for leaders and includes instruction in Special Forces tactics, techniques, and procedures and mission planning. This training is all about innovation in the face of uncertainty. Susan Marquis, a researcher and author on the subject of U.S. Special Operations Forces, notes, "Special Forces training emphasizes creativity and innovation under physical stress, and leadership and problem solving in the middle of isolation and uncertainty."[61] In effect, they are expected to be at ease when dealing with change and ambiguity.

To develop this ability, training emphasizes planning and students (Army captains and their NCO team members) take the data and mission given to them to produce a detailed mission analysis and plan over the course of some days. This leads to what is commonly referred to as the "brief back" where each member of the team stands up and details his specific aspect of the plan and how it will support the overall mission. This is an important aspect of the leader's conditioning process. Training emphasis is on the leader being able to delegate work relying on each member of the team doing his part. In this case success or failure will be in front of the boss. Over time, the adaptive leader gains confidence in the abilities of his subordinates and becomes comfortable with the idea of sharing control to achieve team objectives. It is only then that the true potential of the team is realized.

The ability of SOF to move its leaders from a transactional to a transformational style of leadership will require a constant emphasis and development. However, history has shown it is worth the effort. After all, as Walter F. Ulmer has stated, "Transformational leaders have been identified in both military and commercial settings as more effective than are leaders who rely heavily on transactional or management-by-exception leadership styles."[62] Leading well-trained, experienced and technically competent soldiers in the increasingly complicated operational situations now being experienced by SOF puts far more emphasis on finding better educated and more sophisticated leaders.

In fact, the leaders SOF is looking for to command these special individuals have changed little from the early days. In a broad sense, these leaders must have basic leadership traits that include critical evaluation and problem detection, envisioning, communication skills, impression management, the capacity to empower followers, physical fitness, the ability to lead by example, the ability to maximize available resources, and the capacity to take criticism and advice from subordinates.[63] These traits have been a hallmark of successful SOF leadership from the initial creation of these forces and it will be the foundation that moves them forward into the future.

## NOTES

1.   Bernard M. Bass, *Transformational Leadership* (New Jersey: Lawrence Erlbaum Associates, Publishers, 1998), 3.

2.   Lieutenant-Colonel Bernd Horn, "Complexity Squared: Operating in the Future BattleSpace," *Canadian Military Journal*, Vol. 4, No. 3 (Autumn 2003), 14.

3.   William S. Cohen, secretary of defense, United States, *Annual Report to the President and Congress, 1998*, April 1998, accessed at *www.dtic.mil/execsec/ adr98/index.html*. Special Operations Forces (SOF) are specialized military units designed to deal with a variety of situations. According to the report "They offer a range of options to decision makers confronting crises and conflicts below the threshold of war, such as terrorism, insurgency, and sabotage. Second, they are force multipliers for major conflicts, increasing the effectiveness and efficiency of the U.S. military effort. Finally, they are the forces of choice in situations requiring regional orientation and cultural and political sensitivity, including military-to-military contacts and non-combatant missions like humanitarian assistance, security assistance, and peacekeeping operations."

4.   Susan L. Marquis, *Unconventional Warfare: Rebuilding U.S. Special Operations Forces.* (Washington, DC: Brookings Institution Press, 1997), 15. This abstract originally came from Charles M. Simpson III, *Inside the Green Berets: The First Thirty Years: A History of the U.S. Army Special Forces* (New York: Berkley Books, 1983), xv–xvi, and 29. These were the precise circumstances faced by many American junior SOF officers and NCOs in Vietnam. Their experience in that conflict not only illustrates the depth of their responsibilities but the quality of their command ability. These leaders commanded their detachments during operations and their missions often included advising veteran soldiers and leaders of a host nation's military force, training military units of between 400 to 500 men to be operationally effective in combat, being responsible for millions of dollars worth of equipment and monthly payrolls, as well as supervising the distribution of intelligence funds. In addition, these leaders oversaw the expenditure of thousands of dollars for monthly supplies, while conducting tasks including psychological and intelligence operations, and civic action projects

5.   John Parker, *Commandos: The Inside Story of Britain's Most Elite Fighting Force* (London: Headline Book Publishing, 2000), 7–8. Parker provides a good account of the concept behind the Commandos. In the book he states "the British army agreed at last to the formation of 'guerrilla forces' whose recruitment was based initially on the region in which they lived.

The idea was derived from small special military units that first made their appearance among the Boers in the late nineteenth century and which had been the subject of several studies by British military strategists in the intervening years, including the Madden Committee. The guerrillas were originally used in raids and assaults first against hostile African tribes and then in the Boer War against the British. They were hit-and-run troops who raided installations, sabotaged machinery and communications, and attacked enemy troops. The Boers raised them through electoral districts, each area supplying its own force. Because the men had been 'commandeered' by the military, they soon took the name commandos, and self-sufficiency was their trademark: each man was responsible for providing his own horse, they received no pay or uniform and had no permanent headquarters or base. Their tactics centred around lightning strikes on the British forces, and then they melted back into the veldt before the British could react. The Boer War was extended by at least a year by the activities of the commandos."

6.   In contemporary literature the leadership model SOF is attempting to foster is commonly referred to as transformational leadership. The reason for this heavy emphasis on transformational leadership development is not difficult to understand. The style of leadership necessary to command the more mature and highly skilled soldiers that are found in SOF units is different from the transactional leadership model commonly used by conventional units to lead inexperienced soldiers in combat. This challenge is exacerbated by the fact that SOF organizations generally draw their soldiers and leaders from conventional military forces, which arrive with a heavily ingrained transactional leadership style. The problem for SOF is to develop leadership selection and training programs that will identify and produce a much more rounded leader who is capable of maximizing the skills and knowledge possessed by the SOF soldier and enhancing the team's overall performance. Military leaders trained in conventional warfare have never fully understood this concept and this lack of understanding often leads to the perception of SOF as a bunch of cowboys or prima donnas who lack discipline.

7.   Yukl, Gary, *Leadership in Organizations: Fourth Edition* (Englewood Cliffs, NJ: Prentice Hall Inc., 1998), 2–3.

8.   *Ibid.*, 2.

9.   *Ibid.*, 3.

10.  Land Force Command, *Junior NCO Course Training Plan Volume 1* (Ottawa: Department of National Defence, 1996).

11. Accessed at *www.adtdl.army.mil/cgi-bin/atdl.dll/fm/22-100/ch3.htm#3-1 FM 22-100*, Chapter 3.

12. *Ibid.*, Volume 1. Also see Lieutenant-Colonel Peter Bradley and Dr. Danielle Charbonneau. "Transformational Leadership: Something New, Something Old," *Canadian Military Journal*, Vol. 5, No. 1 (Spring 2004), 7–8. According to Lieutenant-Colonel Peter Bradley and Dr. Danielle Charbonneau, literature on the subject of leadership is vast; "Joseph Rost found 221 definitions of leadership in his review of the area. A scan through any university leadership textbook will reveal a variety of theories. Yukl classified these theories into five broad approaches. First, the trait approach studies the qualities of great leaders. Second, behavioral approaches examine the activities and responsibilities of leaders for the purpose of identifying effective leadership behaviours. Third, the power-influence approach is concerned with the types of power leaders possess and how they exercise this power to influence followers (i.e., in a participative manner or in a more directive manner). Fourth, the situational approach investigates the influence of contextual factors like the nature of the task, followers' characteristics, and type of organization on leadership. Finally, the fifth approach is an integrative perspective that attempts to combine elements of the above-mentioned models."

13. This assumption is changing and many military forces are beginning to realize the need to change their leadership approach towards soldiers. See Bernard M. Bass, *Transformational Leadership* for a complete explanation of this thought process.

14. Bass, 35.

15. *Ibid.*, 6–7.

16. *Ibid.*, 7.

17. United States Field Manual. 22–100. *The Army: Leadership Framework* (Washington, DC: Department of Defense, 1999),9–11, accessed at *www.adtdl.army.mil/cgi-bin/atdl.dll/fm/22-100/ch5.htm.* The manual provides a good definition for each level of leadership. It states, "Strategic leaders are responsible for large organizations and can influence several thousand to hundreds of thousands of people. They establish force structure, allocate resources, communicate strategic vision, and prepare their commands and the Army as a whole for their roles." Organizational leaders, on the other hand, can influence several thousand people. They do so indirectly, generally through a number of levels of subordinates. "The additional levels can make it more difficult for them to see results. Organizational leaders have staffs to help them lead

their people and manage their organization's resources. They establish policies and the organizational climate that support the activities of their subordinate leaders at the next level down."

18. *Ibid.*, 10.

19. *Ibid.*, 15–18.

20. Walter F. Ulmer, "Leadership into the 21st Century: Another 'Bridge Too Far?'" *Parameters, US Army War College Quarterly* (Spring 1998), 10.

21. Land Force Command, *Junior Leadership Training Manual* (Ottawa: DND, 2001). This document provides an outline of these tasks.

22. William Darryl Henderson, *Cohesion: The Human Element in Combat* (Washington, DC: National Defense University Press, 1985), 114.

23. *Ibid.*, 114.

24. Anthony Kemp, *The SAS at War: The Special Air Service Regiment 1941–1945* (London: John Murray Publishers, Ltd., 1991), Appendix D.

25. Kennedy Shaw, *The Long-Range Desert Group* (Novato, CA: Presidio Press, 1989). On page 22, Shaw provides a good description stating "man did not need his courage so often as the unfortunate infantryman suffering constant bombing and shelling up on the coast. But when, caught by enemy aircraft in open desert, he did need it — he needed it badly." However, he goes on to say that "toughness without intelligence was of no use to us, nor was extreme youth essential; speaking without statistics I should say that the twenty-five-year-olds or the nearer-thirties lasted longest and did best." This comment mirrored the experience of other SOF organizations. For example, in the First Special Service Force (FSSF) the average age of the soldiers that went through and passed training was 26 years of age. See FSSF, *Report No. 5, 1st Canadian Special Service Battalion* (National Defence Historical Section), 10–12.

26. Tom Clancy and Carl Stiner, *Shadow Warriors: Inside the Special Forces* (New York: Penguin Putnam, 2002), 132–133. In the case of the American Special Forces, soldiers are trained in a wide variety of skills and according to Clancy must be "an expert marksman on his individual weapon (a pistol) and his M-16 rifle, and be familiar with weapons, such as AK-47s ... He had to be able to shoot them with reasonable accuracy, and to take them apart and maintain them. In the case of larger weapons such as mortars and machine guns, he had to be able to emplace and employ them properly ... Each soldier was trained in explosives. He learned the kind of

charge, the shape, and the placement for bringing down a bridge or power lines, for cratering charges or breaching, for getting inside a sealed and defended building with the minimum damage to the structure ... If he had no explosives of his own, he was taught how to obtain what needed to make them from local sources. Each soldier received communications training — sending and receiving Morse code, and code writing ... [and] was capable of operating any kind of communications gear they might be using. Each soldier received advanced first-aid training."

27. Shaw also points out, "There can be no doubt whatever that much of the early and continued success of L.R.D.G.was due to the speed and thoroughness with which the New Zealanders learned desert work and life. For it is not enough to have learned how to operate, in the military sense, in the desert, though that may be half of the battle. Naturally the driver must be able to drive in conditions entirely new to him, the signalman to keep in touch, the navigator to find his way, the gunner to have his sand-filled Vickers ready ..." Shaw, 18.

28. *FM 22–100 Chapter 3, www.adtdl.army.mil/cgi-bin/atdl.dll/fm/22-100/ ch3.htm#3-1,* accessed 15 January 2004. Interestingly, this trend towards team-centred leadership is now starting to interest conventional military forces, as the nature of modern warfare changes and the need for highly skilled subordinates becomes more important to success in future operations. As such, conventional military forces are moving towards the concept of a proactive small team approach where there is mutual respect between leader and follower. This command philosophy is starting to appear in modern military doctrine. Current U.S. Army doctrine dictates, "This team identity doesn't come about just because people take an oath or join an organization; you can't force a team to come together any more than you can force a plant to grow. Rather, the team identity comes out of mutual respect among its members and a trust between leaders and subordinates. That bond between leaders and subordinates likewise springs from mutual respect as well as from discipline. The highest form of discipline is the willing obedience of subordinates who trust their leaders, understand and believe in the mission's purpose, value the team and their place in it, and have the will to see the mission through. This form of discipline produces individuals and teams who — in the really tough moments — come up with solutions themselves."

29. Kemp, 1–5.

30. After the war, Bagnold continued his research into the movement of sand, carrying out research into water-borne sand. Bagnold was a Fellow of the Royal Society and was awarded the Founders' Gold Medal of the Royal Geographical Society, the Wollaston Medal of the Geological Society of

CASTING LIGHT ON THE SHADOWS

London, the G.K. Warren Prize of the U.S. National Academy of Science, the Penrose Medal of the Geological Society of America, and the Sorby Medal of the International Association of Sedimentology. In 1978, he was the keynote speaker at a NASA sponsored conference on eolian processes on Earth and Mars.

31. According to Shaw, once the "decision was taken to organise the Long Range Desert Group for operations behind the enemy lines a call was sent out to all units of the desert army for volunteers." The call stated, "only men who do not mind a hard life, with scanty food, little water and lots of discomfort, men who possess stamina and initiative, need apply." Shaw, 22.

32. Bradford Roy and Dillon Martin, *Rogue Warrior of the SAS* (London: John Murray Publishers Ltd., 1987), 33–34. Much the same situation existed within the Special Air Service (SAS). Paddy Mayne, David Stirling's right-hand man and commander of the SAS after Stirling's capture, was a Belfast lawyer before the war, and played international rugby for the British Isles. His athletic prowess was incredible as he was also the heavyweight-boxing champion of the Irish Universities. Mayne joined the Commandos as a second lieutenant in 1940, and went to the Middle East with Layforce (British Commandos commanded by Lieutenant-Colonel Robert Laycock) where he was mentioned in dispatches for his gallantry in action.

33. In fact, their lack of formal military training was not that unusual. In the recently mobilized armies of the Allies many officers entered the conventional forces having little formal training.

34. Bass, 99.

35. Canadian leadership doctrine defines transformational leadership as "a general pattern of influence based on shared core values and mutual commitment and trust between the leader and led, and intended to effect significant or radical improvement in individual, group, or system capabilities and performance; sometimes discussed in the context of social-exchange theory." Canada, *Leadership in the Canadian Forces: Conceptual Foundations* (Kingston: Department of National Defence, 2005), 133.

36. *Ibid.*, 5. According to Lieutenant-Colonel Peter Bradley, head of the Military Leadership and Psychology department at the Royal Military College of Canada, "There are four classes of transformational leadership behaviors, referred to as the factors of transformational leadership. Each of these is summarized below. Called idealized influence, the first transformational factor is sometimes referred to as Charisma. This factor consists of behaviors in which the leader acts as a role model, cultivating faith, trust and respect in followers. This factor is probably the cornerstone of trans-

formational leadership, for without the example of a strong role model who imbues trust and loyalty into followers, the other factors of transformational leadership will not take root. Inspirational motivation refers to those behaviors in which the transformational leader communicates a vision of a desired future state with fluency and confidence, sets high standards and convinces individuals that they can achieve beyond their expectations. In this way, the transformational leader exhorts followers to transcend themselves. The transformational factor of intellectual stimulation represents those actions in which the leader promotes the development of future leaders, challenging subordinates to think for themselves and to think about old problems in innovative ways. In this way, the leader creates an atmosphere that encourages creative thinking, careful reasoning, and methodical problem solving instead of acting on unsupported opinions. Individualized consideration refers to those transformational leadership behaviors that focus on the relationship between the leader and each follower, placing special emphasis on paying personal attention to followers. Transformational leaders who are strong on this factor treat each follower individually, investing time for one-on-one communication, coaching and advising them, and recognizing subordinates' achievements." Lieutenant-Colonel Peter Bradley, "Distinguishing the Concepts of Command, Leadership and Management," in *Generalship and the Art of the Admiral: Perspectives on Canadian Senior Military Leadership*, Bernd Horn and Stephen Harris, eds. (St. Catharines, ON: Vanwell Publishing Limited, 2001), 116.

37. James Burns, *Leadership* (New York: 1978), 287.

38. *Ibid.*, 287–291.

39. *Ibid.*, 99.

40. Shaw, 27–28.

41. Layforce was a commando force commanded by Lieutenant-Colonel Robert Laycock, which consisted of 7, 8, and 11 Commandos, Nos. 50 and 52 Middle East Commandos and the Special Boat Section.

42. Alan Hoe and Eric Morris, *Re-Enter the SAS: The Special Air Service and the Malayan Emergency* (London, Leo Cooper, 1994), 3.

43. *Ibid.*, 3. Hoe and Morris provide an excellent account of the logic of Stirling's assessment. They state, "One of these special sub-units of 12 men could cover a target previously requiring the deployment of 5 troops of a Commando (200 men). Using such a force should mean that up to 50 aircraft could be destroyed by any sub-unit. It therefore followed that a prop-

erly trained and equipped special unit of 200 men could attack up to 10 different targets at the same time on the same night compared to only one objective using current Commando techniques This means that only 25 percent success with the special unit would be equivalent to many times the maximum result of a Commando raid. The effect on German morale would be very significant."

44. *Ibid.*, 16. Hoe and Morris give an interesting perspective on the selection on the original members, "his immediate priority, though, was to weld a disparate group of men into a cohesive fighting force. He had no track record himself in combat and the men he was to lead in battle were a pretty tough crowd, all of them individualists and likely to be highly critical of any officer who did not come up to their own standards." Looking back after 45 years had elapsed, he had the following to say about the 'Originals' of L Detachment, "In a sense they weren't really controllable. They were harnessable and all had a sense of individuality. The object was to give them a sense of purpose and once they were harnessed to that proposition, they policed themselves, so to speak. And that goal had to be a very exacting one.... That bag of vagabonds had to grasp what they had to do in order to get there, which included discipline." Although most of them were escaping from conventional regimental discipline, they didn't fully appreciate that they were running into a much more exacting type of discipline. There is no real common denominator that can be used to classify the Originals, the first fifty-odd recruits to the SAS, most of them had done their basic training in one of the Guards regiments and most had completed the Commando course. Few had any experience of combat.

45. *Ibid.*, 99. An emphasis on this type of critical evaluation and problem detection is now a critical component within SOF training. It allows both the leader and the group to come up with creative ideas to complex problems. This requires both planning and organizational skills as well critical evaluation and problem detection skills.

46. Bass, 100.

47. The concept of operations for the Commandos was "to collect together a number of individuals trained to fight independently and not as a formed military unit. For this reason a commando organization is really intended to provide nothing more than a pool of specialized soldiers from which irregular units of any size and type can be very quickly created to undertake any particular task." See John Parker, *Commandos: The Inside Story of Britain's Most Elite Fighting Force* (London: Headline Book Publishing, 2000), 35–37.

48. Shaw, 51–52.

49. Hoe and Morris, 3–9.

50. *Ibid.*, 3–9.

51. It should also be noted that most SOF units were never given priority in equipment issue and generally got what was left over or what they could scrounge,

52. *Ibid.*, 11.

53. That in itself meant that a certain number of the soldiers were undesirable characters who would never have been any use in any regiment; it was the usual Army principle of getting rid of the bad hats.

54. Adrian Weale, *Secret Warfare: Special Operations Forces from the Great Game to the SAS* (London: Hodder Headline PLC, 1998), 160.

55. Hoe and Morris, 11–15.

56. Bass, 99.

57. Shaw, 20.

58. Bass, 7. According to Bass, laissez-faire leadership "is the avoidance or absence of leadership and is, by definition, most inactive, as well as most ineffective according to almost all research on the style. As opposed to transactional leadership, laissez-faire represents a non-transaction. Necessary decisions are not made. Actions are delayed. Responsibilities of leadership are ignored. Authority remains unused."

59. Some of these traits also form the basis of Bass's transformational leadership model.

60. Tony Geraghty, *Who Dares Wins: The Special Air Service — 1950 to the Gulf War* (London: Time Warner Paperbacks, 1993), 507.

61. Marquis, 24–26.

62. Ulmer, 8.

63. Burns, 20.

# 5

## When Cultures Collide:
### *The Conventional Military/SOF Chasm*

### Bernd Horn

The culmination of the evolution of Special Operations Forces (SOF) and their ultimate legitimacy became evident in the aftermath of the terrorist attacks in New York on 11 September 2001. The immediate reliance on SOF by political and military decision makers to strike back at those responsible for the unprecedented attack signalled that SOF had completed their transformation from a force of desperation to the force of choice. Nonetheless, the road to this point for SOF was a difficult one. Throughout their relatively short history there have been constant themes, such as the competition for scarce resources, unorthodox concepts of discipline and accountability, and divergent cultural and philosophical methodologies of operation, that have always been, and remain, associated with the debate on their existence.

Ironically, the unique attributes and characteristics of SOF that have made them the potent capability that they are today are in some ways their Achilles heel. Their uniqueness and definable difference from the conventional military, has always created a barrier, if not a chasm. As such, although SOF are now positioned to be the workhorse of asymmetrical operations, they must educate themselves, as well as others, and strive to work in an interdependent manner with the conventional military. If they fail do so, they risk again becoming constrained and marginalized at a time when they are needed most.

## WHO ARE THESE SHADOW WARRIORS?

Special Operations Forces are generally defined by journalists as "the toughest, smartest, most secretive, fittest, best-equipped and consistently lethal killers in the U.S. [or any other] military."[1] However, a more traditional definition spawned from SOF's Second World War and postwar beginnings describes them as forces that are "specially selected, specially trained, specially equipped, and given special missions and support."[2] But this somewhat simplistic description has been eclipsed by a more comprehensive and nuanced explanation that better captures their shadowy role in the international security environment. It is generally accepted that modern SOF are specially selected, organized, trained, and equipped military and paramilitary forces that conduct high-risk, high-value special operations to achieve military, political, economic, or informational objectives by generally unconventional means in hostile, denied, or politically sensitive areas, in peace, conflict, or war.[3]

Not surprisingly, as with most military concepts, equipment, and organizations, the United States normally sets the standard. It is no different with SOF. As such, the Americans look to SOF to conduct nine core tasks:

- Counterterrorism (CT) — actions taken to preclude, preempt, and resolve terrorist actions throughout the entire threat spectrum, including antiterrorism and counterterrorism[4]
- Special Reconnaissance (SR) — reconnaissance and surveillance actions conducted as special operations in hostile, denied, or politically sensitive environments to collect or verify information of strategic or operational significance, employing military capabilities not normally found in conventional forces.
- Direct Action (DA) — short-term seize, destroy, exploit, capture, damage, or recovery operations.
- Unconventional Warfare (UW) — organizing, training, equipping, advising, and assisting indigenous and surrogate forces in military and paramilitary operations of long duration.

- Counter-proliferation (CP) — combating the proliferation of nuclear, biological and chemical weapons; intelligence collection and analysis; support of diplomacy; arms control; and export controls.
- Foreign Internal Defence (FID) — organizing, training, advising, and assisting host-nation military and paramilitary forces to enable these forces to free and protect their society from subversion, lawlessness, and insurgency.
- Civil Affairs Operations (CAO) — activities that establish relations between military/civil authorities to facilitate military operations.
- Psychological Operations (PSYOP) — planned operations to influence behaviour of foreign forces and governments.
- Information Operations (IO) — actions taken to achieve information superiority by affecting adversary information and information systems while defending one's own information and information systems.[5]

## EVOLUTION OF SPECIAL OPERATIONS FORCES

The nine core tasks represent the mandate of modern SOF. However, those principal missions have evolved over time. Special Operations Forces are largely a phenomena of the Second World War. Paradoxically, they were largely born in crisis from a position of weakness. In the immediate aftermath of the early German victories, the Allies found themselves devoid of major equipment, with questionable military strength, and on the defensive throughout the world. Nonetheless, combative British Prime Minister Winston Churchill gave direction that action be taken by "specially trained troops of the hunter class" to create a reign of terror on the coast line of the occupied territories based on the "butcher and bolt" principle scant days after the dramatic withdrawal from Dunkirk. Churchill realized that this offensive capability, limited though it might be, would be a tonic to public morale, maintain an offensive spirit in the military, and force the Germans to dedicate resources to the defence.

As such, during the early years of the war a plethora of SOF units and organizations such as the British Commandos, Long Range Desert Group (LRDG), the Special Air Service (SAS), Special Operations Executive (SOE), and American Rangers, emerged, creating a means to strike back at the seemingly invincible German military machine. As the tide of the war shifted, they evolved to provide specific capabilities not resident with the larger conventional military and perform distinct tasks such as raiding, sabotage, and economy of effort missions to tie down enemy forces. But these activities were soon eclipsed by tasks such as strategic reconnaissance and unconventional warfare.

In the end, despite the overall success and value of special operations, SOF never fully received acceptance by the larger military community. The irregular nature of the tactics, the unconventional, if not rakish nature of the operators, who were often seen as lacking discipline and military decorum, as well as the almost independent status of the SOF organizations were alien and distasteful to the more traditional and conservative-minded military leadership. Not surprisingly, at the end of the war most SOF organizations were disbanded.

However, in the post-war world unique circumstances that called for specific skill sets not readily available in the conventional military once again necessitated the resurrection of special operation forces. The savage wars of peace in Malaya, Oman, and Yemen, to name but a few, highlighted the strength of specially trained and highly skilled SOF manned by intelligent, adaptive, and highly capable individuals. Increasingly, these relatively small units were very effective and successful against countering insurgencies and other low level conflict.

Their success also became in some ways a handicap. It generated increased antagonism and jealousy between SOF and the conventional military. In addition, it led to them being offered as a panacea in all kinds of situations. For instance, as America became more involved in Vietnam there was an explosion of SOF-type units in response to the war's escalating and complex nature. As unique tasks emerged, such as long-range reconnaissance and interdiction, riverine operations, and unconventional warfare, new units were created to address each requirement. Unfortunately, the sudden spike in demand was met in many cases by lowering selection standards, where in fact they existed, which inevitably led to a lowering of the overall standard of individuals serving in those units. This resulted, rightly or wrongly, in the reputation of SOF as largely a collection of "snake eaters," cowboys, and soldiers of questionable quality running amok. This legacy would haunt them for decades.

Not surprisingly, much like the experience in the Second World War, SOF were still, if not increasingly, marginalized by the mainstream Army. Very few saw the utility of SOF in the Cold War paradigm of "Air Land Battle" which pitted large heavily armoured mass formations against one another on the North European plain. But despite the conventional force bias, a fundamental shift in the threat picture to Western industrialized nations erupted in the early 1970s ensuring SOF received renewed support. Terrorism became recognized as a significant "new" menace that required specific skills that were not resident within the military institution at large. Once again, specially selected individuals who were capable of agility in thought, adaptable in operations, blessed with superior martial skills, and able to conduct high-risk operations provided the solution.

This turn of events provided an increased impetus for SOF. Relatively small, highly skilled, and mobile units that proved extremely effective in operations, and that presented a relatively small footprint, provided the political and military leadership with a viable response. Moreover, they soon realized that SOF could be employed in a myriad of potentially politically sensitive operations. As such, SOF underwent a renaissance in the late 1980s and early 1990s, most visibly represented by the creation of the United States Special Operations Command (USSOCOM) in 1987. American Special Operations Forces now had a unified command, control over their own resources and representation in the highest levels of the U.S. Department of Defense (DoD). SOF, in the American case at any rate, seemed to have been finally accepted as a fundamental component of the military. This was solidified to some extent in the Gulf War of 1990–91. SOF provided strategic reconnaissance, rear area interdiction, and direct action raids, and carried out the politically charged task of hunting Scud missiles. In the process they seemed to earn a new respect from the mainstream military.

But their acceptance, utility, and relevance became even more pronounced in the new millennium. The devastating terrorist attack on the twin towers of the World Trade Center in New York City on 11 September 2001 transformed the perception of SOF and resulted in their acceptance as a core element of any military. Faced with an elusive foe that relied on dispersion, complex terrain, and asymmetric tactics, many key political and military decision makers quickly realized that only a flexible, adaptive, and agile response would suffice. SOF, with its organizational flexibility, rapid mobility, and underlying strength of exceptionally trained personnel answered the call yet again.

## CONSTANT THEMES

But the rise of Special Operations Forces to its current preferred status was not an easy road, and its future is not necessarily assured. Quite simply, there has always existed a cultural and philosophical chasm between the conventional military and SOF. Their differences are substantial, fuelling an ever smouldering fire. In essence, detractors argue that SOF are "expensive, independent, arrogant, out of uniform, [operate] outside normal chains of command, and [are] too specialized for [their] own good."[6] Major-General Julian Thompson, captured the essence of the traditional argument when he stated that "descending on the enemy, killing a few guards, blowing up the odd pillbox, and taking a handful of prisoners was not a cost-effective use of ships, craft and highly trained soldiers."[7] Similarly, renowned American military analyst Tom Clancy observed that SOF "units and their men are frequently seen as "sponges," sucking up prized personnel and funds at the expense of "regular' units."[8] In essence, the criticisms and enmity are long-standing. They are also based on constant themes that revolve around competition for scarce resources, concepts of discipline and accountability, and a distinct difference in cultural and philosophical methodologies.

### Competition for Resources — "Skimming the Cream"

Nothing flames institutional enmity more than the competition for scarce resources. A nation's treasure allows for expansion, modernization, organizational well-being, and training. Simply put, it dictates effectiveness, power, and status. However, there is never enough — and access to it is always tenaciously guarded. From the beginning SOF were seen as interlopers that siphoned off scarce personnel, equipment, and money.

No issue engenders animosity between conventional forces and SOF more than the "poaching" of personnel. It is not surprising that commanders are resentful that some of their best officers and men are attracted to, or recruited by, SOF units. "Almost invariably the men volunteering," explained historian Philip Warner, "are the most enterprising, energetic and least dispensable."[9] The "poachers" themselves conceded as much. "In the first place, there is probably quite a bit of understandable jealousy that any newly formed unit should be given priority as to men and equipment," acknowledged Major-General David Lloyd Owen, the commander of the LRDG. He added, "It is only the normal reaction of any good Commanding Officer to resent having his best men attracted to such 'crackpot' outfits."[10]

It was for this reason that Field Marshal Sir Alan Brooke, Chief of the Imperial General Staff, never agreed with Churchill's special forces policy. He felt that it was "a dangerous drain on the quality of an infantry battalion."[11] The legendary Field Marshal Viscount Slim was in strong agreement. He noted that special units "were usually formed by attracting the best men from normal units by better conditions, promises of excitement and not a little propaganda ... The result of these methods was undoubtedly to lower the quality of the rest of the Army, especially of the infantry, not only by skimming the cream off it, but by encouraging the idea that certain of the normal operations of war were so difficult that only specially equipped *corps d'élite* could be expected to undertake them."[12]

The post-war attitudes were no different. SOF "ate up far too many junior leaders who were badly needed in the infantry battalions," criticized Lieutenant-Colonel J.P. O'Brien in an article in the *Army Quarterly*, in 1948.[13] Former serving Canadian officer and historian John A. English agreed. He argued that Moshe Dayan's emphasis on expanding the Israeli airborne force, during his tenure as chief of staff, actually detracted from the effectiveness of the Israeli infantry as a whole. He believed that the expanded recruitment had a strong "skimming effect" that lowered the quality of soldier that was received by the standing force Golani Brigade.[14] Similarly, Tom Clancy in his ongoing analysis of American combat capability wrote, "a private in an airborne unit might well be qualified to be a sergeant or squad leader in a regular formation."[15] To exacerbate this problem, SOF units most often utilize a higher proportion of senior non-commissioned officers (NCOs). This has the result of reinforcing the claim that the quality of the Army suffers from the deficiency of good NCOs.[16]

Another problem with the "skimming effect" was the negative consequences the process was thought to have on those who failed to pass the high standards normally imposed during selection. Alan Brooke and Slim were two of many who were convinced that those rejected had their confidence undermined by failure.[17] Furthermore, the nature of these highly selective units created an impression that everyone else was second-best. But it is more than just an impression. It is a belief. "I was glad they [those not selected] left camp immediately and didn't say any awkward farewells," confessed one SOF operator, "They were social lepers and I didn't want to risk catching the infection they carried."[18] This attitude is a dangerous one. As one former SAS member noted, "elitism is counter-productive, it alienates you from other people."[19]

But the condemnation of SOF does not rest solely on the issue of purloined personnel. Another general complaint, as voiced by Field Marshal Slim, was that "the equipment of these special units was more generous than that of normal formations."[20] One historian observed that "Special forces are often the subject of envy, dislike and misunderstanding because they are ... issued with equipment which is often more lavish than that provided to their parent units."[21]

There is a timelessness to this issue as demonstrated by the comments of General Fred Franks in regards to the expansion of American SOF in the mid-eighties, specifically the Rangers. "As an elite force [Rangers]," observed Franks, "they were given ample training budgets, stable personnel policies (less rotation in and out than normal units), their pick of volunteers, and leaders and commanders who were already experienced company commanders."[22] This type of special status generated continual complaints. The core of the argument was always that the investment of valuable, highly skilled, and scarce personnel, combined with the lavish consumption of material resources, failed to provide a worthwhile return for the costs incurred. The efforts of special units were likened to "breaking windows by throwing guineas (gold coins) at them."[23]

In short, conventional commanders, whether justified or not, were continually incensed at the cost of SOF. Special Operations Forces were perceived to receive the best personnel and too much funding, despite the fact that they normally spent less actual time in combat. But what incensed the conventional military even more was the fact that when SOF did undertake combat operations their casualty rates were often horrendous, reinforcing their argument of wastefulness. On the surface their argument seems to be justified. A brief sampling of operations during the Second World War quickly demonstrates the high-risk nature of SOF endeavours. For example, the British Commando raid at Tragino suffered a 100 percent casualty rate;[24] the first SAS raid in North Africa 64 percent;[25] the mission to kill Rommel 96 percent;[26] and the British Commando landing at Marina, in Italy 48 percent. For the "greatest raid of all," St. Nazaire, the cost was 79 percent of the commandos and 52 percent of the naval force, who were either killed or captured.[27] In total, British Commandos suffered a significantly higher wartime mortality rate than the rest of the Army.[28] The experience of the Australian commandos was similar. They incurred a wartime casualty rate of 34 percent.[29]

In addition, naval combat demolition units suffered a casualty rate of 52 percent[30] and the First Special Service Force suffered an incredible 78 percent casualty rate in Italy. In the same theatre, during the attempted break-in at Cisterna, of 767 American Rangers who crawled forward in the early morning of 30 January 1944, only 6 returned.[31] In summary, it is generally accepted that SOF suffered a higher percentage of casualties although normally employed for less time in actual combat.

More contemporary SOF operations reinforce the trend. During Operation Eagle Claw, the attempt to rescue the American hostages in Iran, in 1980, all casualties at Desert One were SOF. During Operation Urgent Fury, the invasion of Grenada in 1983, 47 percent of American casualties were SOF and six years later during the action in Panama, Operation Just Cause, the number stood at 48 percent. SOF casualties in Desert Storm in 1991, represented 17 percent of those suffered and 62 percent in Mogadishu in 1993. As of 2003, 63 percent of American casualties suffered as part of Operation Enduring Freedom were SOF.[32] "The commandos [SOF]," calculated one military analyst, "are statistically nine times as likely to die as regular soldiers...."[33]

### Concepts of Discipline and Accountability

Although the apparent preferred staffing and wastefulness of SOF engenders ill will, nothing creates more contention then the perceived lack of discipline and military decorum of SOF. To those on the outside, units that do not fit the conventional mould, specifically those described as elite, special, or unique, are often criticized for being a "law onto themselves." Sociologist Charles Cotton, in his studies of military culture, noted that "their [SOF/elite] cohesive spirit is a threat to the chain of command and wider cohesion."[34]

This is often a result of the fact that the leadership and discipline are informal within SOF and the normal protocol and emphasis placed on ceremony and deportment relaxed. Professor Eliot Cohen revealed, "an almost universally observed characteristic of elite [SOF] units is their lack of formal discipline — and sometimes a lack of substantive discipline as well." His research determined that "elite units often disregard spit and polish or orders about saluting."[35]

He was not mistaken. General de la Billière recalled that as a junior officer in the SAS, "The men, for their part, never called me 'Sir' unless they wanted to be rude."[36] Historian Eric Morris noted, "the LRDG and other like units did offer a means of escape from those petty tediums and irritants of everyday life in the British Army. Drills, guards, fatigues and inspections were almost totally absent."[37] Another military historian observed that "[mad Mike] Calvert, [Commander 2 SAS Brigade] like many fighting soldiers was not particularly concerned by the trivia of, for example, military appearance [since] uniformity and smartness have little bearing on a unit's ability to fight."[38] But without a doubt this "trivial" aspect has an enormous impact on how the respective unit is perceived by others, namely outsiders.

This was not lost on the special operators. "We were already conspicuous by our lack of dress code," confessed one SAS non-commissioned officer (NCO), "The green army always dresses the same."[39] One new American special forces operator recalled his amazement on arriving at his unit. "Sergeants Major are the walking, breathing embodiment of everything that's right in the US Army," he explained. Yet his first glimpse of his new sergeant-major caught him unprepared. "This guy looked like Joe Shit the Ragman," he exclaimed, "His shirt was wide open and he wore no T-shirt. His dog-tags were gold plated. His hat was tipped up on the back of his head, and he wore a huge, elaborately curled and waxed handlebar moustache."[40] in Afghanistan a reporter observed, "Few complete uniforms were in evidence" in the company of SOF soldiers. "These troops," he wrote, "wore jeans, T-shirts, and photojournalist vests, plus fleece jackets to shield themselves from the harsh Afghan winter [and] their hair hung lank around their ears." He added, "All had thick, bushy beards."[41] A Canadian staff officer in Afghanistan observed, "all [SOF] wore beards like it was part of their uniform." He added, "you couldn't recognize who they were from a distance — whether they were friendly or enemy. They had different vehicles, no uniforms — you could spot them a mile away."[42]

The fact of the matter is that SOF realize that their lax discipline and dress codes irritate the conventional Army. This is part of the SOF appeal, as is their need to clearly differentiate themselves from the "regular" Army. This is also why it generates such enmity from the conventional hierarchy. Nonetheless, much of this dynamic is based on the type of individuals that actually join these units. David Stirling, the founder of the SAS, reflected that the "Originals" were not really "controllable" but rather "harnessable."[43] Sergeant Dave Richardson, conceded the Marauders, "hated the GI routine of garrison life, standing formations and inspections."[44] The Rangers were acknowledged to consist largely of "mavericks who couldn't make it in conventional units."[45] William Darby, the Ranger's first commanding officer, said commanding them "was like driving a team of very high spirited horses. No effort was needed to get them to go forward. The problem was to hold them in check."[46]

American Special Forces ("Green Berets"), were later similarly described as those "who wanted to try something new and challenging, and who chafed at rigid discipline."[47] Furthermore, General de la Billière observed that "Most officers and men here do not really fit in normal units of the Army, and that's why they're here in the SAS, which is not like anything else in the Services."[48] He assumed, most of the volunteers, like himself, "were individualists who wanted to break away from the formal drill-machine discipline" which existed in the Army as a whole.[49] This fits a similar pattern. According to General Peter Schoomaker, who joined Delta under its founding commander Colonel Charlie Beckwith, "Beckwith was looking for a bunch of bad cats who wanted to do something different."[50]

This element of self-selection, combined with the feeling of accomplishment, as one of the few who has successfully passed selection; and the self-confidence born from challenging, difficult, and hazardous training, creates an aura of invincibility and an intense loyalty to what is perceived as a very exclusive group. An intimate bond is deepened further through shared hardship and danger. Members of these "special" groups frequently develop an outlook that treats those outside the "club" as inferior and unworthy of respect. Often, this sense of independence from the conventional Army, as well as the lack of respect for traditional forms of discipline, spawn what some analysts describe as the emergence of units that are more akin to militant clans than military organizations.[51] Needless to say, this type of organization and institutional attitude is anathema to a military that prides itself on decorum, tradition, and uniformity.

Not surprisingly, the arrogance and deliberate insubordination of SOF operators often fuels the fire. No image is more representative than the scene from *Black Hawk Down* when a captain gives direction to a group of senior NCOs. Upon completion, the group, less one, acknowledges the orders. The captain quickly confirms with the recalcitrant NCO if he understood the direction. The Delta Force sergeant replies nonchalantly, almost contemptuously, "yeah, I heard ya." This is a classic of art reflecting reality. One operator laughingly described how he had failed to salute two "crap-hat" [regular Army] captains. He explained that he "couldn't because he was smoking and couldn't do two things at once."[52] Similarly, while en route to the Falkland Islands in 1982, an SAS NCO recalled that naval officers in the fleet expected people to move when they came through the narrow passageways of the ship. However, he amusedly recounted, "our guys did not — it caused problems." He explained, "Our guys were not used to being talked to that way."[53]

In another case, a former support officer of a CT organization revealed, "assaulters would refuse to listen to others regardless of rank because 'you hadn't done selection.'"[54] A staff officer overseas complained that a clear double standard existed between SOF and conventional troops. For example, the fraternization policy was aggressively enforced — troops were punished, but the SOF were not touched. Similarly, an executive assistant to a sector commander in Bosnia disclosed that "whenever they [SOF operators] didn't like what they were told they went in to see [circumvented the chain of command] the commander."[55]

In the end, the arrogance and aloofness, bred from a cult of elitism that is often endemic within groups that are specially selected, develops and nurtures an "in-group" mentality that is dangerously inwardly focused. They trust only themselves, that is those who have passed the rigorous selection standards and tests. Anthropologist Donna Winslow confirmed the negative aspects that often arise from an emphasis on the exclusivity of this "warrior cult." It nurtures an unassailable belief, she insisted, that "only those who have done it know, or can be trusted, or more dangerously yet, can give direction."[56] Alan Bell, formerly of the SAS, confessed that we "tended to have an arrogance that we knew it all, did it all, and had nothing to learn." Moreover, he acknowledged that they would work only with Delta Force or Sea Air Land (SEAL) Team Six — no one else. "We figured it wasn't worth our time," he confessed, "we doubted their capabilities."[57] In the Falklands War in 1982, the refusal of some SAS operators to listen to civilian experts cost them dearly when they crashed their helicopters during the retaking of South Georgia Island. "We didn't take their advice," conceded a member of the SAS, "because they were civilians [British Antarctic Survey team]."[58]

As shown in the example above, this type of attitude has consequences. Aside from the operational impact is the often ignored institutional effect. "Too often," observed Tom Clancy, "there's friction, competition, and rivalry — a situation often made worse by the sometimes heavy-handed ways of the SOF community."[59] In the end, this reluctance to work with others, compounded by arrogance, breeds animosity, mistrust, and barriers to cooperation and information sharing with outside agencies. In the end, everyone loses.

### Divergent Cultural and Philosophical Methodology

Competition for scarce resources and disagreement on comportment and discipline were not the only basis for conflict, disagreement and antagonism. Rather, these elements only support the larger issue — the divergent cultural and philosophical methodology of SOF and the conventional Army. General Leslie Hollis captured the essence of the debate when he stated that there existed a misconception within the conventional Army that special formations are "a lot of resolute but irresponsible cut-throats, who roam around the campaign area, spreading confusion amongst their own troops and consternation amongst those of the enemy."[60]

But part of the problem is generated from a limited and restrained philosophical understanding of war. M.R.D. Foot, a Second World War intelligence officer for the SAS and British historian, stated that special operations "are unorthodox coups ... unexpected strokes of violence, usually mounted and executed outside the military establishment of the day."[61] For those trapped in a dogmatic conventional doctrinal mind set — SOF, almost by definition, become problematic. "To the orthodox, traditional soldier," explained Colonel Aaron Banks, "it [UW] was something slimy, underhanded, illegal, and ungentlemanly. It did not fit in the honor code of that profession of arms."[62] Almost 50 years later, the same sentiment remains. "There is a cultural aversion on the part of conventional soldiers, sailors, and airmen," explained Lieutenant-General Samuel Wilson, "to things that smell of smoke and mirrors and feats of derring do.... It's a little too romantic.... It's not doing it the hard way."[63]

The nature of war and how it is fought was not the only issue of concern. Commanders often likened SOF to "Private Armies," that often tend to "become an object of suspicion to the public army."[64] This is often due to the fact that SOF value action and have little institutional patience for bureaucracy. Coupled with an "ends justifies the means attitude" conventional feathers are likely to get ruffled. "One danger of the private army [SOF]," commented one senior officer, "is certainly that it gets into the habit of using wrong channels."[65] He was not wrong. Calvert conceded that "A private army ... short-circuits command."[66]

This is not surprising since SOF-type units have often owed their existence or survival to a powerful mentor who is well-positioned to look after his wards. For instance, Prime Minister Winston Churchill took great interest in the development of the commandos and he supported other similar, aggressive, unorthodox units. General George C. Marshall personally pushed his subordinates to support the establishment of the American Rangers, and his political master, President Franklin D. Roosevelt allowed the director of the Office of Strategic Services (OSS) to maintain a direct pipeline to the White House. Later,

President John F. Kennedy heaped lavish attention on the American Special Forces much to the chagrin of his conventional chiefs of staff, and recently, it was former Secretary of Defense Donald Rumsfeld who personally ensured that American SOF received starring roles in U.S. operations, as well as hefty increases in personnel and budgets. Not surprisingly, SOF are more than willing to use their special connections to further their cause. Equally evident, this type of special access and privilege infuriates conventional commanders who often try to even the score whenever possible.

The refusal to cooperate or work with conventional forces, due to "security concerns" creates another impediment to co-existence. Often SOF operators arrive in theatre to conduct secret missions without informing the "in-place unit." Their presence normally generates suspicion with belligerent forces who recognize "new players," as well as subsequent negative consequences if SOF action occurs. However, at the end of the normally short operation the "in-place" conventional force must deal with the brunt of the belligerent reaction. To add insult to injury, the need for "operational security" is normally used as the reason for completely ignoring conventional forces. Yet, paradoxically, the compulsion to ensure that they are easily recognized from their conventional military brethren, in all settings, seems to override the need for secrecy. In fact, it compels them to utilize exotic equipment, uniforms, and dress codes completely apart from the normal military patterns, even when not required to do so for operational purposes. As a result, paradoxically, they are routinely easily identified.[67]

A corollary detrimental effect to their exaggerated emphasis on secrecy and refusal to work with conventional forces is the fact that they are often misunderstood or not understood at all. "I was appalled," conceded former SAS Commander Major-General Tony Jeapes, "by the lack of understanding of the Regiment's capabilities by those in high positions." He conceded that the "Regiment's insistence upon secrecy in all it did had become counterproductive."[68] Although operational security is paramount, secrecy in and of itself often becomes a tool to avoid scrutiny and build barriers to the outside world. This security consciousness has also led in some cases to a refusal to use computers that are connected to the outside world. This inflated sense of secrecy is not only laughable at times but more important, an impediment to progress and a contributor to the gulf between SOF and conventional forces.

But it is not only practices and overt attitudes that elicit conflict. The philosophical outlook of individuals that are drawn to SOF also creates tension. "Of course, we're all concerned with people who are different," exclaimed a former commander of the 75th Ranger Regiment, "We are uncomfortable with it ... in particular in the military because it is so structured and when all of a sudden you have unstructured beings, people are not comfortable with them.... We had some people who had tremendous capabilities, tremendous skills, but people didn't want to be around them ... These free thinkers. These people who did things in an unconventional manner."[69] This has always been a major issue that is not always understood. Mavericks, critical thinkers, individuals who are capable of conceptualizing innovative tactics, equipment, and methodologies that are alien to the conventional wisdom were, and still are, often marginalized. Yet their ideas and contributions, once properly harnessed and allowed to flourish, provide incredible pay back. This is the strength of SOF.

This was evident from the start. "You'd volunteered for the Commandos," explained one recruit, "they realised that you were human beings and you had a bit of sense, that you didn't need to be roared at and shouted at, screamed at all the time." He added, "Not only that, if you did anything, even in training, everything was explained to you. If you'd a different idea, even as a lowly Private, you could say 'Well, sir, don't you think if we went that way instead of this way it would be easier?' If you were right that was the method that was adopted."[70] One SAS commander explained the concept. "I never had a roll call or kit checks before operations [in Malaya]," he stated, "If a man could not look after himself our opinion was that he had no place in the SAS." He added, "The men responded to this trust and never once did I have cause to regret it."[71]

It is this philosophy that is so alien to the conventional Army but resonates so strongly with SOF. It is SOF's greatest strength. It is the greatest cause for the chasm between SOF and conventional forces — the individual operators.

## THE STRENGTH OF SOF: THE MAN AND THE ORGANIZATION

Nothing better encapsulates the essence of the individual operator than an anecdote from the Vietnam War. An American Studies and Observations Group (SOG) team was completely surrounded by North Vietnamese Army (NVA) forces. In response to the forward air controller's grim assessment that "It sounds pretty bad," the SOG team leader replied, "No, no. I've got them right where I want 'em — surrounded from the inside."[72] This mix of confidence, bravado, and single mindedness of purpose highlights the essence of the SOF operator.

From the beginning the SOF warrior was distinctly different from his conventional brethren. "In truth," explained a Second World War journal, "they [SOF] have the best qualities of the modern soldier to a high degree — intelligence, initiative, skill and cool, calculating courage."[73] Undeniably, SOF operators are a breed apart. "In the Regiment," confided one SAS member, "we thrived on impossible missions. They were our lifeblood. Our job was to make the impossible possible."[74] To achieve that goal meant adaptability, intelligence, tenacity, and toughness. "The reality is quiet, often tired, but determined bodies of men, working together to overcome adversity," explained one former commando, "their most important quality is the ability to keep going until the job is done."[75]

And, it is not just anyone who is capable of such a feat. The focus on the individual, specifically their capability is not surprising when one considers the rigorous selection process and the subsequent standards achieved. As such, SOF can be broken down into roughly three tiers that correspond to both the rigour of the selection standards, and the respective role equated with each level. For example, "Tier 1" SOF consists of primarily "Black Ops," or counterterrorism. Normally, only 10 to 15 percent of those attempting selection are successful. What makes this number so impressive is that a large percentage of those trying are already second or third tier SOF members. Organizations that fall into this category include the U.S. 1st Special Forces Operational Detachment — Delta, the German Grenzschutzgruppe-9 (GSG 9), the Canadian Joint Task Force Two (JTF-2), and the Polish Commandos — Grupa Reagowania Operacyjno Mobilnego (GROM) (Operational Mobile Response Group).[76]

"Tier 2" SOF reflects those organizations that have a selection pass rate of between 20 to 30 percent. They are normally entrusted with high value tasks such as strategic reconnaissance and unconventional warfare. It is at this level that selection is separated from training because the skill sets are considered so difficult, that the testers are looking only for attributes that cannot be inculcated. The actual skills required can be taught later during the training phase. Some examples include the American Special Forces (also referred to as Green Berets), the American SEALs, and the British, Australian and New Zealand SAS.[77]

The final grouping, or "Tier 3," consists of those units, such as the American Rangers that have a selection success rate of 40 to 45 percent, and whose primary mission is "Direct Action." At this level selection is mixed with training. However, the quality control line is drawn here. Generally units below this line are not considered SOF.[78]

Undeniably, selection is all important. "Our assessment and selection programs," explained General Wayne Downing, a former USSOCOM commander, "are designed to get people who do things in an unconventional manner. Who are accustomed to working in scenarios and in situations that are very unstructured.... Our people will generally come up with a very novel approach of how to solve problems, and many times people on the conventional side of the armed forces are very uncomfortable because our people do not do things in the traditional ways."[79] Rear-Admiral Ray Smith, a former commander of the Naval Special Warfare Command was more to the point. "We want a kid who can think," he asserted, "who can make decisions on his own ... under very stressful conditions."[80] As such, it is no surprise then that USSOCOM commander General Charles Holland proclaimed that "The SOF warrior is one of our Nation's great assets: Superbly trained, physically tough, culturally aware, an independent thinker — a quiet professional."[81]

In the end, the SOF soldier is defined by his intellect, role, and philosophical approach to warfare. Moreover, they are capable of operating in an environment of ambiguity, complexity, and change. Undeniably, SOF operators have evolved from the toughened commando killers of the Second World War to warriors capable of adapting to and thinking through the complex environment that the military now finds itself in. These are surroundings that require a warrior ethos combined with language proficiency, cultural awareness, political sensitivity, and the ability to use Information Age technology — in essence, warrior-diplomats.[82]

## A HISTORY OF INSTITUTIONAL HOSTILITY

But, as already elucidated, there exists a historic chasm between the SOF operator and his unit, almost by virtue of their characteristics and practices, and the conventional military (and their dogmatic and limited mind-set). "Almost all of the elite [SOF] units we have studied," revealed Professor Cohen, "faced considerable bureaucratic hostility — enmity translated into effective harassment."[83] Noel Koch, a key DoD proponent of SOF reform in the 1980s, resignedly acceded that "I have discovered in critical areas of the Pentagon, on the subject of special operations force revitalization, that when they [DoD officials] say no, they mean no;

when they say maybe, they mean no; and when they say yes, they mean no, and if they meant anything but no, they wouldn't be there."[84]

This attitude has always been the case. Even the authoritative Prime Minister Churchill had a difficult time establishing commandos and other unconventional organizations. "The resistances of the War Office were obstinate," reflected Churchill, "and increased as the professional ladder was descended." He explained that "the idea that large bands of favoured 'irregulars,' with their unconventional attire and easy-and-free bearing, should throw an implied slur on the efficiency and courage of the Regular battalions was odious to men who had given all their lives to the organization and discipline of permanent units." He added, "The colonels of many of our finest regiments were aggrieved."[85] One official report acknowledged, "Home Forces have consistently used their predominating influence at the War Office to thwart the efforts of those well disposed to us."[86] In trying to raise the SAS, Stirling admonished that "I found during this and subsequent stages, that the A.G. [Adjutant General] Branch was unfailingly obstructive and uncooperative."[87]

Field Marshal Sir William Slim was representative of the traditional military mind set at the time. "Private armies," he proclaimed, "are expensive, wasteful, and unnecessary."[88] His disdain for their ideas and what they represented was clearly evident in the profile he painted. He stated that these "racketeers" were in essence of two kinds, "those whose acquaintance with war was confined to large non-fighting staffs where they had had time and opportunity to develop their theories, and tough, cheerful fellows who might be first-class landed on a beach at night with orders to scupper a sentry-post, but whose experience was about the range of a tommy-gun ... Few of them had anything really new to say, and the few that had, usually forgot that a new idea should have something to recommend it besides just breaking up normal organization."[89]

The American case was no different. General Douglas MacArthur successfully refused to allow OSS operations in the Pacific.[90] American Army historian David Hogan observed that "except for some isolated instances, conventional U.S. generals discarded special operations in Europe and focused almost totally on conventional warfare once their forces had consolidated beachheads in North Africa, Italy, and France."[91] The institutional hostility towards SOF flourished as the war drew to a close. As hostilities neared completion SOF organizations were quickly disbanded or severely curtailed. Among the casualties were such well-known organizations as the LRDG, SAS, British "Phantom," Layforce (British Commandos commanded by Lieutenant-Colonel Robert

Laycock), First Special Service Force (FSSF), OSS, the U.S. Army Rangers and the U.S. Marine Corps Raider Battalions.

Later, in the post-war period, when Colonel Aaron Banks arrived at Fort Bragg to begin work on establishing Special Forces, he was warned that he would "have to work carefully and not step on toes, since there was not only apathy about a UW army capability but also actual resistance to elite special units."[92] In 1952, when Bank began recruiting, he attributed his initial difficulty to the "less than enthusiastic Army wide support for the program."[93] His experience was not unique. The rejuvenated post-war SAS also found itself short of recruits because "the Regiment's reputation stood so low that Commanding Officers of other units were making it difficult for their people to go on selection course."[94]

This attitude was also mirrored in 1963, when the French Foreign Legion (2nd REP) attempted to radically reform some of its elements into a rapid deployable SOF-type unit. As the unofficial unit historian noted, "This was a revolutionary concept at the time and not one to please desk bound conservatives in the French military. To these officers the word 'special' conjured up nonconforming, rogue units."[95] Even in the depths of Africa, torn by internal strife and rampant with insurgency, a lethargy to new ideas remained. Lieutenant-Colonel Ron Reid Daly, in his efforts to establish the Selous Scouts in the former Rhodesia, observed, "I began to get the feeling of a distinct resistance block against me personally, and the scheme as a whole."[96]

Even during the Vietnam War, institutional prejudices within DoD worked against SOF. General Maxwell Taylor recalled that despite President Kennedy's urging, "not much heart went into [the] work [of placing greater emphasis on SOF]." Taylor, like many senior commanders, believed that Special Forces were not doing anything that "any well-trained unit" could not do.[97] Major-General Harold Johnson agreed. Then acting Army deputy chief of staff for Military Operations, he acknowledged that the Kennedy regime was pushing Special Forces and that the "Army agreed that this was a good idea." However, he also conceded that the Army "sort of yawned in backing it up."[98] In 1963, several attempts to transfer a list of officers with known ability and experience to Special Forces were ignored and the "talent received was almost invariably inferior."[99] Once the war was over, a virtual blood-bath occurred. By the mid-1970s the Army slashed special forces manning by 70 percent and its funding by 95 percent.[100] At its lowest point in 1975, the SOF budget represented one tenth of one percent of the total American defence budget.[101]

133

Neither its budget, nor its future improved substantially in the short term. Lingering images and hostility continued. The antipathy towards SOF was particularly resilient. "Over the years in the United States," confessed Secretary of the Army John Marsh in 1983, "there has been resistance among leaders of conventional forces towards unconventional methods."[102] This was clearly evident a year later, when in the fall of 1984, a three-star U.S. Air Force general testifying before a classified session of a Senate Special Operations Panel repeatedly referred to Delta Force as "trained assassins" and "trigger happy." In addition, he aired his personal concerns that Delta might "freelance" a coup d'état in a nation friendly to the USA.[103] Fours years later at the activation ceremony of the USSO-COM, Admiral William J. Crowe, Jr., the chair of the Joint Chiefs of Staff, beseeched those assembled to "break down the wall that has more or less come between special operation forces and other parts of our military."[104] This appeal, however, had limited impact. The Gulf War revealed that ingrained resentment still existed against the concept of SOF.

Journalist and author Douglas Waller observed, "No one nurtured the animosity more than CENTCOM's [Central Command] commander General H. Norman Schwarzkopf III. 'Stormin' Norman Schwarzkopf despised special operators." The reason was almost predictable. Firstly, he had a negative image of SOF operators because of his experience with them in Vietnam and later in Grenada.[105] Secondly, "In an Army now giddy over light divisions and paratroopers," explained Waller, "Schwarzkopf was somewhat of an anachronism — a tank officer whose first love was heavy armored units."[106] As a result, he initially refused their inclusion in his force. But the animosity went both ways. Officers in USSOCOM considered Schwarzkopf a "meat and potatoes thinker, a pompous, plodding tactician who knew little about unconventional warfare and didn't care to learn much more."[107] He seemed to ably represent the conventional military. And it would seem that the sentiment remains smouldering under the surface. As recently as the fall of 2001, General Tommy Franks, the commander-in-chief of CENTCOM who was responsible for prosecuting the war in Afghanistan, questioned the use of special forces, reportedly believing it was a conflict for "heavy metal conventional units."[108]

Not surprisingly, throughout the evolutionary process most SOF operators, particularly officers and senior NCOs felt that SOF employment was career limiting. They were not wrong. For instance, "Marine Officers assigned to the Joint Special Operations Command or to USSOCOM," conceded one former high-ranking officer, "for the most part have not fared well before promotion boards."[109] But this was not a revelation; after all, there has always existed a cultural chasm that was difficult to breach.

## CONCLUSIONS

But the dismal assessment is not entirely without a happy ending. As stated, SOF has evolved and has actually achieved acceptance by political and military decision makers. Consequently, the divide between SOF and conventional forces is now less of a barrier. The creation of USSO-COM in 1987, was an important factor. SOF now had control over their own resources so they could better modernize their organizations. They had a single commander who could promote inter-operability and ensure all SOF assets could operate effectively together. Finally, the provision of a "four-star" commander-in-chief and an assistant secretary of defense for Special Operations and Low Intensity Conflict gave SOF representation in the highest councils of the DoD. Quite simply, SOF could defend themselves in the halls of power. They had come of age.

In addition, the positive image of SOF continued to grow. Internationally in the 1980s and beyond, SOF units scored repeated successes against terrorists. But of great importance, during the Gulf War of 1990–1991, coalition SOF made a significant, publicly recognized contribution to the war effort (i.e., strategic reconnaissance, direct action raids, economy of effort activities such as deception operations, and liaison/training missions with the less advanced non-NATO coalition partners), as well as their most well-known, public mission of "Scud busting" — a strategically essential task that was critical to maintaining the Coalition, because it kept Israel from retaliating against Saddam Hussein's Scud missile attacks on its cities.[110] In the execution of these tasks, SOF received enormous favourable press. Their public image soared.

Clearly, internationally, SOF was on the rise. They proved themselves effective in the murky war against terrorists, in the blowing sands of a conventional war in the Gulf, as well as in the savage peace that prevailed. Globally, they were used for the traditional roles of unconventional warfare, strategic reconnaissance, and direct action raids as well as for their other core missions. In addition, they also successfully conducted the capture of war criminals in the "former" Yugoslavia.[111]

Their importance increased because political decision makers and senior military commanders finally realized their true value. Quite simply, relatively small, highly skilled, and mobile units that proved extremely effective in operations, and that presented a relatively small footprint, provided the political and military leadership with a viable response. SOF could be employed in a myriad of potentially politically sensitive operations without the risk or negative optics that would come with the deployment of a large number of troops. Mass could be replaced by quality. This was not only an economic factor but one of effectiveness. In the volatile, uncertain, and ambiguous environment of conflict, SOF were normally more agile and adaptable. Their higher levels of intelligence, skill, and ingenuity provided a better chance of success. Importantly, conventional commanders, stuck in the reality of today's complex security environment, also began to realize the benefits of SOF. As such, acceptance, albeit reluctant at times, emerged.

The change in momentum became obvious. Using the Americans as a case study, SOF deployments, manning, and budgets have been on the rise since the early 1990s. The U.S. SOF budget was increased yet again in 2004, reaching a staggering $6 billion.[112] As of May 2003, there were approximately 20,000 special operators, representing almost half of the entire Special Operations Forces of 47,000, involved in ongoing conflicts in Afghanistan and Iraq alone.[113] Moreover, U.S. SOF are joined there by a large number of allied SOF contingents.

The acceptance of SOF, particularly their qualities of utility and relevance, by the mainstream military and political decision makers has finally become pronounced in the new millennium. The tragic terrorist attack of 9/11 finalized the transformation of the perception of SOF and represented the culmination of their acceptance as a core element of any military. Although their future is not certain, SOF have seemingly evolved from a force of desperation, born in the initial crisis of the Second World War, to a force of choice in the aftermath of 9/11. Once marginalized and considered as a nuisance to real soldiering, SOF have become the workhorses of the future. They will provide decision makers with the needed political and cultural astuteness and military finesse required to succeed in an increasingly complex and chaotic world.

However, traditional barriers and prejudices will not die easily. Although the cultural divide has apparently been spanned, it is but a footbridge that must be carefully maintained and improved upon. This will take the continued efforts of both the conventional and SOF communities. To progress, both must learn to understand the characteristics, needs, and roles of the other. Only if a more cooperative, informed, and transparent relationship develops will the chasm be permanently closed.

## NOTES

1. William Walker, "Shadow Warriors: Elite Troops Hunt Terrorists in Afghanistan," *Toronto Star*, 20 October 2001, A4.

2. Tom Clancy and John Gresham, *Special Forces: A Guided Tour of the U.S. Army Special Forces* (New York: Berkley Books, 2001), 3. See Bernd Horn, "Special Men, Special Missions: The Utility of Special Operations Forces," in Bernd Horn, David Last, J. Paul de B. Taillon, eds., *Force of Choice: Perspectives on Special Operations* (Montreal: McGill-Queen's Press, 2004), Chapter 1 for a discussion on the myriad of definitions and perspectives on the meaning of SOF.

3. This definition is not original. It takes its root from Thomas K. Adams, *US Special Operations Forces in Action: The Challenge of Unconventional Warfare* (London: Frank Cass, 1998), 7, and adds other critical components drawn from chapter 1.

4. CT measures are the offensive measures, whereas antiterrorism (AT) measures are the defensive measures. SOF CT operations encompass both CT and AT.

5. U.S. Special Operations Command, *US Special Operations Forces: Posture Statement 2000* (Washington, DC: Department of Defense, 2001), 5. In 2003, USSOCOM decided to drop the six collateral activities that included: Coalition Support, Combat Search and Rescue, Counter Drug activities, Humanitarian Demining activities, Security Assistance, and Special Activities. Special Operations Commanders' Conference, 14 April 2003.

6. Adams, 162.

7. Julian Thompson, *War Behind Enemy Lines* (Washington, DC: Brassey's, 2001), 2.

8. Clancy, *Special Forces*, 3–4.

9. Philip Warner, *Phantom* (London: William Kimber, 1982), 11.

10. Major-General David Lloyd Owen, *The Long Range Desert Group* (London: Leo Cooper, 2000), 12. The LRDG were publicly described as "the pick of the seasoned desert fighters of the Eighth Army." "Long Range Desert Patrol," *Illustrated*, 24 October 1942, 14–15.

11. Eric Morris, *Churchill's Private Armies* (London: Hutchinson, 1986), 90.

12. Field Marshal Sir William Slim, *Defeat into Victory* (London: Cassell and Company Ltd., 1956), 547.

13. Brigadier T.B.L. Churchill, "The Value of Commandos," *Royal United Services Institute (RUSI)*, ,Vol. 65, No. 577 (February 1950), 86.

14. John A. English, *A Perspective on Infantry* (New York: Praeger, 1981), 188.

15. Tom Clancy, *Airborne* (New York: Berkley Books, 1997), 54.

16. See Eliot A. Cohen, *Commandos and Politicians* (Cambridge: Center for International Affairs, Harvard University, 1978), 56–58.

17. Slim, 546; and Morris, *Churchill's Private Army*, 243.

18. Command Sergeant Major Eric L. Haney, *Inside Delta Force: The Story of America's Elite Counterterrorist Unit* (New York: A Dell Book, 2002), 97.

19. Andy McNab, *Immediate Action* (London: Bantam Press, 1995), 381.

20. Slim, 546.

21. Philip Warner, *The SAS: The Official History* (London: Sphere Books, 1971), 1.

22. Tom Clancy, *Into the Storm: A Study in Command* (New York: Berkley Books, 1997), 119.

23. Cohen, 61.

24. Hilary St. George Saunders, *The Green Beret: The Story of the Commandos 1940–1945* (London: Michael Joseph, 1949), 193; and Lieutenant-Colonel Robert D. Burhans, *The First Special Service Force: A History of the North Americans 1942–1944* (Toronto: Methuen, 1975), 162.

25. Warner, *Secret Forces*, 17.

26. Adrian Weale, *Secret Warfare: Special Operations Forces from the Great Game to the SAS* (London: Hodder and Stoughton, 1997), 104.

27. Denis and Shelagh Whitaker, *Dieppe: Tragedy to Triumph* (Toronto: McGraw-Hill Ryerson, 1992), 48; and Saunders, 82–101.

28. Cohen, 56.

29. A.B. Feuer, *Commando! The M/Z Unit's Secret War Against Japan* (Westport, CT: Praeger, 1996), 159.

30. Susan L. Marquis, *Unconventional Warfare: Rebuilding US Special Operations Forces* (Washington, DC: Brookings Institution Press, 1997), 23.

31. Christopher Hibbert, *Anzio: The Bid for Rome* (New York: Ballantine Books, 1990), 75–76.

32. John T. Carney and Benjamin F. Schemmer, *No Room for Error* (New York: Ballantine Books, 2003), 236, 283.

33. "Ground Troops Cream of Crop," *Toronto Star*, 21 October 2001, A9.

34. Charles A. Cotton, "Military Mystique" (Canadian Airborne Forces Museum files, n.d.).

35. Cohen, 74. Although the term *elite* is consistently used, the study was specifically on SOF-type units. This is a common phenomenon. The term *elite* is often used interchangeably with *SOF* by authors.

36. General Sir Peter de la Billière, *Looking for Trouble: SAS to Gulf Command* (London: HarperCollins Publishers, 1995), 117.

37. Eric Morris, *Guerillas in Uniform* (London: Hutchinson, 1989), 15.

38. Weale, 154.

39. Cameron Spence, *All Necessary Measures* (London: Penguin Books, 1997), 43. One journalist in the Second World War reported, "A law unto themselves [SOF] in many ways ... dress is always very much a matter of personal taste with the men who venture far behind the enemy's lines." "Long Range Desert Patrol," *Illustrated* (24 October 1942), 14–15.

40. Haney, 20.

41. Sean Naylor, *Not a Good Day to Die: The Untold Story of Operation Anaconda* (New York: Berkley Books, 2005), 29. He noted, "Most of the Dagger troops appeared to be NCOs but it was hard for Larsen to tell, because none of the long-haired, bearded men wore a uniform, and all called each other by their first names." *Ibid.*, 61.

42. Interview with author, 14 September 2005, Ottawa, Ontario.

43. Anthony Kemp, *The SAS at War* (London: John Murray, 1991), 11.

44. Sergeant Dave Richardson, "The Dead End Kids," *Yank*, Vol. 3, No. 3 (2 July 1944), *www.benning.army.mil/rtb/HISTORY/mkids.htm*, accessed 20 November 2003.

45. Charles M. Simpson III, *Inside the Green Berets: The First Thirty Year* (Novato, CA: Presidio Press, 1983), 14; and Charles W. Sasser, *Raider* (New York: St. Martin's Press, 2002), 186.

46. William O. Darby and William H. Baumer, *Darby's Rangers: We Led the Way* (Novato, CA: Presidio Press, reprint 1993), 184.

47. *Ibid.*, 21.

48. De la Billière, 236.

49. *Ibid.*, 98.

50. Greg Jaffe, "A Maverick's Plan to Revamp Army Is Taking Shape," *Wall Street Journal*, 12 December 2003.

51. John Talbot, "The Myth and Reality of the Paratrooper in the Algerian War," *Armed Forces and Society* (November 1976), 75; Cohen, 69; and Donna Winslow, *The Canadian Airborne Regiment in Somalia: A Socio-Cultural Inquiry* (Ottawa: Commission of Inquiry into the Deployment of Canadian Forces to Somalia, 1997), 135–141.

52. Spence, 43.

53. Alan Bell, presentation on Special Air Service (SAS) operations in the Falklands, 1982, 19 March 2004, Fort Frontenac, Kingston, Ontario.

54. Interview with a former SOF member, September 2002.

55. Interview with a Canadian infantry captain, 25 October 2002.

56. Winslow, 126–133.

57. Alan Bell, formerly of 22 SAS, presentation to the RMC Special Operations Symposium, 5 October 2000, and WS 586 class, 19 March 2004. This mind-set has created potential failures. For instance, some analysts have suggested that the U.S. military may have missed chances to capture Mohammad Omar (Taliban leader) and Ayman Zawahiri (deputy to Osama bin Laden) during the past two years because of restrictions on

Green Berets in favour of Delta Force and SEAL Team Six. As a result, during several credible sightings of the fugitives, even though a Green Beret team was just minutes away and ready to deploy, commanders called on Delta Force, which was hours away in Kabul. See Gregory L. Vistica, "Military Split on How to Use Special Forces in Terror War," *Washington Post*, 5 January 2004, A1.

58. Alan Bell, presentation on SAS operations in the Falklands, 1982, 19 March 2004, Fort Frontenac, Kingston, Ontario.

59. Clancy, *Special Forces*, 281.

60. Colonel J.W. Hackett, "The Employment of Special Forces," *RUSI*, Vol. 97, No. 585 (February 1952), 41.

61. Colin S. Gray, *Explorations in Strategy* (London: Greenwood Press, 1996), 151, 156.

62. Aaron Bank, *From OSS to Green Berets: The Birth of Special Forces* (Novato, CA: Presidio Press, 1986), 147.

63. Quoted in Susan L. Marquis, *Unconventional Warfare: Rebuilding US Special Operations Forces* (Washington, DC: Brookings Institution Press, 1997), 6.

64. Hackett, 35.

65. *Ibid.*, 39.

66. *Ibid.*, 39.

67. One need only look at recent pictures from Afghanistan or Iraq to understand the point. Long hair, beards, no rank epaulets, no military headdress (although ball caps are often a favourite), mixed dress — civilian and military, fashionable sunglasses, and an array of exotic weaponry and equipment normally give away the secretive SOF operator.

68. Major-General Tony Jeapes, *SAS Secret War* (Surrey, Eng.: The Book People Ltd., 1996 ), 12.

69. Quoted in Marquis, 7.

70. Will Fowler, *The Commandos at Dieppe: Rehearsal for D-Day* (London: HarperCollins, 2002), 29.

71. John Leary, "Searching for a Role: The Special Air Service (SAS) Regiment in the Malayan Emergency," *Army Historical Research*, Vol. 63, No. 296 (Winter 1996), 269.

72. John L. Plaster, *SOG* (New York: Onyx, 1997), 246.

73. "The Long-Range Desert Group," *The Fighting Forces*, Vol. 19, No. 3 (August 1942), 146.

74. Spence, 151.

75. Hugh McManners, *Commando: Winning the Green Beret* (London: Network Books, 1994), 12.

76. See Colonel C.A. Beckwith, *Delta Force* (New York: Dell Publishing Co., 1985), 123 and 137; interview with Major Anthony Balasevicius, former SOF standards officer (and recognized expert on SOF selection and training theory and practice); Leroy Thompson, *The Rescuers: The World's Top Anti-Terrorist Units* (London: A David & Charles Military Book, 1986), 127–128; General Ulrich Wegener, presentation to the RMC Special Operations Symposium, 5 October 2000; and Victorino Matus, "The GROM Factor," *www.weeklystandard.com/content/public/articles/000/000/002/653hsdpu.asp*, accessed 18 May 2003.

77. Actual selection pass rates vary somewhat between different sources. However, even with the variances, the groups all fit into the Tier 2 range. See Judith E. Brooks and Michelle M. Zazanis, "Enhancing U.S. Army Special Forces: Research and Applications," *ARI Special Report*, Vol. 33 (October 1997), 8; General H. H. Shelton, "Quality People: Selecting and Developing Members of U.S. SOF," *Special Warfare: The Professional Bulletin of the John F. Kennedy Special Warfare Center and School*, Vol. 11, No. 2 (Spring 1998), 3; Marquis, 53; Commander Thomas Dietz, CO Sea Air Land (SEAL) Team 5, presentation to the RMC Special Operations Symposium, 5 October 2000; Leary, 265; James F. Dunnigan, *The Perfect Soldier: Special Operations, Commandos and the Future of US Warfare* (New York: Citadel Press, 2003), 269 and 278; and Michael Asher, *Shoot to Kill: A Soldier's Journey Through Violence* (London: Viking, 1990), 205.

78. It is for this reason that airborne forces are more often than not considered SOF. Contemporary airborne success rates are approximately 70 percent. See Colonel Bill Kidd, "Ranger Training Brigade," *US Army Infantry Center Infantry Senior Leader Newsletter* (February 2003), 8–9. However, this can be problematic as airborne units generally share some attitudinal, cultural and philosophical traits — i.e. tenacity of purpose, no mission too daunting, disdain for those outside the group, et cetera ... In addition, many early

airborne units also had rigorous selection and training standards which would easily fall into the Tier 3 and sometimes Tier 2 levels.

79. Marquis, 47–48.

80. *Ibid.*, 47.

81. General Charles Holland, USAF, "Quiet Professionals," *Armed Forces Journal International* (February 2002), 26.

82. General Peter J. Schoomaker, *Special Operations Forces: The Way Ahead*, USSOCOM, 2000, 7.

83. Cohen, 95.

84. Quoted in Marquis, 107.

85. Winston S. Churchill, *The Second World War: Their Finest Hour* (Boston: Houghton Mifflin Company, 1949), 467. See also Saunders, *The Green Beret*, 29–30.

86. "Role of the Special Service Brigade and Desirability of Reorganization," 2. Public Record Office, DEFE 2/1051, Special Service Brigade, role, reorganization, 1943–1944.

87. Kemp, 10.

88. Slim, 548.

89. Field Marshals Alan Brooke and Sir Archibald Wavell and General Sir Bernard Paget were three prominent British commanders who deeply resented SOF organizations. See Charles Messenger, *The Commandos 1940–1946* (London: William Kimber, 1985), 408; Morris, *Churchill's Private Armies*, 172, 243; Brigadier T.B.L. Churchill, "The Value of Commandos," *RUSI*, Vol. 65, No. 577 (February 1950), 85–86.

90. Adams, 40.

91. Gray, 223.

92. Bank, 155.

93. Alfred H. Paddock, *U.S. Army Special Warfare: Its Origins* (Washington, DC: National Defense University Press, 1982), 148.

94. De la Billière, 102.

95. H.R. Simpson, *The Paratroopers of the French Foreign Legion* (London: Brassey's, 1997), 39. The author noted a similar mentality in the Pentagon that tended to "label U.S. Special Forces 'snake eaters' and to shortchange the budget for Special Operation Forces."

96. Peter Stiff, *Selous Scouts: Top Secret War* (Alberton, South Africa: Galago Publishing Inc., 1982), 54. Only 15 percent of candidates passed the Selous Scouts selection course. *Ibid.*, 137.

97. Quoted in Adams, 70, 148. See also Michael Duffy, Mark Thompson, and Michael Weisskopf, "Secret Armies of the Night," *Time*, Vol. 161, No. 25 (23 June 2003).

98. *Ibid.*, 75.

99. *Ibid.*, 69.

100. Marquis, 4, 35, 40, 78. Special Forces manning went from the tens of thousands to 3,600 personnel.

101. *Ibid.*, 68.

102. Dr. Terry White, *Swords of Lightning: Special Forces and the Changing Face of Warfare* (London: Brassey's, 1997), 1.

103. *Ibid.*, 117.

104. Major-General J.L. Hobson, "AF Special Operations Girds for Next Century Missions," *National Defense* (February 1997), 27.

105. Clancy, *Special Forces*, 12; Waller, *Commandos*, 231; D.C. Waller, "Secret Warriors," *Newsweek* (17 June 1991), 21.

106. Waller, *Commandos*, 231; D.C. Waller, "Secret Warriors," 21.

107. Waller, *Commandos*, 230. In the end, despite his initial reluctance to use SOF, he later singled out those forces as critical to the Allied victory. Approximately 7,705 SOF personnel participated.

108. Robin Moore, *The Hunt for Bin Laden: Task Force Dagger* (New York: Ballantine Books, 2003), 21, 31–32.

109. Colonel (Retired) W. Hays Parks, "Should Marines 'Join' Special Operations Command?" *US Naval Institute Proceedings*, Vol. 129 (May 2003), 4. See also Tom Clancy, *Shadow Warriors: Inside Special Forces* (New York: Putnam, 2002), 221.

110. See Department of Defense, *United States Special Operations Command History* (Washington, DC: USSOCOM, 1999), 34–42; Waller, *Commando*, 225–352; Marquis, 227–249; Adams, 231–244; Carney and Schemmer, 224–236; B.J. Schemmer, "Special Ops Teams Found 29 Scuds Ready to Barrage Israel 24 Hours Before Ceasefire," *Armed Forces Journal International* (July 1991), 36; Mark Thompson, Azadeh Moaveni, Matt Rees, and Aharon Klein, "The Great Scud Hunt," *Time*, Vol. 160, No. 26 (23 December 2002), 34; William Rosenau, *Special Operations Forces and Elusive Ground Targets: Lessons from Vietnam and the Persian Gulf War* (Santa Monica, CA: Rand, 2001), and Spence, *Sabre Squadron*. Although no Scuds were reportedly destroyed, the provision of the Coalition's best troops provided the Israelis with the confidence that everything possible was being done to eradicate the threat.

111. Department of Defense, *USSOCOM History*, 44–69; Carney and Schemmer, 245–282; *US SOF Posture Statement 2000*, 15–23; Robin Neillands, *In the Combat Zone: Special Forces Since 1945* (London: Weidenfeld and Nicolson, 1997), 105–154, 298–315; Adams, 244–286.

112. James C. Hyde, "An Exclusive Interview with James R. Locher III," *Armed Forces Journal International* (November/December 1992), 34; Lieutenant-General Peter J. Schoomaker, "Army Special Operations: Foreign Link, Brainy Force," *National Defense* (February 1997), 32–33; Scott Gourlay, "Boosting the Optempo," *Janes Defence Weekly* (14 July 1999), 26; Hyde, 34; Ray Bond, ed., *America's Special Forces* (Miami: Salamander Books, 2001); Kim Burger, "US Special Operations Get Budget Boost," *Jane's Defence Weekly*, Vol. 37, No. 8 (20 February 2002), 2; Glenn Goodman, "Expanded Role for Elite Commandos," *Armed Forces Journal International*, (February 2003), 36; Duffy et al., "Secret Armies of the Night"; Harold Kennedy, "Special Operators Seeking a Technical Advantage," *National Defense*, Vol. 87, No. 594 (May 2003), 20; and *US SOF, Posture Statement 2000*, 41. Despite the significant capability they represent, proven by their steadily growing operational tempo and record of success, their funding envelope still represents only about 1.3 percent of the (DoD) total budget. Burger, 2.

113. Roxane Tiron, "Demand for Special Ops Forces Outpaces Supply," *National Defence*, Vol. 87, No. 594 (May 2003), 18. There were more than 12,000 deployed to Iraq and approximately 8,000 deployed to Afghanistan.

# 6

## When the Guns Stop:
### *Leveraging SOF for Post-Conflict Success*

### Bernd Horn

The brazen terrorist attacks on the United States on 11 September 2001 undeniably became a defining moment of the new millennium. Arguably, those acts ushered in a new era, an epoch that changed Western views on security, terrorism, and the manner in which warfare is waged. In the aftermath of those tragic events, the United States embarked on a war against terrorism that continues to this day. Of note, was the immediate and principal reliance on Special Operations Forces (SOF).

This in itself was surprising. Although an obvious choice, based on their ability to respond to the ambiguous, elusive, and asymmetric nature of the threat, SOF have traditionally been marginalized by political and military decision makers and shunned by their conventional military brethren. They have largely been the black sheep of the family.

This phenomenon was evident when they were created in the chaos of the Second World War when the Allies were devoid of the ability or means to strike back at the seemingly invincible German military machine. Then, small specialized forces became the primary tool for limited offensive action. The image of SOF that developed these early days was that of tough hardened killers and desperate cut-throats capable of violence and efficient killing, but virtually uncontrollable and lacking any sense of military decorum. Moreover, their operations were judged by many conventional commanders to be resource intensive, but lacking in substantive value to the larger war effort.

Despite the opposition, SOF were established and provided tangible results. Born from crisis, they filled a pressing need. They enabled the Allies, particularly the British, to operate offensively from a position of weakness as an economy of effort weapon. However, as the tide of the war shifted so did their support, as feeble as it was. Raiding and direct action were soon eclipsed by the less glamorous tasks of unconventional warfare and strategic reconnaissance. And, as the large conventional forces achieved a foothold in the respective theatres of operation, SOF were largely ignored or simply utilized as normal ground troops. Predictably, SOF units were largely disbanded by the end of the war.

The post-war era was no more friendly to SOF. They were consistently marginalized until a specific need arose, at which time they were directed to fill the void. Even then, they failed to be embraced by the larger institution. As such, SOF evolved during the Cold War from their raiding roots, towards tasks associated with unconventional warfare, counter-insurgency and counterterrorism.

But legitimacy for Special Operations Forces did not begin to solidify until the post–Cold War period that generated an entirely new geopolitical environment that was laden with new threats. Gone was the stability and predictability of the Cold War that was managed by two global superpowers. Instead the world became fragmented and increasingly dangerous as flash points erupted worldwide. In this volatile climate, SOF evolved once again. Their specialization, small organizational footprint, and ability to conduct missions that fell into the grey area of political/military operations that are normally politically sensitive, expanded their utility.

As such, the culmination of the evolution of SOF and its ultimate legitimacy became evident with the reliance on SOF in the aftermath of 9/11. It became clear that they had completed their transformation from a force of desperation to a force of choice. Their importance increased because political decision makers and senior military commanders finally realized their true value. Quite simply, relatively small, highly skilled, and mobile units that proved extremely effective in operations, and who presented a relatively small footprint, provided the political and military leadership with a viable response. SOF could be employed in a myriad of potentially politically sensitive operations but without the normal risk or negative optics of a large-scale deployment of troops. Mass could be replaced by quality. This was not only an economic factor but one of effectiveness. In the volatile, uncertain, and ambiguous environment of conflict, SOF were normally more agile and adaptable. Their higher levels of intelligence, skill, and ingenuity provided a better chance of success.

These attributes and strengths are critical. They provide governments with a powerful tool to not only win the war, but also the peace. Quite simply, SOF's new legitimacy and acceptance, positions them to become the workhorses of the future, particularly in the realm of post-conflict resolution. The unique skill sets and abilities of SOF, namely their small footprint, cultural awareness, adaptive and flexible mindset, greater intelligence, aptitudes, experience, and training, provide political and military decision makers not only with a lethal force that is normally the first in during conflict, but also with warrior-diplomats capable of ensuring the hard won gains of combat are not lost in the power and security vacuum that normally follows the cessation of hostilities. As such, the expansive capabilities of SOF must be leveraged once the guns stop, if the peace is to be won.

## SPECIAL OPERATIONS FORCES IN POST-CONFLICT RESOLUTION

As outlined in the previous chapters, SOF has proven its capabilities, by their performance, both in the murky war against terrorism, as well as on the conventional battlefield. In the process, they have earned the acceptance of the mainstream military and political decision makers. Quite simply, the American response to 9/11, which centred on Special Operations Forces, finalized the transformation of SOF from a force of desperation to a force of choice. However, SOF's utility is not only best served as a "first in" combat force used to prepare the battlefield for those who follow. The very attributes, characteristics, and strengths that make them such a potent warfighting force also make them the ideal choice for post-conflict resolution.

This is often overlooked. Undeniably, nations, regardless of their intent, have a moral and legal obligation to ensure the safety and security of a population once hostilities cease. Quite simply, the in-place force must provide an environment conducive to the reestablishment of government, public safety, and the well-being of society (i.e., prevent starvation and the spread of disease, enforce law and order, et cetera). In the end, it is in their best interest to do so. A failure to "win the peace" could be catastrophic — leading to anarchy, political discord, social unrest, and potentially insurgency, thus, lengthening the conflict and adding to its cost in lives and national treasure.

The stakes are clearly high. Unfortunately, conventional forces, although numerous and well-equipped, are often not capable of conducting successful post-conflict resolution. They are normally combat troops that are equipped and trained to deliver violence. They are not always attuned or sensitive to cultural differences, or the nuances of "diplomacy." As a result, they are often unable to effectively implement the necessary actions or behaviours necessary to winning the "hearts and minds" of a population struggling to rebuild their lives. Their actions in an ambiguous, chaotic, media-filled, and politically charged environment are often clumsy and appear heavy-handed.

It is for this exact reason that SOF must be leveraged to win the peace. As already articulated, the specially selected SOF soldiers are highly intelligent, adaptable, and capable of independent decision in an environment that is characterized by ambiguity, change, uncertainty, and volatility. Although SOF has been used in the past during peace to assist with training other military and paramilitary forces (i.e., counter-insurgency in Vietnam, Central America), anti-drug operations (e.g., South America), as well as demining operations, and the pursuit of war criminals (e.g., Bosnia-Herzegovina), the focus has always been minimal, almost a sideshow to keep busy until something more substantial arose. The requirement now demands far more resources and emphasis. As such, the SOF warrior is ideally suited to meeting the political and social challenges that are inherent in the aftermath of armed conflict in chaotic future security environment.

For instance, SOF can be instrumental in stabilizing a country after the fighting has stopped by assisting in the creation of a favourable environment for political and social reconstruction. They normally operate in small teams, thus, SOF present a small footprint yet a powerful presence. As a small organization, they are more capable of rapid change and can more easily adapt to ambiguous or fluid situations. More importantly, SOF's role in the shadows avoids the stigma of an occupying force. This is critical in respecting the sensitivities of the host nation as can be currently seen in Iraq. Moreover, the low profile makes it far more difficult for belligerents to target friendly forces or governments, whether by propaganda or physical attack.

Despite its small footprint their contribution far outstrips that of conventional forces. Their knowledge of cultural, social, and behavioural patterns of their allies and enemies, is a key force multiplier. SOF are normally regionally focused, possess language skills, and more often than not have worked closely with elements of the in-place government.[1] The level of established trust and credibility that emanates from these skills and experiences allows SOF to accomplish much more, with less resources in a fraction of the time. This dynamic is clearly evident in the report of one SF team that was deployed in Afghanistan:

> We work closely with the muj [mujahadeen], advising them on military, security, and humanitarian assistance matters. We directly negotiate with local commanders for the place-ment of multinational humanitarian assistance teams to be stationed at Herat airfield. We are instrumental in assessing the population and the situation both inside the city of Herat and in the surrounding towns to the south and east. Without our presence and perseverance, Ismail Khan and his followers would not be as supportive of the interim government as they currently are.[2]

SOF's ability and experience in training and assisting host nation military and paramilitary forces in security operations is another key enabling issue. It allows indigenous forces to provide for their own security and create the necessary stable environment for reconstruction and political, economic, and social renewal. SOF's information and psychological warfare capabilities also assist in this endeavour by helping host nations to convey necessary information to the public to explain humanitarian assistance, policies, regulations, political decrees, and reforms, or simply to counter or deny enemy propaganda.

Clearly the creation of a stable and secure environment is all important in post-conflict reconstruction. Once again, SOF is a force multiplier. Its close rapport with host government forces, its small size, and often irregular appearance, combined by its in-depth com-prehension of the local culture and attitudes allows them to access information that would not normally be available.[3] Better intelligence has a spiral effect. It allows for more rapid response or pre-emptive strikes, greater precision, and less collateral damage. In short, more effective action. This in turn promotes credibility and confidence in the host government and reconstruction efforts, which conversely lessens the appeal of extremists or insurgents attempting to derail the process. In the end, it is results that are all important and it matters not whether the intelligence is provided to conventional forces (whether host nation or coalition) or whether it is used by SOF themselves. However, their special skills and training does position them to be the ideal force to track down insurgents or terrorist networks or perform other direct action missions. For example, since 9/11, in Afghanistan "roughly one-third of the senior al-Qaeda leaders, as well as 2,000 rank and file members, have been killed or jailed."[4] In Iraq, SOF has been similarly successful with tracking down Saddam and key members of his former regime.[5] Simply put, SOF in a direct action role are key to eliminating emerging threats or those elements that stand in the way of achieving security and stability for the population at large.

In addition, SOF can be used, as was done in Afghanistan, Bosnia-Herzegovina and Iraq, to track down war criminals. This is an important task. Firstly, as in the example of Iraq and the capture of Saddam Hussein and a large number of his key senior military and security leaders, it removes lingering doubt in the minds of the population and promotes the support of a new political process. Furthermore, it acts as a strong message, if not deterrent, to others. The realization that committed countries will dedicate resources to ensure that justice will be served and that war criminals will be held accountable may potentially cause military and political leaders to think twice before authorizing, instigating, or allowing crimes against humanity.

In the end, SOF are key to post-conflict reconstruction. Although small in number they are an invaluable force multiplier. Born from chaos from a position of weakness in the Second World War, modern SOF has evolved from a force of desperation to a force of choice in the aftermath of 9/11. Significantly, SOF's adaptabiltity, as well as their highly skilled, intelligent and mature operators who are capable of working in an environment characterized by ambiguity, change, uncertainty, and volatility, positions them to readily meet the exigencies of winning the peace. As such, SOF must be leveraged not only during conflict but especially once the guns have stopped.

## NOTES

1. Robin Moore, *The Hunt for Bin Laden: Task Force Dagger* (New York: Ballantine Books, 2003), 90 and 193.

2. *Ibid.*, 200.

3. See Anna Simons and David Tucker, "United States Special Operations Forces and the War on Terrorism," *Small Wars and Insurgencies*, Vol. 14, No. 1 (Spring 2003), 83–84.

4. Paul Moorcraft, "Can Al-Qaida Be Defeated?" *Armed Forces Journal International* (July 2004), 30.

5. See Robin Moore, *Hunting Down Saddam: The Inside Story of the Search and Capture* (New York: St. Martin's Press, 2004).

# PART II

*Historical Context*

# 7

---

# "Avenging Angels":
## The Ascent of SOF as the Force of Choice in the New Security Environment

### Bernd Horn

> This is not war as you have ever known it before. This is
> vengeance for the women and children they murdered on 9/11.
> Our responsibility is to implement that vengeance. Fight as
> though your own families were killed in New York. You are
> America's avenging angels. Your goal is justice and you are
> authorized to use all means necessary towards that end.
> — U.S. Special Forces Officer During a Classified Briefing,
> October 2001[1]

The terrorist attacks against the United States on 11 September 2001 remain vivid in the collective memory. In the aftermath of those tragic events, the United States embarked on a war against terrorism that continues to this day. Of note was the immediate and principal reliance on Special Operations Forces (SOF). Although this development should not have been unexpected due to SOF's ability to respond to the ambiguous, elusive, and asymmetric nature of the threat, many people were still surprised.

The reason behind this apparent paradox is the fact that SOF have often, if not almost always, been the black sheep of the military family. They were created largely in the chaos of the Second World War when the

Allies were devoid of the ability or means to strike back at the seemingly invincible German military machine as a result of years of doctrinal stagnation, unpreparedness, limited resources, and catastrophic initial defeats. As a means of response, small specialized forces became the primary tool for limited offensive action. However, the image of SOF that developed was that of the tough hardened killer commandos and desperate cut-throats capable of violence and efficient killing, but virtually uncontrollable and lacking any sense of military decorum. Moreover, their operations were judged by many conventional commanders to be resource intensive, yet without any substantive value to the larger war effort.

This image, cultivated by a traditional and conservative military institution, continued in the post-war era. Predictably, SOF units were largely disbanded by the end of the war. Those units that remained were consistently marginalized until a specific need arose, at which time they were directed to fill whatever void emerged, whether unconventional warfare, counter-insurgency, or counterterrorism. Even then, they failed to be embraced by the larger institution.

Legitimacy for SOF did not begin to solidify until the post–Cold War period that generated an entirely new geo-political environment that was full of new threats. As the stability of the Cold War disappeared and the world became fragmented and increasingly dangerous, SOF evolved once again to fill the gap. Their specialization, small organizational footprint and ability to conduct missions that fell into the grey area of political/military operations that are normally politically sensitive expanded their utility. As such, the culmination of the evolution of SOF and its ultimate legitimacy became evident with the reliance on SOF in the aftermath of 9/11. It became clear that they had completed their transformation from a force of desperation to a force of choice. Simply put, they now represent the leading military edge in the new security environment.

## WHO ARE THESE SHADOW WARRIORS?

Special Operations Forces are generally defined by journalists as "the toughest, smartest, most secretive, fittest, best-equipped, and consistently lethal killers in the U.S. [or any other] military."[2] However, a more traditional definition originating from SOF's Second World War and post-war beginnings describes them as forces that are "specially selected, specially trained, specially equipped, and given special missions and support."[3] But this somewhat simplistic description has been eclipsed by a more comprehensive and nuanced explanation that better captures their shadowy role in the international security environment. It is generally accepted by political, military, and scholarly circles that modern SOF are "specially organized, trained and equipped military and paramilitary forces that conduct special operations to achieve military, political, economic or informational objectives by generally unconventional means in hostile, denied or politically sensitive areas."[4]

Not surprisingly, as with most military concepts, equipment, and organizations, the United States normally sets the standard. It is no different with SOF. As such, the Americans look to SOF to conduct nine core tasks:

- Counterterrorism (CT) — actions taken to preclude, preempt, and resolve terrorist actions throughout the entire threat spectrum, including antiterrorism and counterterrorism.[5]
- Special Reconnaissance (SR) — reconnaissance and surveillance actions conducted as special operations in hostile, denied, or politically sensitive environments to collect or verify information of strategic or operational significance, employing military capabilities not normally found in conventional forces. These actions provide an additive capability for commanders and may supplement other intelligence collection when conventional reconnaissance and surveillance actions are limited by weather, terrain, or adversary counter-measures.
- Direct Action (DA) — short-term seize, destroy, exploit, capture, damage, or recovery operations.
- Unconventional Warfare (UW) — organizing, training, equipping, advising, and assisting indigenous and surrogate forces in military and paramilitary operations of long duration.[6]
- Counter-Proliferation (CP) — combating the proliferation of nuclear, biological and chemical weapons; providing intelligence collection and analysis; and supporting diplomacy, arms control, and export controls.
- Foreign Internal Defence (FID) — organizing, training, advising, and assisting host-nation military and paramilitary forces to enable these forces to free and protect their society from subversion, lawlessness, and insurgency.
- Civil Affairs Operations (CAO) — activities that establish relations between military/civil authorities to facilitate military operations.

- Psychological Operations (PSYOP) — planned operations to influence behaviour of foreign forces and governments.
- Information Operations (IO) — actions taken to achieve information superiority by affecting adversary information and information systems while defending one's own information and information systems.[7]

## EVOLUTION OF SPECIAL OPERATIONS FORCES

The nine core tasks represent the mandate of modern SOF. However, those principal missions have evolved over time. Special Operations Forces are largely phenomena of the Second World War. Paradoxically, they were largely born in crisis from a position of weakness. In the immediate aftermath of the early German victories, the Allies found themselves devoid of major equipment, of questionable military strength, and on the defensive throughout the world. Nonetheless, combative British Prime Minister Winston Churchill gave direction that action be taken by "specially trained troops of the hunter class" to create a reign of terror on the coastline of the occupied territories based on the "butcher and bolt" principle scant days after the dramatic withdrawal from Dunkirk. Churchill realized that this offensive capability, as limited as it might have been, would be a tonic to public morale, maintain an offensive spirit in the military, and force the Germans to dedicate resources to the defence. As such, he refused to accept a "defensive" war despite the looming threat of invasion in 1940, instead pushing for the establishment of Commandos.[8] These hand-picked volunteers who encapsulated courage, endurance, initiative, and resourcefulness, as well as self-reliance and aggressiveness, were expected to capture strong points, destroy enemy services, neutralize coastal batteries, and wipe out any designated enemy target through raiding operations.[9]

Their standards were unrelenting. Individuals who failed to meet the requisite training requirements were immediately returned to their original units. In the end, despite a slow start and relative short history, commando raids were successful and achieved their aim. They not only raised public morale, but they forged a record for perseverance and toughness, as well as tactical, and at times, arguably, strategic success.[10] In the process, the ground was prepared for the birth, if not near explosion, of modern Special Operations Forces. The idea of specially organized and specially trained units, made up of intrepid individuals who revelled in challenging and highly dangerous small-unit action that called for innovation, individualism, and independent action became more widely accepted, or at least tolerated, in an institution known for its conservatism and traditionalism. However, this limited, if not conditional acceptance existed largely only at the beginning of the war. During this chaotic period of despair, a few desperate men were able to fill a void — an ability to strike out from a position of seeming impotence. And so, special units were raised to cover for weakness, as well as to meet specific needs that conventional forces were seen as too unwieldy or poorly trained to accomplish.

As such, a myriad of other relatively small raiding and reconnaissance units such as the Long Range Desert Group (LRDG), the Special Air Service (SAS), the American Rangers, "Phantom" regiments, Layforce (British Commandos commanded by Lieutenant-Colonel Robert Laycock), the First Special Service Force (FSSF), Popski's Private Army, the Special Boat Service emerged to prop up the war effort until larger conventional forces could crush the German war machine. As the tide of the war shifted, so too did the emphasis on SOF. Direct action raids were marginalized and strategic reconnaissance and unconventional warfare, conducted by the Office of Strategic Services (OSS), the Special Operations Executive (SOE) and the SAS gained in relative importance. Nonetheless, once the large conventional armies were established in Europe, particularly after the Normandy campaign in the summer of 1944, SOF forces were ignored and forgotten, or relegated to the status of a nuisance to "real soldiering."

However, the post-war era did not provide the war-weary and debt-ridden governments or their public with a prolonged period of peace and tranquility. The onset of the Cold War forced Western nations to create large peacetime standing armies. It also established the spectre of two large, heavily armed camps facing off in Europe.

The fact that the seemingly aggressive and very belligerent Soviet Union maintained a buffer of occupied territories and peoples between itself and the West clearly presented an opportunity for unconventional warfare. This was not lost on strategic planners and commanders, particularly those with recent OSS and SOE experience, and as a result SOF capability was once again mobilized to fill this specialized requirement. As such, the evolutionary process begun in the Second World War from a primary focus on direct action raids towards strategic reconnaissance and unconventional warfare continued.

The British and American examples provide a case in point. The SAS was transformed into a Territorial Army unit — 21st SAS Regiment (Artists).[11] Their role was to provide lay-back patrols that would stay hidden as the Soviet forces swept by and then report on enemy movements and troop concentrations. The Americans resurrected their SOF capability in the same direction — strategic reconnaissance and unconventional warfare. In April 1952, the U.S. Army created the Psychological Warfare Center at Fort Bragg, North Carolina, the name of which was later changed to the Special Warfare Center. At roughly the same time, the 10th Special Forces Group (SFG) was activated. The following year the bulk of the 10th SFG was deployed to Bad Tolz, West Germany, and the soldiers who were left behind in Fort Bragg were reorganized into a new unit, the 77th SFG.[12]

For the troops of the 10th SFG, the officers of which were largely drawn from Second World War SOF organizations such as the OSS, Rangers, and airborne units, their mission in Europe was extremely sensitive and secret. They were tasked, in the event of the expected Soviet invasion, with developing and exploiting the resistance potential of the population in those areas behind the enemy lines, namely the Soviet-occupied territories. In addition, the Special Forces (SF) teams were responsible for reconnaissance and potential sabotage missions. In essence, the teams were expected to train and advise resistance movements in the art of guerrilla warfare, as well as conduct strategic reconnaissance to locate Soviet headquarters and nuclear weapon installations.[13] But this European focus, set in the context of a high-intensity conventional war akin to the Second World War, was somewhat misplaced. The nature of conflict would take on a different face.

During the Cold War, wars of nationalism and Communist insurgency, two concepts that were often not always properly delineated by the West, ushered in a period frequently referred to as the savage wars of peace. Once again, the complex nature of such conflicts, which were of long duration; required political, not simply military solutions; and that were normally conducted in complex terrain that provided cover, concealment, and protection for the less heavily armed and equipped insurgents, overwhelmed the conventional capability. The regular soldier was often unaccustomed to operating in hostile environments for prolonged periods of time. In addition, they had neither the training, nor the innovative, adaptable tactics or methodology of thought to counter and defeat elusive, wily insurgents.

To the British this became evident during the Malaya Emergency from 1947 to 1960. The immediate unwieldy, unsophisticated, and limited response of conventional forces failed to destroy the guerrillas or increase the level of security within the country. Although they succeeded in killing some insurgents they just as often alienated segments of the population through heavy-handedness. But more important, the regular forces were incapable of operating in the austere and hostile jungles for any length of time. As a result, they failed to deny sanctuary and breeding grounds to the guerrillas. Fortuitously, a recognized expert, Major "Mad" Mike Calvert, a former commando, Chindit battalion commander, and wartime 2 SAS Brigade commander, was summoned to investigate the problem and devise a solution. Not surprisingly, he recommended the establishment of a special unit, the Malayan Scouts (SAS) as a means to penetrate the jungle and chase down the guerrillas.[14]

Their success, combined with the growing realization that SOF, when employed correctly, revealed a "comparatively low cost in lives set against results achieved" provided a new lease on life for SOF.[15] Quite simply, frugal bureaucrats realized that SOF provided an inexpensive means of waging war against insurgents in distant jungles and deserts, often largely on their own. Savings realized by replacing generic capability backed with quantity, with specific skill sets reinforced by quality, became an attractive option. Therefore, SOF began to evolve once again to a force that was concentrated on unconventional warfare and counter-insurgency. For example, SOF forces were utilized by a myriad of nations during low-level conflict in Malaya, Oman, Brunei, Borneo, Aden, Indochina, Algeria, and Chad, to name but a few.[16]

But once again, despite the arguable success of SOF during this period, they were never fully accepted by the larger institution.[17] Ironically, the very attributes that furnished SOF with its greatest strength also generated enmity from the conventional forces. The ability to outwit their adversaries and endure austere and hostile environments inherently required unconventional tactics, an independence of thought and initiative by the operators, mental agility, specialized training, as well as a level of aggressiveness, fitness, and general toughness not found in regular Army units. Quite simply, these were the secrets to SOF success.

However, their success continued to generate antagonism and jealousy between themselves and the conventional military. But it also produced the panacea of a silver bullet. For instance, the eventual American involvement in Vietnam witnessed another explosion of SOF-type units as a component of the American response to the escalating and complex nature of the war. As unique tasks such as unconventional warfare, long-range reconnaissance and interdiction, and riverine operations emerged in the politically restrictive and environmentally hostile theatre of operations, new units were created, or existing ones expanded exponentially, to address the requirement.

For example, the U.S. Special Forces, or "Green Berets," were dramatically increased in size. They were initially tasked with the Strategic Hamlet Program and later became responsible for the Civil Irregular Defence Group (CIDG) program, which revolved largely around training indigenous populations in self-defence by raising local defence forces capable of defending their villages. In addition, the SF soldiers undertook basic civil affairs programs such as improving agricultural practices, sanitation, and water supply. However, they also built and occupied fortified camps from which fighting patrols by SF and CIDG soldiers could be mounted. The CIDG program was later abused and its personnel used to form multipurpose reaction forces and Mobile Strike Forces in support of conventional, as well as covert operations.[18]

The dramatic growth of SOF during this period was reflected in the fact that all three services were getting into the SOF business. In 1961, the Air Force redesignated existing units as "Air Commandos" and trained them specifically for counter insurgency operations using diverse fixed-wing and rotary-wing aircraft. A year later, the Navy created Sea Air Land (SEAL) teams and sent some to Vietnam where they initially acted in an advisory role to the Vietnamese Navy, but later became responsible for the interdiction of all waterway supply routes from North Vietnam and Cambodia, by ambush, patrols, sabotage, and mines. In addition, they were entrusted with conducting raids on Viet Cong bases and headquarters.[19]

Further SOF developments included the decision by Military Assistance Command Vietnam (MACV) in April 1964, to create the Studies and Observation Group (SOG) that was tasked with strategic reconnaissance and special operations. Specifically, they were responsible for covert cross-border reconnaissance operations against the Ho Chi Minh Trail, inserting and running agents and complex deception operations in the North, psychological operations, and covert maritime interdiction, capture, and destruction of North Vietnamese naval craft and fishing boats.[20]

But this was only part of the expansion. In 1965, 13 Long Range Reconnaissance Patrol (LRRP) companies were formed. Four years later, they were collectively designated the 75th Infantry Regiment (Ranger).[21] In addition, Projects Delta, Omega, and Gamma were sequential programs undertaken to create battalion-sized SOF units, comprised of both U.S. and Vietnamese personnel that were capable of long-range reconnaissance and raiding. Australian and New Zealand SAS forces were also employed in this capacity.[22] Finally, throughout the conflict, SOF organizations and ad hoc task groups were also tasked with running rescue operations, 119 in total, to rescue American prisoners of war.[23]

Unfortunately, the sudden spike in demand was met in many cases by lowering selection standards, where in fact they existed, which inevitably led to a diminution of the overall standard of individuals serving in those units. For instance, the Special Warfare Centre, which on average graduated less than 400 individuals in a given year, ballooned to eight times that number. By 1962, the attrition rate, which was historically 90 percent, fell to 70 percent. Two years later it plummeted to 30 percent. Incredibly, in 1965, Special Forces accepted for the first time 6,500 first-term enlistees, as well as second lieutenants! Not surprisingly, the emphasis on quality — that is ability, experience, maturity, and skill — was ignored in favour of quantity.[24]

In theatre, the SOF culture of lax discipline, deportment and "unconventional" tactics, exacerbated by the type of inexperienced, and often immature, individuals who were now serving in SOF, created difficulties. Rightly or wrongly, the reputation of SOF suffered. They became viewed by the conventional military, as well as by much of the public, as largely a collection of "snake eaters," cowboys, and soldiers of questionable quality who were running amok without adequate control mechanisms.

This legacy would haunt the special operators for decades, even though SOF arguable demonstrated, as it had always done, that it was in fact a force multiplier and a very economical tool. For example, between January/February 1969, SOG maintained a kill ratio of almost 100:1. This compares to the conventional unit kill ratio of 15:1. Moreover, the SOG kill ratio jumped to 153:1 in 1970. Equally important, the SOG activity required the North Vietnamese Army (NVA) to allocate approximately three full divisions, approximately 30,000 men, to rear area security. This was achieved by about 50 American SOG members and their indigenous soldiers.[25] An NVA officer later conceded that SOG effectively attacked and weakened their forces and hurt their morale because "they were unable to stop the SF attacks."[26]

Nonetheless, much like the Second World War experience, SOF units were still, if not increasingly, marginalized by the mainstream Army. General Maxwell Taylor recalled that despite President John F. Kennedy's urging, "not much heart went into [the] work [of placing greater emphasis on SOF]." Taylor, like many senior commanders, believed that Special Forces were not doing anything that "any well-trained unit" could not do.[27]

And so, although SOF missions had undergone an evolutionary shift, not much had changed. In the post-Vietnam era, the American SOF witnessed their budgets and organizations slashed unmercifully. By the mid-1970s the Navy was considering moving its remaining special warfare forces to the reserves, and the Air Force cut its Air Commandos, which were a separate Air Force during the Vietnam War, down to a few squadrons and a handful of aircraft. The Army reaction was even greater. It slashed special forces manning by 70 percent and funding by 95 percent.[28] At its lowest point in 1975, the SOF budget represented one-tenth of one percent of the total American defence budget.[29]

Not surprisingly, most operators, particularly officers and senior non-commissioned officers felt that SOF employment was career limiting. Predictably, not everyone, in fact very few, saw their utility in the Cold War paradigm of "Air Land Battle," which pitted large heavily armoured mass formations against one another on the North European plains. Low-intensity warfare and insurgencies were seen as an inconvenient nuisance that distracted the military from the real business of high-intensity warfare. A classified research project in the mid-1970s entitled the "Multi-Purpose Force Study: US Army Special Forces" confirmed that "there is a pervasive lack of understanding, interest and support of unconventional warfare and Special Forces as a valid national response option."[30] Despite this reality, the allure of SOF still drew those individuals who were attracted to its reliance on individual initiative and adaptability, as well as its unconventional methodology and tactics.

But once again, despite the overwhelming institutional prejudice, the "unexpected" forced conventional-minded military commanders to turn to SOF yet again. A fundamental shift in the threat picture to Western industrialized nations erupted in the late 1960s to early 1970s and provided SOF with another area of specialization.

Terrorism became recognized as a significant "new" menace. Bombings, kidnapping, murders, and the hijacking of commercial aircraft were suddenly frequent occurences, and not just in the Middle East. European countries were thrust into a state of violence as both home-grown and international terrorists waged a relentless war that recognized no borders or limits. Israeli targets, particularly EL AL, its national airline, were struck at Athens, Rome, Zurich, and elsewhere. Other international airlines such as Swissair, TWA, and Pan Am, and their passengers, also became victims of terrorism. The murder of Israeli athletes at the 1972 Olympics in Munich, West Germany, became one of the defining images of the crisis, as did the 1975 terrorist assault on the headquarters of the Organization of the Petroleum Exporting Countries (OPEC) in Vienna, Austria.[31] The scope of the problem was such that in the 1970s, in Italy alone, there were 11,780 terrorist attacks.[32]

But the problem went beyond a spillover of Middle Eastern conflict and politics. In Germany, groups such as the Baader-Meinhof gang (or Red Army Faction) created death and destruction. Holland was besieged by Moluccan terrorists, and Britain struggled with the Irish Republican Army (IRA) and the Northern Ireland question. Even in North America, terrorism raised its ugly head. The Americans saw the growth of radical groups such as the Weathermen, New World Liberation Front, and Black Panther Party, to name but a few. In Canada, the Front de libération du Québec (FLQ) began a reign of terror that culminated in the October Crisis of 1970. In addition, foreign terrorists imported their political struggles and launched attacks against targets in Canada.[33]

One common theme quickly emerged. No country was immune. The terrorist threat was a global phenomenon. Whether home-grown or imported, every state had to mount a response. That realization spawned the next major evolutionary step for SOF. To fight terrorism required specific skills that were not resident within the military institution at large. Consequently, SOF were once again targeted to provide the solution. And who better than specially selected individuals who were capable of agility in thought, adaptability in operations, and who possessed superior martial skills. Not surprisingly, SOF were once again in demand. Predictably, new units were created or existing ones assigned new tasks. For example, the Germans established Grenzshutzgruppe 9 (GSG 9) in September 1972; the British assigned the counterterrorist (CT) role to the SAS that same year; the French formed the Groupe d'Intervention de la Gendarmerie Nationale (GIGN) two years later; the Belgiums created the Escadron Special D'Intervention (ESI) also in 1974; the United Stated formed its premier CT unit, the 1st Special Forces Operational Detachment (DELTA), in 1977; and the Italians raised the Gruppo d'Intervento Speziale (GIS) in 1978. In the end, most countries developed specialist CT organizations to deal with the problem.[34]

In fact, SOF stock rose even more in May 1980. The SAS response to the seizure of the Iranian embassy at Princes Gate by the Democratic Revolutionary Movement for the Liberation of Arabistan (DRMLA) in full view of the world media brought instant respect and credibility to the organization.[35] This success, contrasted by the utter failure and humiliation of the American attempt to rescue its hostages in Iran weeks earlier, sparked a renaissance for Special Operations Forces.[36] It became evident that SOF had a role in the turbulent new era. Although this lesson was not easily accepted by conventional military commanders, further problems with the cooperation, integration, performance, and utilization of SOF in Operation Urgent Fury, the invasion of Grenada in 1983, finally broke the proverbial back of the camel. American legislators now intervened and assisted those within the military institution in breaking down the barriers that impeded SOF. American senators Sam Nunn and William Cohen, both members of the Armed Services Committee, as well as Noel Koch, principal deputy assistant secretary of defense for international security affairs, were instrumental in pressing for change. In 1987, after a long struggle, Congress mandated that the president create a unified combatant command. And on 13 April of that year, United States Special Operations Command (USSOCOM) was activated.[37]

The creation of USSOCOM provided an important benchmark in SOF evolution. The Americans who, in the post–Second World War era, were normally the trendsetters in military affairs — whether oriented towards equipment, doctrine, organization, or technology — recognized SOF as an independent joint command. SOF now had control over their own resources so they could better modernize their organizations. They had a single commander who could promote inter-operability and ensure all SOF assets could operate effectively together. Finally, the provision of a "four-star" commander-in-chief and an assistant secretary of defense for Special Operations and Low Intensity Conflict gave SOF representation in the highest councils of the U.S. Department of Defense (DoD). Quite simply, SOF had come of age.

The universal image of SOF continued to grow. Internationally, SOF units scored repeated success against terrorists. But of great importance, SOF forces gained the limelight once again during the Gulf War in 1990–1991. Coalition SOF conducted strategic reconnaissance, direct action raids, economy of effort activities such as deception operations, and liaison/training missions with the less-advanced non-NATO coalition partners.[38] But their best-known public mission was "Scud busting" — a strategically essential task that was critical to maintaining the Coalition by keeping Israel from retaliating against Saddam Hussein's continued Scud missile attacks on Israeli soil. SOF were given the difficult task of locating and destroying the mobile launchers.[39]

In the end, of the 540,396 American troops deployed to Operation Desert Storm, approximately 7,000 were SOF personnel.[40] Paradoxically, General H. "Stormin'" Norman Schwarzkopf III, who actually despised special operators because of his negative experience with them in Vietnam and later in Grenada, initially refused their inclusion in his force.[41] Yet, in the end, he singled out those forces as critical to the Coalition victory.[42]

Special Operations Forces were now on the rise. They proved themselves effective in the murky war against terrorists, in the blowing sands of a conventional war in the Gulf, as well as in the savage peace that prevailed. Globally, they were used for the traditional roles of unconventional warfare, strategic reconnaissance, and direct action raids. However, they now also specialized in counterterrorism, foreign internal defence (i.e., training foreign militaries in counter-insurgency and CT), counter-proliferation (i.e., combating the proliferation of nuclear, biological, and chemical weapons; intelligence collection and analysis; support of diplomacy, arms control, and export controls), civic affairs, psychological operations, and information operations. They were also used to hunt down war criminals in the former Yugoslavia.[43]

Their importance increased because political decision makers and senior military commanders finally realized their true value. Quite simply, relatively small, highly skilled, and mobile units that proved extremely effective in operations, and that presented a relatively small footprint, provided the political and military leadership with a viable response. SOF could be employed in a myriad of potentially politically sensitive operations, but without the normal risks or negative optics that came with deploying a large number of troops. Mass could be replaced by quality. This was not only an economic factor but one of effectiveness. In the volatile, uncertain, and ambiguous environment of conflict, SOF were normally more agile and adaptable. Their higher levels of intelligence, skill, and ingenuity provided a better chance of success.[44]

## POST-9/11

The growing reliance on SOF continued to grow. Their budget for fiscal year (FY) 2001 was $3.7 billion.[45] Their budget for FY 2003 was approximately $4.9 billion, an increase of 21 percent.[46] This figure was expected to increase again in 2004 to an estimated $6.6 billion.[47] But despite the significant capability they represent, proven by their steadily growing operational tempo and record of success, their funding envelope still represents only about 1.3 percent of the (DoD) total budget.[48] By 2001, 5,141 SOF personnel were deployed to 149 countries and foreign territories.[49] However, this number skyrocketed in the aftermath of 9/11 and the invasion of Iraq. As of May 2003, there were approximately 20,000 special operators, representing almost half of the entire Special Operations Forces of 47,000, involved in ongoing conflicts in Afghanistan and Iraq.[50] Moreover, U.S. SOF are joined there by a large number of Coalition SOF contingents.

SOF very quickly proved themselves to be "avenging angels." Their impact became clearly evident in the early hours after 9/11. Americans were justifiably enraged and looked for a means to strike back at their attackers. SOF once again provided the answer. As part of Operation Enduring Freedom in Afghanistan, it took only 49 days following the insertion of the first Special Forces teams with Northern Alliance forces to the fall of Kandahar. This was achieved with approximately 300 U.S. SF. These operators rallied and forged cohesive teams out of the unorganized anti-Taliban opposition groups and, more important, using a small amount of sophisticated targeting equipment, brought the weight of American airpower down on Taliban and al-Qaeda fighters. Air strikes brought down by one of the first SF teams in the country, aided by a lone Air Force combat controller, are credited with killing as many as 3,500 fighters and destroying up to 450 vehicles.[51] Another Team, "Tiger Team 2," was credited with 2,500 enemy killed, over 50 vehicles destroyed, and over 3,500 prisoners captured, as well as the liberation of over 50 towns and cities.[52] At one time just 10 American SF sergeants were responsible for 120 miles of battlefront.[53] As Major-General Robert Scales explained, "A few well-trained and properly equipped special operations soldiers on the ground armed with the authority to call for and direct aerial precision missions from the ground made the difference between success and failure in the fire-power campaign in Afghanistan."[54] His assessment was not unique. "Success in this campaign has come not just from our remarkable ability to fly bombers from bases in Missouri halfway around the world to strike targets with great precision," revealed Deputy Secretary of Defense Paul Wolfowitz, "success has also come from putting extraordinarily brave men on the ground so they could direct that air power and make it truly effective."[55]

SOF proved incredibly useful during the invasion of Iraq in 2004, as well. Major-General Duncan Lewis, commander of Australian Special Operations Command, revealed that "the duration of patrols, the distances to be covered, the long-range communication requirements, the calling of precision air strikes, the use of stealth and agility, and the liaison role with Afghan indigenous forces demanded skills that are not generally available in conventional forces."[56] Their application was clearly successful. One strategic assessment insisted, "raids by special operations forces were more impressive than the early air campaign." It went on to explain that "dozens of small special operations teams disrupted Iraqi command-and-control, seized oil infrastructure, prevented dams from being demolished and took hold of airfields in regions where Scud missiles might have been launched at Israel. They also provided information on the whereabouts of Iraqi leaders, permitting attacks against Saddam Hussein and the notorious General Ali Hassan Majid (Chemical Ali). Special Forces also disrupted internal Iraqi lines of communication in Baghdad and elsewhere, perhaps hastening the collapse of Iraqi forces once urban combat began."[57]

## CONCLUSION

Because of their utility and performance, SOF had finally earned the acceptance of the mainstream military and political decision makers. As such, the terrorist attacks against the United States on 11 September 2001 finalized the transformation of the perception of SOF and represented the culmination of their acceptance as a core element of any military. Faced with an elusive foe that relied on dispersion, complex terrain, and asymmetric tactics, military commanders quickly realized that only a flexible, adaptive, and agile response would suffice. The challenge had now become one of locating and rooting out terrorists and terrorist networks that threatened American and Western interests. It became a question of disrupting their plans, finding and killing or capturing them, and driving them from their safe havens. As such, USSOCOM has "realigned" itself to better "track down and ... destroy terrorist networks around the world" because in the words of General Charles Holland, its former commander, "we are waging a new type of world war, one against transnational terrorists with global reach, and [SOF] play a crucial role in the fight."[58]

This is not surprising. SOF, with its organizational flexibility, rapid mobility, and underlying strength of exceptionally trained personnel are best positioned to answer the call. For example, they swiftly destroyed the Taliban regime in Afghanistan and severely crippled the capability of al-Qaeda in 2001 and proved invaluable in Iraq in 2003. As the war on terror continues unabated, so too does the reliance on special operations and those who undertake them. SOF, armed with aggressive, intelligent, and highly motivated individuals who are rigorously selected and specially trained and equipped, provide political and military decision makers with an expanded range of options that though normally high-risk are also high-value and capable of significant payoff.

As such, SOF provide a self-contained, versatile, and unique capability, whether employed alone or complementing other forces or agencies to attain military, strategic, or operational objectives. In contrast to conventional forces, SOF are generally small, precise, adaptable, and innovative. As a result, they can conduct operations in a clandestine, covert, or discreet manner. They are capable of organizing and deploying rapidly and can gain entry to and operate in hostile or denied areas without the necessity of secured ports, airfields, or road networks. In addition, they can operate in austere and harsh environments and communicate worldwide with integral equipment. Moreover, they deploy rapidly at relatively low cost, with a low profile, and have a less intrusive presence than larger conventional forces.

Although the future is not certain, SOF have seemingly evolved from a force of desperation, born in the initial crisis of the Second World War, to a force of choice in the aftermath of the 9/11 terrorist attack. Once marginalized and considered as a nuisance to real soldiering, Special Operations Forces will become the workhorses of the future. They will provide decision makers with the needed political and cultural astuteness and military finesse required to succeed in an increasingly complex and chaotic world. It is for this reason that Donald Rumsfeld, the American secretary of defense, asserted, "in an emergency, we dial 911 and ask for Fort Bragg."[59]

NOTES

1. Robin Moore, *The Hunt for Bin Laden: Task Force Dagger* (New York: Ballantine Books, 2003), 233.

2. William Walker, "Shadow Warriors: Elite Troops Hunt Terrorists in Afghanistan," *Toronto Star*, 20 October 2001, A4.

3. Tom Clancy and John Gresham, *Special Forces: A Guided Tour of the U.S. Army Special Forces* (New York: Berkley Books, 2001), 3. See Bernd Horn, "Special Men, Special Missions: The Utility of Special Operations Forces," in Bernd Horn, David Last, J. Paul de B. Taillon, eds., *Force of Choice: Perspectives on Special Operations* (Montreal: McGill-Queen's Press, 2004), Chapter 1 for a discussion on the myriad of definitions and perspectives on the meaning of SOF.

4. Thomas K. Adams, *US Special Operations Forces in Action: The Challenge of Unconventional Warfare* (London: Frank Cass, 1998), 7. Canada has adopted the NATO definition for Special Operations which says they are "military activities conducted by specially designated, organized, trained and equipped forces, using operational techniques and modes of employment not standard to conventional forces. These activities are conducted across the spectrum of military operations independently or in co-ordination with operations of conventional forces." Colonel W.J. Fulton, DNBCD, "Capabilities Required of DND, Asymmetric Threats and Weapons of Mass Destruction," Fourth Draft 18 March 2001, 16/22.

5. CT measures are the offensive measures, whereas antiterrorism (AT) measures are the defensive measures. SOF CT operations encompass both CT and AT.

6. UW is a broad spectrum of military and paramilitary operations that normally includes guerrilla warfare and other direct-offensive, low-visibility, covert, or clandestine operations, as well as the indirect activities of subversion, sabotage, intelligence activities, and unconventional assisted recovery. Special Operations Commanders' Conference, 14 April 2003.

7. U.S. Special Operations Command, *US Special Operations Forces: Posture Statement 2000* (Washington, DC: Department of Defense, 2001), 5. In 2003, USSOCOM decided to drop the six collateral activities that included: Coalition Support, Combat Search and Rescue, Counter Drug activities, Humanitarian Demining activities, Security Assistance, and Special Activities. Special Operations Commanders' Conference, 14 April 2003.

8. David Jablonsky, *Churchill: The Making of a Grand Strategist* (Carlisle Barracks: Strategic Studies Institute, U.S. Army War College, 1990), 125; Cecil Aspinall-Oglander, *Roger Keyes: Being the Biography of Admiral of the Fleet Lord Keyes of Zeebrugge and Dover* (London: Hogarth Press, 1951), 380; John Terraine, *The Life and Times of Lord Mountbatten* (London: Arrow Books, 1980), 83; Winston S. Churchill, *The Second World War: Their Finest Hour* (Boston: Houghton Mifflin Company, 1949), 246–247. See also Colonel J.W. Hackett, "The Employment of Special Forces," *Royal United Services Institute (RUSI)*, Vol. 97, No. 585 (February 1952), 28; and Colonel D.W. Clarke, "The Start of the Commandos," 30 October 1942, Public Record Office (PRO), DEFE 2/4, War Diary Combined Operations Command (COC) 1.

9. "Hand-Out to Press Party Visiting the Commando Depot Achnacarry, 9–12 January 1943," PRO, DEFE 2/5, War Diary COC, 2.

10. See Hilary St. George Saunders, *The Green Beret: The Story of the Commandos 1940–1945* (London: Michael Joseph, 1949); *Combined Operations: The Official Story of the Commandos* (New York: Macmillan Company, 1943); Peter Wilkinson and Joan Bright Astley, *Gubbins and the SOE* (London: Leo Cooper, 1997), 50–68; John Parker, *Commandos: The Inside Story of Britain's Most Elite Fighting Force* (London: Headline Book Publishing, 2000); Brigadier John Durnford-Slater, *Commando* (Annapolis, MD: Naval Institute Press, reprint 1991); Brigadier Peter Young, *Commando* (New York: Ballantine Books, 1969); Brigadier T.B.L. Churchill, "The Value of Commandos," *RUSI*, Vol. 65, No. 577 (February 1950), 85; Tony Geraghty, *Inside the SAS* (Toronto: Methuen, 1980); and Charles Messenger, *The Commandos 1940–1946* (London: William Kimber, 1985).

11. See Ken Connor, *Ghost Force* (London: Orion, 1998), 13–14; Anthony Kemp, *The SAS: Savage Wars of Peace 1947 to the Present* (London: Penguin, 2001), 37–41; and Adrian Weale, *Secret Warfare: Special Operations Forces from the Great Game to the SAS* (London: Coronet, 1997), 145.

12. See Thomas K. Adams, *US Special Operations Forces in Action: The Challenge of Unconventional Warfare* (London: Frank Cass, 1998), 47, 56; Mark Lloyd, Special Forces, *The Changing Face of Warfare* (London: Arms and Armour, 1995), 117–119; and Charles M. Simpson III, *Inside the Green Berets: The Story of the US Army Special Forces* (New York: Berkley Books, 1984), 35.

13. See Simpson, 35–54; Weale, 147–148; and Joseph Nadel, *Special Men and Special Missions* (London: Greenhill Books, 1994), 33–34.

14. See Geraghty, *Inside the SAS*, 23–39; Kemp, *The SAS: Savage Wars* ...,15–35; Conner, 149–55; and Weale, 149–159.

15. See Kenneth Macksey, *Commando Strike: The Story of Amphibious Raiding in World War II* (London: Leo Cooper, 1985), 208; and Conner, 84–85; Kemp, *The SAS: Savage Wars* ..., 38; Conner, 54–55 and 84–86; and Geraghty, *Inside the SAS*, 49.

16. See Geraghty, *Inside the SAS*, 23–85; Kemp, *The SAS: Savage Wars* ..., Chapters 2, 4–6; Conner, 56–262; Lloyd, 100–119; Robin Neillands, *In the Combat Zone: Special Forces Since 1945* (London: Weidenfeld and Nicolson, 1997), 105–154; Peter Dickens, *SAS: The Jungle Frontier* (London: Arms and Armour Press, 1983); and David Charters and Maurice Tugwell, *Armies in Low-Intensity Conflict* (New York: Brassey's, 1989).

17. A perennial problem and complaint by SOF has been the misemployment of the highly trained but lightly equipped and armed SOF by commanders who do not understand their role or who simply just do not like them. For example, in Korea, eventually 17 Ranger companies were created. However, they "became nomads attached to various infantry regiments for various periods of time during which they were normally used as shock troops in the most dangerous parts of the front." Thomas K. Adams, *US Special Operations Forces in Action: The Challenge of Unconventional Warfare* (London: Frank Cass, 1998), 51.

18. See Colonel Scott Crerar, "The Special Force Experience with the Civilian Irregular Defence Group (CIDG) in Vietnam," in Bernd Horn, J. Paul de B. Taillon, and David Last, eds., *Force of Choice: Perspectives on Special Operations Forces* (Kingston: McGill-Queen's Press, 2004), Chapter 5; Robin Moore, *The Green Berets* (New York: Ballantine, 1965); 99–119; Susan Marquis, *Unconventional Warfare: Rebuilding US Special Operations Forces* (Washington, DC: Brookings Institutions Press, 1997), 14–20; and Neillands, 154–172.

19. Alan and Frieda Landau, *US Special Forces* (Osceola, WI: MBI Publishing Company, 1992), 288–295; Marquis, 20–33; Neillands, 168–169; and Nadel, 60–75.

20. See John L. Plaster, *SOG* (New York: Onyx, 1997); Richard H. Shultz, *The Secret War Against Hanoi: The Untold Story of Spies, Saboteurs and Covert Warriors in North Vietnam* (New York: Perennial, 2000); and Adams, chapters 4 and 5.

21. John D. Lock, *To Fight with Intrepidity: The Complete History of the US Army Rangers* (New York: Pocket Books, 1998), 330–438; Landau, 32–33; Neillands, 177–178.

22. D.M. Horner, *SAS Phantoms of the Jungle: A History of the Australian Special Air Service* (Nashville, TN: The Battery Press, 1989), 170–391; Weale, 194–200; and Neillands, 152–153 and 178–181.

23. See Weale, 192–194; William H. McRaven, *Spec Ops: Case Studies in Special Operations Warfare: Theory and Practice* (Novato, CA: Presidio Press, 1995), 287–331; and Benjamin F. Schemmer, *The Raid: The Son Tay Prison Rescue Mission* (New York: Ballantine Books, 2001).

24. Simpson, 72–73; Adams, 158.

25. John L. Plaster, *SOG* (New York: Onyx, 1997), 251, 267, and 355. SEALs had a kill ratio of 50:1 (Nadel, 75). USMC reports indicated that their Force Recon soldiers had a kill ratio of 38:1 as compared to the USMC overall kill ratio of 8:1. Neillands, 38.

26. *Ibid.*, 357.

27. Quoted in Adams, 70, 148. See also Michael Duffy, Mark Thompson, and Michael Weisskopf, "Secret Armies of the Night," *Time*, Vol. 161, No. 25 (23 June 2003).

28. Marquis, 4, 35, 40, and 78. Special Forces manning went from the tens of thousands to 3,600 personnel.

29. Marquis, 68.

30. *Ibid.*, 160.

31. See Peter Harclerode, *Secret Soldiers: Special Forces in the War Against Terrorism* (London: Cassell & Co., 2000); J. Paul de B. Taillon, *The Evolution of Special Forces in Counter-Terrorism* (Westport, CT: Praeger, 2001); Benjamin Netanyahu, *Fighting Terrorism* (New York: Noonday Press, 1995); Christopher Dobson and Ronald Payne, *The Terrorists* (New York: Facts on File, 1995); Landau, 187–201; Marquis, 62–65; and Brian MacDonald, ed., *Terror* (Toronto: The Canadian Institute of Strategic Studies, 1986).

32. Harcelrode, 51.

33. A few examples include the storming of the Turkish embassy by three Armenian men on 12 March 1985 (Armenian Revolutionary Army); the

paralyzing of the Toronto public transit system on 1 April 1985, as a result of a communiqué sent by a group identifying itself as the Armenian Secret Army for the Liberation of Our Homeland in which they threatened death to passengers of the transit system; and the downing of an Air India flight off the coast of Ireland on 23 June 1985, killing 329 people as a result of a bomb that was planted prior to the plane's departure from Toronto's Pearson International Airport.

34. See Major-General Ulrich Wegener, "The Evolution of Grenzschutzgruppe (GSG) 9 and the Lessons of 'Operation Magic Fire' in Mogadishu," in Horn et al., *Force of Choice*, Chapter 7; David Miller, *Special Forces* (London: Salamander Books, 2001), 18–73; Harclerode, 264–285 and 411; Adams, 160–162; Marquis, 63–65; Weale, 201–235; Colonel Charlie Beckwith, *Delta Force* (New York: Dell, 1983); Connor, 262–356; Neillands, 204–246; and Leroy Thompson, *The Rescuers: The World's Top Anti-Terrorist Units* (London: A David & Charles Military Book, 1986).

35. On 30 April 1980, six DRMLA terrorists seized the Iranian embassy located at No. 16 Princes Gate, London, and took 29 hostages. On 5 May, after one of the hostages had been killed, the SAS launched their assault. In 11 minutes, they freed the remaining hostages, killed five of the six terrorists, and arrested the sixth, who was hiding among the released hostages. See Harclerode, 386–408; Connor, 341–355; and Taillon, 41–52.

36. On 4 November 1979, radical Iranian students seized the U.S. embassy in Tehran, capturing 53 U.S. hostages, who they would hold for 444 days. During this period, a very complicated and complex operation with the overall designation "Operation Eagle Claw" was mounted on 24 April 1980. The plan was for six C-130 Hercules to land at "Desert One" in Iran and await helicopters that would refuel and then take the assault force to a landing zone from which vehicles would later be taken to launch the actual rescue attempt. However, mechanical problems with the helicopters necessitated the cancellation of the mission. In addition, chaos struck at Desert One. Two aircraft collided and caused the death of eight SOF members. In the end, the mission was a cataclysmic failure as a result of faulty equipment, planning, and coordination, as well as command and control. See also Beckwith, 216–262; Adams, 163–167; Marquis, 69–73; Taillon, 103–117; and John T. Carney and Benjamin F. Schemmer, *No Room for Error* (New York: Ballantine Books, 2003), 84–100.

37. Department of Defense, (DoD), *United States Special Operations Command History* (Washington, DC: USSOCOM, 1999), 3–16; Marquis, 69–226; Department of Defense, *US Special Operations Forces: Posture Statement 2000* (Washington, DC: USSOCOM, 2000), 11–14; and Clancy, *Special Forces*, 10–27.

38. See DoD, *USSOCOM History*, 34–42; Douglas C. Waller, *Commando: The Inside Story of America's Secret Soldiers* (New York: Simon & Schuster, 1994), 225–352; Marquis, 227–249; Adams, 231–244; Carney and Schemmer, 224–236; Connor, 456–501; and Neillands, 287–297.

39. See previous note. See also DoD, *USSOCOM History*, 42–44; B.J. Schemmer, "Special Ops Teams Found 29 Scuds Ready to Barrage Israel 24 Hours Before Ceasefire," *Armed Forces Journal International* (July 1991), 36; Mark Thompson, Azadeh Moaveni, Matt Rees, and Aharon Klein, "The Great Scud Hunt," *Time*, Vol. 160, No. 26 (23 December 2002), 34; William Rosenau, *Special Operations Forces and Elusive Ground Targets: Lessons from Vietnam and the Persian Gulf War* (Santa Monica, CA: Rand, 2001); and Cameron Spence, *Sabre Squadron* (London: Michael Joseph, 1997).

40. Marquis, 228; and Waller, *Commando*, 34 and 241; Schemmer, 36. Waller states that 7,705 SOF personnel participated.

41. Clancy, *Special Forces*, 12; Waller, 231 and D.C. Waller, "Secret Warriors," *Newsweek* (17 June 1991), 21.

42. Schemmer, 36; and Waller, *Commandos*, 34 and 241. Waller states that 7,705 SOF personnel participated.

43. DoD, *USSOCOM History*, 44–69; Carney and Schemmer, 245–282; *US SOF Posture Statement 2000*, 15–23; Neillands, 298–315; Adams, 244–286.

44. The change in momentum became obvious. Using the Americans as a case study, the assistant secretary of defense for special operations and low-intensity conflict reported, in 1992, that "our deployments between Fiscal Years 1991 and 1992 grew by 83%." This trend continued. "During 1997," revealed General Schoomaker, "SOF deployed to 144 countries around the world, with an average of 4,760 SOF personnel deployed per week — a threefold increase in missions since 1991." During the fiscal year 1997 alone, SOF conducted 17 crisis response operations, 194 counter-drug missions, humanitarian demining operations in 11 countries. They participated in 224 combined exercises for training in 91 countries. The following year, SOF conducted 2,178 missions outside the continental USA in 152 different countries. A point worth noting is that the incredible capability and flexibility provided by the U.S. SOF, which numbers about 45,690 members, came at the cost of only 1 percent of their defence budget. James C. Hyde, "An Exclusive Interview with James R. Locher III," *Armed Forces Journal International* (November/December 1992), 34; Lieutenant-General Peter J. Schoomaker, "Army Special Operations: Foreign Link, Brainy Force," *National Defense* (February 1997), 32–33; Scott Gourlay, "Boosting the Optempo," *Jane's Defence Weekly* (14 July 1999), 26; and Hyde, 34.

45. Ray Bond, ed., *America's Special Forces* (Miami: Salamander Books, 2001).

46. Kim Burger, "US Special Operations Get Budget Boost," *Jane's Defence Weekly*, Vol. 37, No. 8 (20 February 2002), 2.

47. Tom Breen, "US Special Operations Command," *Armed Forces Journal* (July 2004), 47; Glenn Goodman, "Expanded Role for Elite Commandos," *Armed Forces Journal* (February 2003), 36; Duffy et al., "Secret Armies of the Night"; Roxane Tiron, "Demand for Special Ops Forces Outpaces Supply," *National Defence*, Vol. 87, No. 594 (May 2003), 18; Harold Kennedy, "Special Operators Seeking a Technical Advantage," *National Defense*, Vol. 87, No. 594 (May 2003), 20.

48. *Ibid.*, 2. In Australia, their Special Operations Command, which is equally tasked, currently costs their taxpayers a little over two cents of every dollar allocated to defence. Major-General Duncan Lewis (Commander Special Operations Command), "Inside and Outside the Battlespace," *Australian Army Journal*, Vol. 1, No. 2 (2003), 58.

49. Bond, 9. This includes an active force element of 29,164 personnel and a reserve component of 10,043. DoD, *US SOF, Posture Statement 2000*, 41.

50. Tiron, 18. There were more than 12,000 deployed to Iraq and approximately 8,000 deployed to Afghanistan.

51. Glenn Goodman, "Tip of the Spear," *Armed Forces Journal International* (June 2002), 35; Moore, *The Hunt for Bin Laden*, xix and 2; and Carney and Schemmer, 7. This number represents 18 Operational Detachment-Alpha — 12-man teams. Initially only four SF teams were inserted by helicopter in the north to link up with Northern Alliance commanders in late October and early November when the U.S.-backed anti-Taliban offensive appeared to be bogged down. The growing importance of their role as combat control teams is evident. In Afghanistan, 60 percent of munitions dropped were precision-guided compared to 35 percent during the Kosovo air campaign in 1999 and 6 percent in the Gulf War in 1991. Dr. Elinor Sloan, "Terrorism and the Transformation of US Military Forces," *Canadian Military Journal*, Vol. 3, No. 2 (Summer 2002). Currently, these small SOF teams of about a dozen Special Forces personnel are establishing outposts deep in enemy territory and are working with Afghan units approximately 120 strong. Michael Ware, "On the Mop-Up Patrol," *Time* (25 March 2002), 36–37; and Thomas E. Ricks, "Troops in Afghanistan to Take Political Role Officials Say Remaining Fights to Be Taken by Special Forces, CIA, " *Duluth News Tribune*, 7 July 2002, 1. The CIA has unleashed its 150-man covert paramilitary force in Afghanistan to conduct sabotage, collect intelligence, and train Northern Alliance guerrillas. See Calabresi and Ratnesar, 22.

52. Moore, *The Hunt for Bin Laden*, 103–104 and 139.

53. *Ibid.*, 136.

54. Major-General (Retired) Robert H. Scales, Jr., *Yellow Smoke: The Future of Land Warfare for America's Military* (New York: Rowman & Littlefield, 2003), 21. See also Stephen Biddle, *Afghanistan and the Future of Warfare: Implications for Army and Defense Policy* (Carlisle: Strategic Studies Institute, U.S. Army War College, 2002), 1.

55. Quoted in Carney and Schemmer, 8.

56. Lewis, 54.

57. "Lessons from the Iraq War," *Strategic Comments* (7 May 2003), *www.iss.org*, report went on to say "the combination of GPS-guided all-weather bombs, better all-weather sensors and real time joint communications networks denied Iraqi forces any sanctuary." Another account revealed that U.S. SF were "usually ahead of the tip of the spear: as US troops pushed toward Baghdad, secret combat teams zipped into Iraq aboard specially outfitted MC-130 Combat Talon planes that used highways as landing strips, surprising the enemy at its rear. On the road to Tikrit, they fingered Iraqi vehicles fleeing the capital for destruction by M1 tanks. And inside the capital the elite Delta Force slipped into Baghdad's back alleys and into its sewers to eavesdrop on communications, cut fiber-optic cables, target regime leaders and build networks of informants." Michael Duffy, Mark Thompson, and Michael Weisskopf, "Secret Armies of the Night," *Time*, Vol. 161, No. 25, accessed electronically 12 January 2004.

58. Breen, 46.

59. Quoted in Carney and Schemmer, 13.

# 8

## Who Has Seen the Wind?
### *A Historical Overview of Canadian Special Operations*

Sean M. Maloney

Who has seen the wind? Neither you nor I.
— W.O. Mitchell, *Who Has Seen the Wind?*

Media reaction to revelations that Canadian Special Operations Forces, specifically Joint Task Force Two (JTF-2), were conducting operations in Afghanistan in late 2001 and were involved in the capture of Taliban and al-Qaeda personnel in early 2002 was one of profound shock. Since the 1970s, Canadians have been conditioned to believe that the supposedly "underhanded" aspects of national security policy execution — spying, propaganda, subversion, psychological operations, and guerrilla warfare — were activities morally beneath Canada. Indeed, many Canadians firmly believe that the Canadian Forces (CF) exists only to conduct UN peacekeeping operations based on the model of the 1956 United Nations Emergency Force in the Sinai, or to conduct relief operations to aid unfortunate Third World disaster victims. The realities of Canadian history do not support these narrow views. Canada has, in fact, a rich heritage of involvement in special operations, particularly during the Second World War. That this heritage does not conform to the public perception of the more extensive experience in special operations that exist in the British or American contexts speaks volumes about its covert, sporadic, and ad hoc nature.

Here, a note on definitions and parameters. It is not possible to perfectly superimpose the current American definition of special operations onto the Canadian experience. The Canadian experience is a combination of what American doctrine calls "unconventional warfare" (the clandestine conduct of paramilitary and military operations in enemy-held, controlled, or politically sensitive territory), counterterrorism (specifically hostage rescue), security assistance, and irregular support to conventional operations in pursuit of an operational or strategic aim. Unlike the American experience and doctrine, Canadian psychological operation efforts, both strategic and tactical, have been generally separate from these other roles and missions  and will not be discussed in any great detail in this chapter.[1]

## THE SECOND WORLD WAR

The Canadian special operations experience began when Canada was invited to supply personnel to Great Britain's Special Operations Executive (SOE) during the early days of the Second World War. This agency was the amalgamation of three overlapping organizations within the British government: Section D of the Secret Intelligence Service (MI6), General Staff (Research), later called Military Intelligence (Research) (MI[R]), and Electra House (EH). All three organizations independently pursued special operations concepts and issues from 1938, in part because of a belief prevalent in the Chamberlain government that the rapid succession of Axis political victories in the late 1930s were somehow connected to so-called "Fifth Columns" of pro-Nazi traitors embedded in the target nations' societies.[2]

The concepts that emerged bear some elaboration, for they provide excellent embodiments of special operations and the closest thing to a pre-JTF-2 Canadian understanding of special operations. Section D explored ideas of "secret offensives," which included the coordination of sabotage, labour unrest, propaganda, and economic inflation directed against an enemy nation. Later, enhanced Section D concepts called for the creation of a so-called "democratic international" that would conduct industrial sabotage, labour agitation, propaganda, terrorist acts against traitors, the assassination of German leaders, economic boycotts, and the fomenting of riots. It governed the activities of military personnel conducting operations without uniforms.[3]

MI(R), on the other hand, dealt with uniformed activity, and used the term *irregular warfare* to encompass a variety of operations, including the use of guerrilla warfare. This was considered, "[the] preparation of projects involving the employment of special or irregular forces to assist or increase the effect of normally conducted operations, directly or indirectly."[4]

MI(R) postulated that there were three types of guerrilla war that could be conducted in countries occupied by an enemy power: Individuals or small groups working by stealth to sabotage industrial or military targets; larger groups employing military tactics and weapons to destroy a particular target; and large military organizations, such as partisan forces, formed to carry out broad offensive campaigns.[5]

MI(R) tended to focus on the technological and doctrinal developments that would be needed to carry out any sort of program conforming to these concepts. By way of example, the development of plastic explosives and the translation of manuals describing their use, specifications for rudimentary submachine guns, such as the Sten, and discussions on how to employ small raiding groups were prominent MI(R) activities. Indeed, the creation of the first so-called independent companies, later renamed the Commandos, was an outgrowth of MI(R) work.[6]

Finally, there was Electra House (EH), whose specialty was "moral sabotage," better known as propaganda. Led by the Canadian, Sir Campbell Stuart, EH conceptualized techniques which, when combined with the planned activities of Section D and MI(R), would augment the conventional "regular" military efforts to destroy the will of the target enemy nation to continue the fight.

All three organizations, but most particularly MI(R), drew on historical experience for their work. Many of the planners had direct knowledge of some of the original special operations. The favoured experiences were T.E. Lawrence's engagements in the Middle East during the First World War, and specific attention was paid to Michael Collins's campaign against the "Cairo Gang" in Ireland and subsequent IRA urban and rural guerrilla operations. Orde Wingate's organization of the Jewish Special Night Squads to combat the Arab Revolt in the 1930s was another significant influence, as were the operations of Chinese guerrillas against the Japanese in the late 1930s.[7]

On 23 March 1939, Section D, MI(R), and EH merged to form the Special Operations Executive. SOE's importance was enhanced by Winston Churchill in 1940 when Great Britain and its empire were in dire peril after the fall of France. Churchill's quest for positive action, his "set Europe ablaze" dictum, influenced to an extent by his own experience against the Boers in the South African War, gave SOE the catalyst needed to take the war to the Axis powers. It was also intended to keep them off balance until a re-entry by force onto the continent could be accomplished.

Ultimately, two streams of special operations emerged in 1940. SOE was responsible for clandestine subversive and guerrilla operations inside occupied and enemy countries. Uniformed raiding units under the command of Combined Operations Headquarters (COHQ) were responsible for the destruction of military targets on the periphery of the enemy's "Fortress Europe." There was overlap at times: SOE assisted with intelligence gathering, liaison, and training in 1942 for the Bruneval raid against a German radar site, as well as the St. Nazaire raid against the Normandy dock, staged with the intention of denying it to the enemy as a battleship repair facility.[8]

Canadians were involved in both special operations streams, although the first experiences were with SOE. In addition to Campbell Stuart, who was eased out during the war's early innings due to age and obstinacy, the only senior Canadian figure involved with SOE was Sir William Stephenson. This colourful character was in charge of British Security Coordination (BSC), which was essentially a "joint command" handling MI5, MI6, and SOE activities in the Western Hemisphere. BSC was heavily involved in SOE training, particularly the shadowy Camp X located near Oshawa, Ontario. The official SOE history notes, however, that SOE did not operate in the United States and that Stephenson's activities on behalf of the executive were minuscule when compared with his MI5 and MI6 activities and liaison with "Wild Bill" Donovan's American SOE equivalent, the Office of Strategic Services (OSS).[9]

Canada was closely integrated into Great Britain's war effort in every way: Canadians not only served in the indigenous Canadian forces, but also in the British Army, the Royal Air Force and the Royal Navy in great numbers, alongside other British Empire personnel from countries as disparate as Rhodesia and Malaya. Why Canada did not establish her own SOE in the way she maintained her own Air Force, Navy, and Army is unclear, but was most likely due to cost, a lack of experience in the field, and a strategic vision that resulted in Canadian efforts being rolled into broader British imperial efforts. In 1940, SOE asked the senior Canadian Army commander in England, General A.G.L. McNaughton, for Canadian volunteers. McNaughton apparently initially had some reservations, but he acquiesced in 1941. Canadian volunteers from the uniformed services would be "loaned" to the War Office for duty with SOE. This agency recruited three types of Canadians: French Canadians for service in France, Canadians of Eastern European descent for operations in the Balkans, and Chinese Canadians for Asian operations.[10]

One can only estimate the total number of Canadians who served in SOE. Approximately 28 served in France, while another 56 served in Eastern Europe and the Balkans. A further 143 were active in the China-Burma-India theatre. Many more served in training and support capacities in Canada, England, Asia, and the Middle East. Canadian RCAF and RAF personnel also served with some of the Special Duty Squadrons, units used to drop weapons, and insert and extract SOE personnel.[11]

As with all special operations, the relatively small size of the Canadian contribution does not tell the full story nor does it capture the brutal and human nature of the activities. For example, there is the exceptional case of Gustave Bieler from Montreal's Régiment de Maisonneuve. Bieler was inserted into France by SOE in 1942. By the time he was captured in 1943, he had organized several sabotage groups which seriously disrupted German rail communications throughout the St. Quentin region and destroyed at least 40 barges loaded with submarine components headed for the port of Rouen during the height of the Battle for the Atlantic. When captured, Bieler held out against particularly brutal Gestapo torture so steadfastly that the SS guards at Flossenberg concentration camp, where he was ultimately incarcerated, mounted an honour guard as he limped fearlessly to his death by firing squad.

SOE was, by late 1942, desperately short of trained radio operators. Many Canadians serving with SOE hailed from the Royal Canadian Corps of Signals (RCCS). A dangerous job given advanced German direction finding (DF) capabilities, Canadians took great risks to bolster the rudimentary SOE communications system. For example, a Lieutenant Alcide Beauregard, at great personal risk, kept several SOE cells, known as "circuits," in operation until he was captured and tortured to the point of insanity. He was eventually murdered by the Lyon Gestapo along with 120 French resistance fighters. Notably, no Canadian SOE operator who was captured by the Germans survived incarceration.[12]

There were, however, many notable Canadian SOE successes. Canadian-led efforts seriously hindered the ability of the 1st and 2nd SS Panzer Divisions to intervene in Normandy in a timely fashion after 6

June 1944. Also, Canadian-led SOE operations attempted to disrupt the logistic structures supporting the V-1 and V-2 blitz campaign against London in 1944. Canadian SOE personnel, many of them Spanish Civil War veterans of the Mackenzie-Papineau Brigade, also operated in Yugoslavia supporting Tito's partisans by providing weapons training, operations planning, communications, and medical support, and by coordinating arms drops.[13]

The exploits of Force 136, somewhat loosely portrayed in the movie *Bridge on the River Kwai*, included operations in Malaya conducted by Chinese Canadian NCOs, such as Norman Wong and Roger Chung. At least 16 Chinese Canadians dropped or landed in Sarawak to supply, train, and lead native tribes in guerrilla operations against the Japanese, events that formed the basis of another movie, *Farewell to the King*.[14]

The second special operations stream that emerged during the Second World War consisted of the theatre-specific raiding and reconnaissance units. The best known at the time were the Commandos, who conducted raiding operations from Norway to Greece, some of them at the battalion-level of effort. Airborne forces were also employed on occasion for raids, usually at the company level. In time, the employment of large-scale amphibious and airborne operations became standard and thus could be considered conventional military operations conveyed through a different medium, be it air or sea, rather than special operations.

Early in the war, however, regular infantry units were used in strategic raiding operations. The first such action involving Canadian forces was Operation "Gauntlet" in August 1941. "Gauntlet's" objective was to land on the island of Spitsbergen, deny coal production facilities to the Germans, destroy key meteorological stations supporting the U-boat war, and evacuate 2,000 interned Russians. The force consisted of the Edmonton Regiment and a company from the Princess Patricia's Canadian Light Infantry, the 3rd Field Company, Royal Canadian Engineers, and a machine gun company from the Saskatchewan Light Infantry. It was known as "111 Force" and was transported aboard the converted liner *Empress of Canada* and supported by two British cruisers and three destroyers.[15]

The bulk of the planning was conducted at COHQ with minimal Canadian input, though the force units received amphibious assault training at the Combined Training Centre Inverary. Landing with minimal resistance, 111 Force conducted its demolitions and withdrew. The Germans were caught completely off guard and subsequently deployed scarce troop resources on other Norwegian islands to deter further raids.[16] The disastrous Dieppe Raid of 1942, a COHQ-planned and predominately Canadian-executed operation, demonstrated that amphibious operations of brigade size or larger were too unwieldy for strategic raiding. British attention shifted to other endeavours, such as the small-scale but effective Operation "Frankton" raid against shipping in the Gironde estuary by the Royal Marines' "Cockleshell Heroes," which also occurred in 1942.

A number of British Special Operations Forces emerged in the Mediterranean theatre, particularly in the Aegean and the Western Desert. These included the Special Boat Squadron (SBS), the New Zealand-dominated Long Range Desert Group (LRDG), and No. 1 Demolitions Squadron. All were involved in some form of clandestine or covert infiltration of enemy lines and the subsequent destruction of military targets deep in rear areas. The LRDG's primary function was as a theatre reconnaissance force, although it transported other special units to their targets. All three units were British formations that had small numbers of individual Canadian volunteers.[17]

The most famous British Special Operations Force to emerge from the Mediterranean that included Canadians was the Special Air Service (SAS). The SAS evolved from a desert raiding force, which had destroyed more German aircraft on the ground than the RAF destroyed in the air over Libya and Egypt, into a partisan support force working alongside SOE in the Balkans. Eventually, it expanded into a full brigade in Northwest Europe and Italy where it operated behind German lines conducting jeep-borne raids as well as supporting and leading resistance groups. An effective operation in northern Italy led by a Canadian, Captain Buck McDonald, significantly disrupted enemy communications and seized the town of Alba deep in German-occupied territory. As with the demolitions squadron, the SBS and the LRDG, Canadian involvement appears to have been on an individual level, as there are no records indicating the existence of a Canadian national SAS sub-unit.[18]

Although no Canadian SAS or SBS equivalent organization existed, Canadian commanders in Northwest Europe were not reluctant to use SAS resources to support the conventional battle as the Canadian Army fought its way through the Netherlands in the spring of 1945. General Harry Crerar, working with Brigadier J.M. Calvert of the SAS, devised Operation "Amherst," whereby 700 men from the SAS Brigade, mostly French and Belgian operators from French SAS paratrooper regiments, would be dropped by air in advance of the ground thrust. They were to "cause confusion in the German rear areas, help the Dutch resistance, and in other ways assist the progress of our divisions.... Their general task was the preservation of canal and river bridges on the 2nd Corps' axis of advance." The Special Air Service was also to raid forward German air bases in order to disrupt enemy fighter cover and to provide operational-level intelligence and battlefield guides to the advancing First Canadian Army.[19]

The SAS units fought continuously for the next seven days, capturing 250 Germans and preventing the destruction of the vital bridges. The Canadian official historian Colonel Charles Stacey noted that at Spier, one of the field unit commanders, "having boldly captured the village with a small party, was rescued from imminent annihilation by far superior German forces by the timely arrival, in the best manner of films, of vehicles from the 8th Canadian Reconnaissance Regiment."[20] Although not a perfect operation, "Amherst" demonstrated to Canadian officers how special operations could have a positive influence on a conventional campaign.

The most famous raiding force from a Canadian perspective was the First Special Service Force (FSSF), better known as the Devil's Brigade. The concept of a combined Canadian-American unit emerged from COHQ deliberations in 1942. Headquarters planners wanted to destroy several of Norway's hydroelectric plants, which were being used to refine a variety of scarce ores needed for the German war effort. An added benefit was presumed to be the concomitant tying down of thousands of German troops because of the threat of future raids, troops that might have been employed against the Allies elsewhere. Additional missions envisioned by COHQ for the FSSF included the destruction of the Ploesti oil fields in Romania and an attack against Italy's hydroelectric capacity, which, it was hoped, could cripple the industrialized regions of the nation.[21]

The FSSF initially mustered about 2,600 personnel, although it usually fought with approximately 1,700 effectives. About one-quarter to one-third of them were Canadian. The Force possessed an exaggerated structure of three "regiments," each consisting of two battalions of 200 to 300 men. Each "battalion" had two companies, with each company consisting of three platoons of two sections. This non-standard structure was designed in part for deception and in part to permit dispersion. The FSSF had a significant demolitions capability, was partially mechanized with tracked over-snow vehicles, could be air dropped by parachute, and its personnel received amphibious, mountain and ski training.[22]

The FSSF was designed, structured, and trained to smash large dispersed industrial targets deep in enemy territory. Several factors conspired to deny the FSSF its primary mission, however. The security of the Norwegian operation was compromised, and in any event, RAF Bomber Command viewed the existence and use of such a force as being contrary to its own interests. Combined Operations Headquarters, led by Lord Louis Mountbatten, did not want to worsen its already strained relationship with "Bomber" Harris in the pursuit of other projects.[23]

The FSSF was also later deployed to Kiska in the Aleutian Islands chain west of Alaska. This became a combined Canadian-American fiasco when several thousand troops landed on a supposedly Japanese-occupied island, which was, in fact, deserted. Supreme Headquarters Allied Expeditionary Forces (SHAEF) then believed that the FSSF might have a role in raiding operations in Italy and the Balkans, perhaps supporting Tito's partisans. In any event, an Allied troop shortage in Italy brought the FSSF into a series of conventional operations. This occurred first at Mount Difensa, where it seized an important terrain feature and broke a strong point in the German defensive line, then at Anzio, where it acted in an economy-of-force role defending the critical Mussolini Canal zone. Aggressive FSSF night raiding, which involved units ranging in size from three men to a battalion, was so effective that the Germans apparently believed that they were up against a reinforced brigade or a reduced division. However, after a number of other missions in Italy and southern France, the casualty rate was so high that the Force could no longer be sustained.[24]

Though extremely able, aggressive, specially trained, and equipped for a unique mission, the FSSF functioned more as a small light infantry brigade rather than as a special operations unit during the Second World War.

What of the Allied use of airborne forces during the war? Canada contributed the 1st Canadian Parachute Battalion, which operated as part of the British 6th Airborne Division. The role of the airborne forces in eastern Normandy included the destruction of shore batteries, the seizure of bridges, and action as a blocking force to prevent the enemy from reinforcing units defending against the amphibious landing. These forces had no role in operating with guerrilla or resistance units and did not operate in a clandestine fashion: SAS units were deployed in Normandy to handle those missions. The types of targets airborne forces were employed against were mostly operational and not strategic in nature.[25]

What is one to make of Canada's Second World War special operations experience overall? For the most part, it consisted of individual efforts incorporated into Allied umbrella units. However, Canada did have significant light infantry experiences that overlapped to some extent with special operations. Notably, the use of Special Operations Forces by Canadian commanders to support the conventional battle was significant towards the end of the war, when the size of Canada's conventional forces in the field permitted access to this capability.

## THE COLD WAR

Canadian interest in Special Operations Forces did not carry over into the Cold War period in any systematic way. Consequently, the Cold War experience is a patchwork of activities, few of which were coordinated in any fashion.

From 1946 to 1955, Canadian defence planners focused some of their efforts on creating an airborne force for North American continental defence. The Mobile Striking Force (MSF) was essentially a light infantry brigade group that could deploy three airborne company groups by parachute, with follow-on battalions coming by glider. The MSF was fundamentally a light infantry force designed for operations in Canada's north, in Alaska, or in Iceland. It possessed a Pathfinder force, but this unit was given traditional airborne-oriented tasks. Embedded was a Canadian SAS company, but its role remains obscure, and in any event, it was not in existence for very long.[26]

The Canadian Army's two main Cold War commitments, 25 Canadian Infantry Brigade serving with UN forces in Korea, and 27 Canadian Infantry Brigade serving with NATO forces in Europe, were conventional formations. Successor formations to 27 Brigade in West Germany did, however, retain for a time a small unit of eight German-born Canadian soldiers who were planned to be used to conduct sabotage and deep reconnaissance missions against Warsaw Pact forces operating against the Canadian brigade. This capability was of an almost tactical nature, however, and had been discontinued by 1970.[27]

The 1950s and 1960s are generally acknowledged to be the Golden Age of Western counter-insurgency efforts, endeavours that produced a plethora of Special Operations Forces in Western armies. There does not appear to have been any doctrinal basis for Canadian special operations during this period, nor any centralized organization to provide Canadian forces with special operations skills.

Many counter-insurgency operations were brought on by decolonization and specialist organizations were created to fight in them. For example, the SAS was reactivated to fight in the Malayan Emergency, while the French deployed the Commandos de Chasse against rebel forces in Algeria.[28] Canada had no colonies and was not directly involved with military forces in assisting Britain, France, or Portugal in their decolonization wars. The use of UN peacekeeping as a surrogate force to fill power vacuums left by decolonization and to prevent Soviet-bloc encroachment was one Canadian contribution to the Third World stabilization effort during the Cold War. Special Operations Forces did not factor in these efforts, given the nature of peace observation and interpositionary peacekeeping prevalent at the time.[29]

The development of the U.S. Army's Special Forces in the 1950s was initially related to the planned conduct of SOE or OSS-like operations in the Soviet-controlled Eastern Bloc in the event of war, while the CIA created clandestine stay-behind organizations in Western Europe, including the NATO and neutral countries, in the event that they were overrun.[30] Canada does not appear to have had any interest in these roles, probably due to budgetary constraints: Most funds were dedicated to the creation and maintenance of Canadian nuclear deterrent forces. Canada, however, did send individual soldiers to undertake Special Forces training in the United States throughout the 1950s, and continues to do so today.[31]

In time, the American Special Forces mission evolved to include security assistance training for allied and friendly forces worldwide to resist Communist expansion.[32] There was similar Canadian activity in the 1960s when the Army deployed Military Assistance Program (MAP) teams to Nigeria, Ghana, and Tanzania. These teams consisted of regular Army officers who, at the "operational" level, trained the military personnel of these new Commonwealth countries to increase their professionalism. The strategic function, particularly of the 83-man team in Tanzania, was to maintain a Western presence to counter Soviet and Chinese-bloc political and military influence. This program was disbanded in 1971, when the Trudeau government disavowed its strategic value.[33]

In the field of hostage rescue, Canadian efforts were ad hoc and situation-specific. The first recorded hostage rescue mission involving Canadian forces occurred in the Congo in 1964. The UN operation was at the time acting as a Western surrogate force to stabilize the country and to prevent Communist interference. Soviet and Chinese-supported insurgents initiated a terror campaign against missionaries and aid workers,

191

which included the seizure of hostages. The senior Canadian UN commander, Brigadier-General J.A. Dextraze, determined that the success of the UN effort lay in the stabilizing influence in the region generated by non-government organizations (NGOs). He then formed a composite Canadian-Nigerian-Swedish airmobile rescue force, which conducted a rescue campaign during which at least 100 people were forcibly extracted from the clutches of the insurgents on several occasions.[34]

Canada's first domestic counterterrorism campaign lasted from 1963 to 1971. While the nation's military forces were somewhat involved in intelligence gathering activities against the leftist Front de Libération du Québec (FLQ) throughout the period, the principle of "police primacy" dominated. There were no Special Operations Forces created specifically for counter-FLQ missions. When the Army was finally deployed en masse in the fall of 1970 after the Pierre Laporte kidnapping, the Canadian Airborne Regiment conducted several airmobile cordon and search operations. These could, however, have also been considered conventional light infantry missions.[35]

The tragic events of the 1972 Munich Olympics were not lost on Canadian planners, but the prevailing belief in the run-up to the 1976 Montreal Olympics was that "police primacy" would dominate and the armed forces would be used in a supporting role. That said, Mobile Command planners responsible for the provision of this support formed several ad hoc quick response groups. Trained on a Special Weapons and Tactics (SWAT)-type model, and incorporating the existing sniper sections assigned to traditional infantry battalions, these 10-man sections were covertly deployed into a number of Olympic Games venues and athlete housing facilities. They were to respond immediately if any violent situation developed. These sections were apparently drawn from the conventional infantry and armour units assigned to security duties in each geographical region. At the end of the Olympic Games, they were integrated back into their parent units.[36]

Special mention should be made of the formation of the Special Service Force (SSF) in 1976. The print media was quick to make what it believed to be connections with the SSF and the SAS when the Canadian Airborne Regiment moved from Edmonton, Alberta to Petawawa, Ontario, and received a new "winged dagger" insignia, which borrowed heavily from British traditions. Rampant speculation about further internal security operations in Quebec followed the move eastward. The SSF, as constituted in the 1970s and 1980s, was actually a rapidly deployable light infantry brigade designed for use on NATO's flanks as part of

Allied Command Europe (ACE) Mobile Force (Land) and the Canadian Air-Sea Transportable (CAST) Brigade. The SSF also functioned as part of the UN Standby Battalion commitment. Despite its name and insignia, the SSF was not a Special Operations Force, although its members did collectively and individually train with the SAS and U.S. Special Forces.[37] Specifically, combat divers from Army engineer units and Fleet Diving Units conducted training exchanges with U.S. Navy Sea Air Land (SEAL) teams and the British Special Boat Squadron in the 1970s.[38]

The astronomical increase in international terrorist incidents in the late 1970s and into the 1980s did not seriously concern the Canadian government in terms of a direct threat to the nation, and therefore there was no impetus to create a special operations capability for counterterrorism. By 1985, that situation changed when terrorist acts were committed on Canadian soil. The response, after some debate, was to create the Special Emergency Response Team (SERT). This agency became a unit of the Royal Canadian Mounted Police (RCMP), although it was supported by Air Force transport resources. It trained with a variety of allied military and police forces for the hostage rescue role.[39]

### ACTIVITIES DURING THE 1990S AND BEYOND

The Canadian Forces entered the post–Cold War world without a special operations capability, but by early in the new millennium, had deployed a dedicated Special Operations Force to fight al-Qaeda and the Taliban in Afghanistan. The publicly available specifics of how this force was created and how it was employed throughout the 1990s are not clear, although some journalistic efforts have delineated the broad outlines and shape of Joint Task Force Two and its activities.[40]

Until the time of the Afghanistan deployment, however, temporary solutions were utilized. An incident involving the seizure of Canadian soldiers in Bosnia led to the creation of an ad hoc hostage rescue force, which was embedded within the United Nations Protection Force (UNPROFOR II) in 1994. At the time, individual Canadians serving in UNPROFOR, who had been on exchange with the SAS, SBS, Special Forces and SEALs, were brought together with SAS and SBS personnel who were already operating in the region under British national control. Some refresher training was conducted and rudimentary plans were made to effect a rescue of captives, had the situation further deteriorated.[41]

In addition to the hostage rescue role, increased national demand for the collection of timely, covert information, and the direction of precision engagements emerged throughout the 1990s. It was evident to those examining the future of the Canadian Army that a gap existed in these capabilities and that the expansion of Special Operations Forces was the best means to address the shortcomings. Pre-emptive action against terrorist threats directed against deployed Canadian forces might also be necessary, since relying upon allied capabilities in this arena compromised independent action and sovereign control. Consequently, more and more effort was spent on expanding JTF-2's capabilities, and the unit's eventual deployment to Afghanistan reflects this state of affairs.

## CONCLUSION

How should one define the Canadian special operations experience overall? Until the formation of JTF-2 in the 1990s, it was ad hoc, reactive, and sporadic in its execution. In many ways, special operations are a strategic weapon — they demand a strong political context in which to operate effectively. During the Second World War, Canada was a young and very junior partner in the Allied camp and chose to follow Great Britain's lead in strategy formulation and execution with resultant effects on the lack of development of an independent Canadian special operations capability. Coherent and consistent Canadian strategic context was lacking. Though there were unstated strategic traditions that emerged in the 1940s, Canadian policymakers during the Cold War were struggling with the fundamental building blocks of strategic policy, such as nuclear weapons, naval forces, and air defence, and the associated problems of coordinating these elements with foreign policy aims. The more sophisticated analysis necessary for Special Operations Forces to develop and thrive was simply not being done. A series of reactive or situation-specific attempts at a special operations capability followed, but there was no defined requirement for separate and independent means given Canada's strategic context.

When Canada was confronted with the realities of the post–Cold War world in the 1990s, formal and dedicated Special Operations Forces were finally established, and they are now part of the country's ability to help protect Canadian national interests at home and abroad. The nature of conflict today and in the future should dictate that Special Operations Forces have a permanent place in Canada's reservoir of operational capabilities.

## NOTES

1. Note that these comments on the Canadian experience come nowhere close to reflecting the 13-line, all-inclusive official American definition of special operations. See William H. McRaven, *Spec Ops: Case Studies in Special Operations Warfare: Theory and Practice* (Novato, CA: Presidio Press, 1995), 2.

2. William Mackenzie, *The Secret History of SOE: The Special Operations Executive 1940–1945* (London: St. Ermin's Press, 2000), xix.

3. M.R.D. Foot, *SOE: The Special Operations Executive 1940–1946* (London: Pimlico Books, 1999), 5, 18–19; and Mackenzie, 4–5.

4. Mackenzie, 10.

5. *Ibid.*, 32.

6. Foot, 9–10, 14.

7. *Ibid.*, 5–6; and Mackenzie, 32.

8. See William Seymour, *British Special Forces* (London: Sidgewick and Jackson, 1985), Ch. 1; and Mackenzie, 362.

9. See H. William Hyde, *The Quiet Canadian: The Secret Service Story of Sir William Stephenson* (London: Constable Books, 1962); and Mackenzie, 329. See also Bill Macdonald, *The True Intrepid: Sir William Stephenson and the Unknown Agents* (Vancouver: Raincoast Books, 2001).

10. Due to the paucity of literature on Canadian Special Operations Executive (SOE) operations, the author is forced to rely upon Roy MacLaren's superbly researched *Canadians Behind Enemy Lines 1939–1945* (Vancouver: University of British Columbia Press, 1983) for most of this section, although there is some information available in C.P. Stacey, *The Victory Campaign: The Operations in North-West Europe 1944–1945* (Ottawa: The Queen's Printer, 1960), 635–637.

11. MacLaren, 147, 172, 200.

12. *Ibid.*, 65–67.

13. *Ibid.*, 80 and 114. See also Brian Jeffrey Street, *The Parachute Ward: A Canadian Surgeon's Wartime Adventures in Yugoslavia* (Toronto: Lester, Orphen and Dennys, 1987).

14. MacLaren, Chapter 13.

15. C.P. Stacey, *Six Years of War: The Army in Canada, Britain and the Pacific* (Ottawa: Queen's Printer, 1957), 301–305.

16. *Ibid.*

17. Alastair Timpson, *In Rommel's Backyard: A Memoir of the Long Range Desert Group* (London: Leo Coopers, 2000); Vladimir Peniakoff, *Private Army* (London: Jonathan Cape, 1950); William Seymour, *British Special Forces* (London: Sidgewick and Jackson, 1985); and Maclaren, 287–299.

18. Peter Macdonald, *SAS im Einsatz: Die Geschichte der Britishen Spezialeinheit* (Stuttgart: Motorbuch Verlag, 1990), 1–30; and Barry Davis, *The Complete Encyclopedia of the SAS* (London: Virgin Publishing Ltd., 1998), 57.

19. C.P. Stacey, *The Victory Campaign*, 552–556.

20. *Ibid.*, 553.

21. Joseph A. Springer, *The Black Devil Brigade: The True Story of the First Special Service Force* (Pacifica: Pacifica Military History, 2001), xxviii; and Robert H. Adleman and George Walton, *The Devil's Brigade* (New York: Chilton Books, 1966), 2, 11–13 and 85.

22. Both the Springer and Adleman/Walton books provide ample details of the structure and training of the FSSF.

23. Springer, 46; Adleman and Walton, 85–86; and C.P. Stacey, *Six Years of War*, 104–107.

24. Springer, 144; and Adleman and Walton, 177, 189.

25. See Bernd Horn and Michel Wyczynski, *Tip of the Spear: An Intimate Portrait of the First Canadian Parachute Battalion, 1942–1945* (Toronto: Dundurn Press, 2002); and Dan Hartigan, *A Rising of Courage: Canada's Paratroops in the Liberation of Normandy* (Calgary: Drop Zone Publishers, 2000).

26. Sean M. Maloney, "The Mobile Striking Force and Continental Defence, 1948–1955," *Canadian Military History*, Vol. 2, No. 3 (Autumn 1993), 75–89; and Bernd Horn, "A Military Enigma: The Canadian Special Air Service Company, 1948–49," *Canadian Military History*, Vol. 10, No. 1 (Winter 2001), 21–30.

27. Sean M. Maloney, *War Without Battles: Canada's NATO Brigade in Germany, 1951–1993* (Toronto: McGraw-Hill Ryerson, 1997), 177.

28. Tony Geraghty, *Who Dares Wins: The Special Air Service, 1950 to the Gulf War* (New York: Warner Books, 1992), 323–354; and Peter Paret, *French Revolutionary Warfare from Indochina to Algeria* (London: Praeger Books, 1964), 37.

29. See Sean M. Maloney, *Canada and UN Peacekeeping: Cold War by Other Means, 1945–1970* (Toronto: Vanwell Publishing, 2002).

30. Alfred H. Paddock, Jr., *US Army Special Warfare: Its Origins* (Washington, DC: National Defense University Press, 1982), Ch. 7; and Jens Mecklenburg, ed., *Gladio: die Geheim Terrororganisation der NATO* (Berlin: Elefanten Press, 1997), 16–22.

31. Ian D.W. Sutherland, *Special Forces of the United States Army 1952–1982* (San Jose, CA: R. James Bender Publishing, 1990), 164.

32. Douglas Blaufarb, "Economic/Security Assistance and Special Operations," in Frank Barnett et al., eds., *Special Operations in US Strategy* (Washington, DC: National Defense University Press, 1984), 203–221.

33. "Canadian Armed Forces World Wide Commitments," *Sentinel* (June 1966), 24–25; and Greg Donaghy, "The Rise and Fall of Canadian Military Assistance in the Developing World, 1952–1971," *Canadian Military History*, Vol. 4, No. 1 (Spring 1995), 75–84.

34. Sean M. Maloney, "Mad Jimmy Dextraze: The Tightrope of UN Command in the Congo," in Bernd Horn and Stephen Harris, *Warrior Chiefs: Perspectives on Senior Canadian Military Leaders* (Toronto: Dundurn Press, 2001), 303–320.

35. Sean M. Maloney, "A Mere Rustle of Leaves: Canadian Strategy and FLQ Crisis," *Canadian Military History*, Vol. 9, No. 2 (Summer 2000), 73–86.

36. Interview with Brigadier-General C. de L. "Kip" Kirby, 17 May 1997. See also Sean M. Maloney, "Domestic Operations: The Canadian Approach," *Parameters, US Army War College Quarterly*, Vol. 27, No. 3 (Autumn 1997), 135–152.

37. Roy MacGregor, "The Armed Forces: In from the Cold," *Maclean's* (6 November, 1978), 20–25; Dick Brown, "Hanging Tough," *Quest: Canada's Urban Magazine*, Vol. 7, No. 3 (May 1978), 12–22. See also Bernd Horn, *Bastard Sons: An Examination of Canada's Airborne Experience, 1942–1995*

(St. Catharines, ON: Vanwell Publishing, 2001); and David Bercuson, *Significant Incident: Canada's Army, the Airborne and the Murder in Somalia* (Toronto: McClelland and Stewart, 1996). Note that the SSF of the 1970s was based on the SSF that existed in the early 1960s, which had the same roles and missions but was incorporated into 2 Canadian Infantry Brigade Group.

38. Author's discussions with FDU and RCE personnel.

39. David Pugliese, *Canada's Secret Commandos: The Unauthorized Story of Joint Task Force Two* (Ottawa: Esprit de Corps Books, 2002), 13–22.

40. *Ibid.*

41. Sean M. Maloney, *Chances for Peace: The Canadians in UNPROFOR, 1992–1995* (Toronto: Vanwell Publishing, 2002).

# 9

## Seamless Black?
### *Observations on the Canadian SOF Experience*

Michael A. Hennessy

The stand-up of the new Canadian Special Operations Forces Command (CANSOFCOM) has been met with the usual skepticism from elements of the Canadian Forces (CF) and the defence policy community. The CF is too small to maintain such forces, they really do not have a role, the Canadian public will not accept such a role, and other similar criticisms have been voiced. Such skepticism has accompanied all prior efforts too. Dissension within the armed forces and external criticism can prove serious checks on new thinking. A healthy dose of skepticism should accompany any change but a review of Canada's experience in generating, supporting, and employing Special Forces can put many of these criticisms to rest. There may well be reasons for concern about sustainability and employability but a review of the history of SOF-type forces in Canada will reveal that where there is the political will there has been the way.

Canada's new force is being built upon the foundation of the Joint Task Force Two (JTF-2), a direct action, counterterrorist strike unit originally formed for hostage rescue incidents. This force routinely conducts close personal protection (CPP), and has since late 2001, been involved in detention and neutralization missions that have taken them far afield to Afghanistan where their actions are very similar to those conducted by commandos in the Second World War. The formation of CANSOFCOM indicates the government's recognition of the utility of such forces at least in the present global struggle against terrorism.

One element of that utility may well be the nearly covert nature of such forces and missions. Operational Security (OpSec) demands high security and thus confidentiality concerning personnel, weapons, methods, and targets. As well, however, it allows the employment of forces with little or no media scrutiny thus minimizing political exposure to questions. JTF-2 is regarded as a "black force" therefore less because of the colour of their counterterrorist uniform and more because of their *sub rosa* nature and profile. It is a force hidden in the shadows designed for fighting in the shadows. Although unique in its table of organization and equipment, the force is not unique in Canadian experience.

## HISTORY WITHOUT LEGACY

Belying its peaceable kingdom epithet, Canada has supported many prior SOF-type enterprises. This chapter will recap some of those efforts to illustrate what has been done within Canada in order to illustrate that SOF forces are not beyond this nation's grasp and to highlight several of the pitfalls that hampered previous efforts.

SOF forces came into their own during the full-spectrum conflict of the Second World War. British Prime Minister Winston Churchill's admonishment to set Europe "ablaze" prompted the rapid expansion of forces designed to take the war to the enemy by striking deep behind enemy lines or raiding across various fronts. The Special Operations Executive (SOE) undertook the recruiting, training, and deployment of military agents in direct operations like assassination missions and for the *encadrement* of resistance forces.

The Canadian contribution to this effort remained very small, however, and very large numbers of those nominated for service failed to complete their training because of poor physical conditioning or other attributes that militated against their deployment. Clearly, when units of the armed forces were charged with nominating volunteers this was used to weed out certain unit members, a problem that bedevilled all Special Service recruiting efforts during the war. Nevertheless, with its large mix of ethnic populations Canada held the potential of becoming a major provider of agents, but very few were actually employed. SOE operators of French Canadian or Chinese Canadian origin enjoyed many successes in forming local guerrilla or resistance bands, conducting strategic reconnaissance, and hampering the enemy's lines of communications in France and the Far East. The selective recruiting of particular agents based on their linguist and ethnic origins proved highly effective.[1] Canada made small contributions to SOE, particularly in providing agents who could speak French, Chinese, or Eastern European languages while operating behind enemy lines. What was true then remains true today. Canada's great ethnic diversity renders it of prime potential for individual agents, but this potential is not explicitly captured in the charge to the new SOFCOM, a point to be returned to later.

Canada also attempted to make larger contributions to commando raiding forces but with mixed results. During the Second World War, Combined Operations Headquarters (COHQ) employed Special Service troops who were more commonly called "commandos," a name adopted from South African Boer formations. Assigning the 2nd Canadian Division to the COHQ raid on Dieppe in August 1942 proved an unmitigated disaster.[2] Support for the joint Canadian-American First Special Service Force (FSSF), formed for an aborted raid into Norway, proved more successful. The FSSF served with great distinction in Italy. However, the Canadian Army failed to provide the necessary reinforcements, particularly after the force was devastated in the daring seizure of a formidable German mountain bastion at La Difensa immortalized in the classic film *The Devil's Brigade*.[3]

Canada also facilitated the training of covert operators for Allied powers by allowing the SOE to run the training school known as Camp X, outside Whitby, Ontario, and some other schools for Asiatic operations elsewhere in Canada.[4] Moreover, Canadian scientists played an important role producing chemical and biological agents for use by the Allies in covert assassination plots and for use against economic targets such as food crops.[5] As well, many Canadians participated in psychological warfare, and for a while a Canadian headed the British propaganda effort at Electra House aimed at "moral sabotage." To use modern parlance, Canada, in short, participated in the Second World War as a full-spectrum conflict.

This rich history left little legacy, however. Efforts to maintain a nucleus of commando operational expertise through a small Special Air Service (SAS) company fell by the wayside in the immediate postwar period. All such special units were disbanded, secret schools closed, and all the hard-won expertise scattered throughout the empire and beyond. Through the long Cold War, specific initiatives tied to NATO defence plans, and then later, the growth of international terrorist incidents, resulted in the re-creation of a large Canadian "airborne" formation and the rapid reaction "Special Service Force," both now since disbanded. The Army did not seek to expand into the counterterrorist role and was content to let the Royal Canadian Mounted Police (RCMP) mount Canada's first national counterterror team in the wake of the 1972 Munich Olympic Massacre and later outrages. Only with the loss of a clear NATO battlefield mission for the Army after the collapse of the Berlin Wall, in 1989, did Army staffs seek to revisit the counterterrorist role. Facing budget cuts and morale problems among their force, the RCMP willingly devolved its mission, but not its force, to the Canadian Forces in the early 1990s, resulting in the JTF-2. But this force did not repeat the RCMP's experience of waiting for Godot. The hot zones of the post–Cold War era soon brought a series of small deployments. Several of these, like the deployment to the Zaire border in 1996,[6] experienced problems not unrelated to one of the chief limitations of Canadian Special Operations Forces during the Second World War.

## THE PROBLEM OF NATIONAL COMMAND

There was an enduring legacy of fundamental importance to current efforts to re-create such forces. SOE, SAS, and Commando activities were conducted at the tactical level and within operations for which Canada provided little to no strategic guidance, planning, or control. That is to say that at the highest levels of national leadership the management of what constituted our Special Operations Forces was left primarily to allied powers, particularly the United Kingdom. The general absence of a command and control organization at the top of the Canadian government to oversee development, planning, and mission execution for these forces can be explained as a legacy of Canada's colonial past but it has never been fully addressed. In the Second World War the Canadian government avoided being responsible for such guidance but that was true of the entire military war effort.[7]

This problem of national command where strategic design and operational employment are managed to achieve national objectives remains a concern. The recent hasty decision to deploy our forces to Kandahar illustrates a certain immaturity in the national command organization.[8] The reorganization of Canadian Forces and Department of National Defence (DND) reporting relationships under new commands like Canada Command, and CANSOFCOM must be considered actions that are *maître chez nous* to DND, which is only one house to put in order.[9] The deeper issue revealed in the manner in which the deployment to Kandahar was taken concerns the tier of command above the defence department. The authority of the Privy Council Office (PCO)/Prime Minister's Office (PMO) to order deployments is not in dispute but how decisions regarding force employment are made within the markedly un-military PCO/PMO nexus is worth consideration. There is within that level no body similar to the War Cabinet in the Second World War, and there is no higher national security planning apparatus above the various departments charged with permanent care and planning for military operations, force employment, or similar activities. There is no doubt a plethora of ad hoc interdepartmental committees addressing various issues but no ad hoc committee can do work comparable to the coordinating function of the U.S. National Security Council,[10] or indeed comparable to the U.S. "country team" concept, which is explored below. This weakness may seem far removed from the sharp end of Special Forces operations but the potential for "blowback" is high and the forces promise a "strategic edge," which may not be fully realized without such "strategic" leadership. Canada's SOF forces provide a sharp tool committed to employment in pursuit of national and alliance policy, but policy is not strategy. This gap cannot be fully closed by the general structure of DND or by the lines of command and control of the Canadian Forces.

## WAR WITHOUT SEAMS?

Whatever the logic of taking on the mission in Afghanistan, many of the types of missions that will be conducted there will require the forces to operate across a wide spectrum of activity. Most of the activities are reflected in American Special Forces doctrine, but not Canadian. The current composition, tasking, and training of the JTF-2 renders it a member of the international Special Operations Forces community. However, the force is too small and too task-specific to cover off all the SOF roles adopted by the U.S. Special Forces community. In American doctrine the principal roles for Special Forces include counter-proliferation of WMD, information warfare, unconventional warfare, psychological operations, special reconnaissance missions, counterterrorism operations, direct action missions, participation in civil affairs, and support for foreign internal defence (FID) missions.[11] The latter two missions involve security assistance, nation building, and local capacity building, usually through training of local forces. Canada has no particular FID doctrine and the current JTF-2 has very limited to no capacity to conduct large raid and strike missions, strategic reconnaissance, operational reconnaissance, humanitarian assistance, civic affairs, information warfare, psychological operations, and sensitive site exploitation.

The new SOFCOM structure will address some of these deficiencies, but not all. Within U.S. doctrine Special Forces are ideally suited for a full-spectrum conflict. Their presence greatly expands a commander's tactical and operational options. They provide the promise of considerable economy of force, once the choice to use force is made. These forces are also designed to be task-tailored and they are markedly suitable for countering or delivering asymmetric threats. These attributes will also pertain to the Canadian force but to a lesser degree because our doctrine is not as expansive and our command and control organization is less developed or articulated.

For instance, Canada has no comparable FID doctrine, a fixture in U.S. force planning since the early 1960s. FID doctrine articulates fully the roles and responsibilities of all aspects of the U.S. government and is an agreed policy document. Canada's effort in Afghanistan will see our forces operating in very much the environment envisioned in U.S. FID doctrine, but we have nothing similar.[12] U.S. national doctrine — not just U.S. Department of Defense doctrine — articulates and ties the roles of the U.S. State Department, country missions (Ambassador), Defense Intelligence Agency, CIA, and USAID agencies into a coordinated whole. U.S. Special Forces operate in such an environment but the level of detailed commitment of other agency assets is no where so solidly articulated in Canadian doctrine. American Special Forces are designed and structured to operate across a spectrum of environments from tactical operations in support of conventional operations to covert operations in support of covert agencies such as the CIA.

This seamlessness extends to a flexible manning policy that allows Special Forces operators to be "seconded" to various covert formations and non–defence department agencies for tactical employment in the field — indeed members routinely surrender their power of attorney to the state so that their legal and physical entities can be divided, thus making assignment to covert operations and agencies truly seamless. From covert operations to human intelligence (HUMINT) development and exploitation, U.S. Special Forces operate across that shadowy environment.[13] It remains unclear as to whether Canada has adopted such seamlessness by commingling Canadian Security and Intelligence Service (CSIS) field agents and HUMINT development and exploitation teams within a continuous but non-conventional effort during current operations. Given Canada's tremendous ethnic diversity, developing a ready pool of covert operators should be easily achieved. Moreover, Canada's current 3D philosophy of Defence, Diplomacy, and Development (or perhaps the less felicitously named "Whole of Government" [WOG!] effort) does broach the potential for such inter-agency coordination but it is far more haphazard and personality dependent because no department has its resources bound by it.

A case in point is the current Provincial Reconstruction Team (PRT) program in Afghanistan. The PRT will require conventional troops for local security and presence operations, covert and overt human intelligence gathering, and more covert Special Forces direct action missions. These various tasks are to be conducted with some sense of ultimate purpose as articulated by Canada and its allied partners. Most of the daily activities can be fairly left to local commanders to manage, but where is the national coordination of effort being done? The origins of the PRT effort are found in U.S. counter-insurgency and FID doctrine. The effort began as a local counter-insurgency effort guided by those doctrines and Canada has inherited the scheme rather *totus porcus*. Canada has taken over a tool developed by others and now finds itself practising a tool-driven science (i.e., experimenting with the tool rather than exploring more fundamental issues),[14] and the national authorities outside the defence department may neither have considered the limitations of such a scheme nor fully agreed with its logic.

These are major seams therefore that our SOFCOM will have to manoeuvre around if it is to find best utility in the full-spectrum conflict the Canadian Forces are now committed to. There is much room for greater horizontal and vertical integration of the Canadian SOF effort to both the national strategy and national effort. This is particularly true in light of the recent American articulation of a "long war strategy" for combating the global terrorist threat.[15]

Who in Canada is responsible for preparing for such a "long war"?

## NOTES

1. The best account of these activities is found in Roy MacLaren, *Canadians Behind Enemy Lines, 1939–1945* (Vancouver: University of British Columbia Press, 1981), but it is rather incomplete. See also Sean M. Maloney, "Who Has Seen the Wind? A Historical Overview of Canadian Special Operations," Chapter 8 in this book.

2. Robin Neillands, *The Dieppe Raid: The Story of the Disastrous 1942 Expedition* (Aurum Press: London, 2005) reveals little new detail but offers a clear assessment of the deficient planning at all levels.

3. See Bernd Horn, *Bastard Sons: An Examination of Canada's Airborne Forces 1942–1995* (St. Catharines, ON: Vanwell Publishing, 2001) for a review of the history of this and similar airborne units. Horn is particularly strong on the failure of the senior officer corps to develop, manage, and maintain this national asset.

4. David Stafford, *Camp X Canada's School for Secret Agents 1941–45* (Toronto: Lester & Orpen Dennys Ltd., 1986).

5. Stanley P. Lovell, the chief science adviser to the Office of Strategic Services (OSS), reveals a series of Canadian biological and chemical special warfare vectors, such as a plan to blind Adolf Hitler and Benito Mussolini, in *Of Lies & Strategems* (New York: Prentice Hall, 1963).

6. See M.A. Hennessy, "Operation ASSURANCE: Planning a Multi-National Force for Rwanda/Zaire," *Canadian Military Journal* (Spring 2001), 11–20.

7. See C.P. Stacey, *Arms, Men and Governments 1939–1945* (Ottawa, 1970).

8. See comments by Lieutenant-Colonel C. Oliviero, in "Tam Marte Quam Minerva: The Web of Western Military Theory (An Intellectual Investigation of Military Theory in the Western World)" (Kingston: Royal Military College of Canada, PhD dissertation, draft, 2006), 59.

9. For a discussion of the Department's reorganization see Charmion Chaplin-Thomas, "Origins and Growth of the DCDS Group" (Department of National Defence, February 2006). On problems of operational command see also T. Fitzgerald and M.A. Hennessy, "An Expedient Reorganization: The NDHQ J-Staff System in the Gulf War," *Canadian Military Journal*, Vol. 4, No. 1 (Spring 2003), 23–28.

10. This is not to indicate that U.S. national strategic command systems are the best model, many would argue they are not, but at least they are well

articulated and relatively transparent to various levels of government and the legislative arm.

11. Modified list extracted from General Peter J. Schoomaker, "CINUSSO-COM Special Operations Forces: The Way Ahead" (USSOCOM, 2000). See also Samuel A. Southworth and Stephen Tanner, *U.S. Special Forces* (Cambridge, MA: Da Capo Press, 2002).

12. On the origins of U.S. FID doctrine see Michael A. Hennessy, *Strategy In Vietnam: The Marines and Revolutionary War in I Corps, 1965–1972* (Westport, CT: Praeger Press, 1997), 13–39.

13. Even in peacekeeping operations. See my "A Reading of Tea Leaves: Toward a Framework for Modern Peacekeeping Intelligence," in David Carment and Martin Rudner, eds., *Peacekeeping Intelligence* (London: Taylor & Francis, 2006), in press.

14. The phrase is attributed to F. Dyson.

15. On this strategy see its articulation in U.S. Department of Defense "Quadrennial Defense Review Report" (Washington, DC: 6 February 2006).

# 10

## Special Operations Forces:
### *Relevant, Ready, and Precise*

### Jamie W. Hammond

Is DoD [The U.S. Department of Defense] changing fast
enough to deal with the new 21st century security environment? ... Does DoD need to think through new ways to organize, train, equip and focus to deal with the global war on terror?
Are the changes we have and are making too modest and incremental? My impression is that we have not yet made truly bold
moves, although we have made many sensible, logical moves in
the right direction, but are they enough?
— U.S. Secretary of Defense Donald Rumsfeld[1]

Are military forces being transformed from Cold War models into
relevant, efficient, and effective forces that are able to deal with
current and future security environments? Secretary Rumsfeld's questions could have been asked by defence ministers in almost every
Western nation, and most of their ministries are reviewing roles and
force structures. The United Kingdom's Ministry of Defence has, for
example, completed five defence reviews or updates in the past six
years, the most recent in July 2004.[2] Canada, however, has not issued a
detailed analysis of its defence requirements since 1994, and the need
to conduct some form of comprehensive review seems to be the one

thing that virtually all defence critics, analysts, and practitioners in Canada agree must be done. However, such a review cannot be just an exercise in re-apportioning the budget and ensuring a fair share for each service. A defence review must tackle the hard questions of the type posed by Secretary Rumsfeld. Are the Canadian Forces (CF) relevant? Are the contemplated changes truly bold? Will the future force structure be effective? The CF of the future must be capable of participating in discretionary operations with our allies not only to show solidarity or to earn a seat at the table; our forces must be capable of dealing effectively with the inevitable and "non-discretionary" asymmetric challenges of the future. In short, the CF must be capable of delivering sophisticated capabilities to protect Canadians at home and abroad. Moreover, those capabilities must be delivered from within reasonable and realistic budget envelopes.

While we pride ourselves on tradition in the CF, we must recognize that the forces of the past may not be appropriate for the future. There are significant capability gaps in the current 1994-model defence structure, furthermore, we retain types of forces that have not been employed in their doctrinal forms for half a century. Hard choices have to be made. While there are many underdeveloped areas within the CF which will merit attention, this article intends to show that Special Operations Forces (SOF) have evolved over the past years and have become an essential and core capability that must be considered very seriously in any defence review. Maligned or ignored in the past, SOF now seem to be in the news daily. Their flexibility and agility demonstrate not only their operational necessity in the post-9/11 security environment, but also their cost-effectiveness. But, prior to deciding what specific SOF capabilities are required by Canada, there needs to be a greater understanding of what these forces are, what they are doing in the world, and what they offer.

## SPECIAL OPERATIONS FORCES TODAY

With the events of the past three years, it can be argued that Special Operations are no longer very "special." Both the overall U.S.-led campaign against terrorism and the operations in Afghanistan and Iraq were conducted using SOF as a primary tool. Certainly, Special Operations are no longer just an adjunct to support conventional operations. A recent internal report by one Commonwealth military force goes so far to suggest that a key role now emerging for conventional forces is to support SOF, a reversal of the traditional relationship. This was certainly the case during the war in Afghanistan, but it can also be seen to be a key aspect of U.S. operations worldwide over the last decade and across the spectrum of conflict. This is particularly true in post-conflict operations in places like Iraq, where conventional forces in large measure conduct "framework" operations and support specialized SOF operations against those who would disrupt the peace process.

Special Operations Forces have, however, become less special in another way. Rather than being the traditional quiet professionals who "neither confirm nor deny," SOF have entered the world of the media spotlight, press releases, recruiting competitiveness, and inter-service rivalry. Even some of the most clandestine forces in the world are now commonly mentioned in open sources. This attention is the direct result of the ongoing tempo of special operations, and politicians have not failed to notice the utility of SOF. In the United States, the United Kingdom, and Australia, significant developments are underway to enhance special operations capabilities.

In the United States, the special operations community is currently about 49,000 strong. Over the next five years it will grow to 52,559, and its budget in 2003 grew by 35 percent to $6.8 billion.[3] Even then, in his election platform, Democratic presidential candidate John Kerry stated that he intended to double the capabilities of the U.S. Special Forces, add a special operations helicopter squadron to the Air Force, and increase the number of active civil affairs and psychological operations personnel.[4] This proposed growth would seem to make sense when one looks at the tempo of operations of U.S. SOF. In one recent week, over 6,500 SOF personnel were deployed around the world, and they have conducted 200 missions in Iraq alone in the past four months.[5] Rather than maintaining a force ratio of one unit deployed to five at home, as we tend to do in Canada, U.S. SOF pick up and go when needed. According to U.S. Special Operations Command (SOCOM), 100 percent of the U.S. Army Special Operations Aviation Regiment have seen action during the past two years, and 90 percent of the personnel in the Air Force Special Tactics Squadrons deployed simultaneously to Iraq.[6]

In the United Kingdom, the situation is the same, albeit on a reduced scale. A Ministry of Defence paper released in July 2004 announced growth in the strength of the U.K. Special Forces (U.K. SF), along with the purchase of new SF equipment and "significant enhancements."[7] While British government statements do not divulge exactly what the enhancements are, the press has speculated that a further Special Forces Squadron is being created,[8] and that a new special forces unit, the Reconnaissance and Surveillance Regiment of 600 personnel, will be established to conduct covert surveillance and work with intelligence agencies.[9] Like their U.S. counterparts, the British Special Forces have been constantly engaged in operations since 2001, although they remain much more tight-lipped about their work than U.S. SOF community.

Although much smaller than either their U.S. or British counterparts, Australia has made the most radical changes to their force structure by establishing the Australian Special Operations Command in 2003. This command, a "joint command with a command status equivalent to Maritime, Land and Air Commands," includes over 2,000 personnel and required the conversion of an infantry unit into a special operations commando regiment and the regrouping of other special operations components.[10] SOF were the primary ground forces committed by Australia to both the Afghanistan and Iraq operations. While the Special Air Service Regiment was the main force in Afghanistan, the Special Forces Task Group sent to Iraq also included elements from the recently rerolled 4th Royal Australian Regiment (Commando), a nuclear, biological, and chemical defence team from the Special Operations Command's Incident Response Regiment, as well as logistics forces and Chinook helicopters.[11] Australia, a middle power, has thus been able to "punch above its weight" in the last four years.

As it is by far the largest, and, from a Canadian point of view, the most important SOF command in terms of inter-operability, the next section of the chapter will examine, in very general terms, the recent history and structure of U.S. Special Operations Command.

## THE DEVELOPMENT OF U.S. SOF ORGANIZATIONS

Although the effectiveness and relevance of U.S. SOF capabilities is today taken for granted across the U.S. military, and a number of key positions are now occupied by senior special operations officers,[12] the establishment of SOCOM was not only unforeseen by most — it was actively opposed by many. As Susan L. Marquis recounts in *Unconventional Warfare: Rebuilding U.S. Special Operations Forces*,[13] today's U.S. SOF capabilities were not developed by the senior leadership of the services, but in spite of them. It was, in fact, the three shocking events in the early

1980s that provided the catalysts for radical change in the U.S. force structure. All three were failures, and showed that U.S. elected representatives, more than their military counterparts, followed Field Marshal Slim's advice to "remember only the lessons to be learned from defeat — they are more than from victory."[14]

The first critical catalyst for review of the U.S. structure was the failure of the attempted rescue of American hostages in Teheran in 1980. Operation "Rice Bowl"/"Eagle Claw" was aborted in the Iranian desert on 25 April 1980 as a result of dust storms and helicopter malfunctions. Following the abort decision, one helicopter collided with a C-130 Hercules aircraft on the ground, resulting in eight deaths. Exploding ammunition from the collision also caused the commander to abandon the rest of the helicopters on the ground and the task force withdrew, leaving the remains of the six helicopters and one C-130 in the desert.[15] While the American hostages continued to be held by the Iranians until negotiations led to their release in January 1981, the U.S. military immediately began an analysis of the failure. The most notable report was from the Holloway Commission, the first external review of an SOF operation. It made two key recommendations: the creation of a standing counterterrorist joint task force to reduce ad hoc responses to terrorism, and the creation of a special operations advisory panel of active or recently retired senior officers to improve oversight.[16]

The recommendations of the Holloway Commission were implemented over the next three years, but it was the death of 247 U.S. Marines in a truck bombing in Lebanon in 1983 that brought home to the U.S. military the requirement for forces designed to deal specifically with low-intensity conflict and terrorism. The need for change was further reinforced by the American operations in Grenada, during which the application of accepted tenets of special operations (such as simplicity, security, repetition, speed, surprise, and purpose)[17] were woefully lacking. In fact, of seven operations during the Grenada invasion that involved SOF, only two were successful, two were marginally successful, and three resulted in the deaths of SOF soldiers for little or no operational benefit.[18] The combination of all these events played a key role in increasing awareness in Congress of the need to better integrate SOF in the U.S. military. After two more years of discussion and debate, an amendment to the 1986 Goldwater-Nichols Defense Organization Act, known as the Nunn-Cohen Amendment, was passed by Congress to establish a four-star joint command headquarters, now the U.S. Special Operations Command. A critical issue for legislators was the importance of ensuring that SOF budgeting and development be fully protected from traditional service priorities. In the end, through civilian intervention, and in spite of military opposition from the Joint Chiefs of Staff, the new command was established with responsibilities for SOF funding, research and development, training, and integration into joint operations.

As in Britain and Australia, Special Operations Command remains independent from the other services. In the U.S., however, the Army, Navy, and Air Force retain SOF commands and units within their force structures, but the primary budgetary and command responsibility for those organizations lies with SOCOM. The three services act as force providers and are responsible for non-SOF specific training, equipment, doctrine, recruiting, and basing. Operationally, the SOF elements normally deploy under the operational command of a regional U.S. combatant commander (i.e., Commander Central Command), each of which has a subordinate special operations command, normally at the one-star level. While SOCOM has always maintained a watch on all worldwide operations, SOCOM did not play a primary role in the command and control of deployed SOF until ordered to take the lead in the global war on terrorism in 2003. Rather, SOCOM and the services together were responsible for developing SOF over the long term and to providing ready SOF forces for employment by the National Command Authorities, by the regional commands, or by U.S. ambassadors. SOCOM retains command of one Joint Special Operations Command, and control over three component commands, as described below:[19]

**Naval Special Warfare Command** — This command is organized around eight Sea Air Land (SEAL) Teams. These teams are made up of six to eight SEAL Platoons (normally 16 personnel each), supported by SEAL delivery vehicles (small submarines) and Special Boat Units. All SEALs are trained to dive, parachute, and conduct missions that range from special reconnaissance of harbours and beaches to ship boarding and inland direct action missions.

**U.S. Army Special Operations Command (USASOC)** — The Army has the largest SOF community of the three services and, within USASOC, the Special Forces are the largest component. Note that within the U.S. SOF, the term *Special Forces* (SF) refers only to the

Army Green Berets, organized into SF battalions and groups (it is worth remembering that the United Kingdom and most Commonwealth countries refer to all of their SOF as SF). The basic building block of the Green Berets is the 12-man Operational Detachment Alpha (ODA — the term *A-Team* has fallen out of favour). This team consists of one officer, one warrant officer, and 10 non-commissioned members (NCMs), all qualified on the SF "Q-course" and also sent on advanced skills courses (i.e., medical assistant, communications, and languages). Normally six Alpha Detachments are grouped as a company (ODB). Three SF companies and a support company constitute a battalion (ODC). A full strength SF battalion consists of less than 400 personnel. Three SF battalions form an SF group. The U.S. Army currently has five regionally focused active SF groups (about 1,400 personnel each) and two National Guard SF groups (both of which have seen recent action). While SF battalions are capable of establishing Forward Operating Bases, SF groups are often used as the framework for a Combined Joint Special Operations Task Force (CJSOTF). SF personnel are capable of conducting direct action and special reconnaissance missions, but their strength lies in unconventional warfare and foreign internal defence (the first seeks to support a revolutionary force through the provision of training, equipment, and advice, while the second seeks to defeat and deter revolutionary forces through the same means).

The 75th Ranger Regiment consists of three battalions (each of approximately 550 men) and a training battalion. Each battalion is structured as a three-company light infantry battalion focused on direct action missions (i.e., raids, airborne, and airmobile assaults). In many ways, each Ranger battalion is similar in structure and capability to the Canadian Airborne Regiment as it existed between 1993 and 1995.[20] While the Rangers are infantry, they are designated as SOF, which gives them certain advantages: The right to select experienced commanders at all levels (i.e., a company commander must have already commanded a company elsewhere); a budget that allows the Rangers to maintain equipment that ensures inter-operability with other SOF elements; overmanning to ensure readiness at full strength; and an SOF-focused and demanding collective training program.

The U.S. Army also maintains three SOF aviation battalions in the 160th Special Operations Aviation Regiment. These battalions primarily operate MH-47 (Chinook), MH-60 (Blackhawk) and MH-6 (Little Bird) helicopters (the M stands for Modified — both the Chinook and

Blackhawk variants are modified to include air-to-air refuelling and enhanced avionics). All three battalions focus primarily on night operations in support of SOF units.

Within the U.S. structure, Civil Affairs, Psychological Operations, Information Operations, and some nuclear, biological, and chemical defence units are grouped within the SOF organizations.

**Air Force Special Operations Command** — The U.S. Air Force maintains six Special Tactics Squadrons (STS), which perform Combat Search and Rescue tasks, establish runways and drop zones, control air traffic, and direct the aerial delivery of ordnance. Though small in numbers, these personnel are highly trained and extend the capability of the U.S. Air Force significantly. Much of the air-to-ground operations during the Afghanistan campaign were directed by the Air Force STS Operators.

The USAF also maintain a number of Special Operations Wings equipped with aircraft ranging from MH-53J Pave Low helicopters to AC-130U/H Spectre gunships, and other C-130 variants for air-to-air refuelling (MC-130P), insertion/extraction operations (MC-130E/H), and electronic warfare (EC-130s).

### U.S. SPECIAL OPERATIONS FORCES IN AFGHANISTAN

Although U.S. SOF have operated in virtually every military operation since the establishment of SOCOM (including the costly and well-publicized operations of Task Force Ranger in Somalia in 1993, where 16 soldiers were killed and 83 injured in a single day),[21] it has been in the past three years that SOF have become the primary actor in the operations, rather than playing a supporting role to conventional forces.

During the early phases of the Afghanistan campaign, U.S. SOF operated mainly from forward operating bases outside Afghanistan. The initial 13 days of air operations were followed by daring raids conducted by U.S. Army Rangers and ground Special Operations Forces. On the night of 19 October, these forces, reportedly operating from the USS *Kitty Hawk* and staging through bases in Oman and Pakistan, attacked Mullah Omar's palace near Kandahar and an airfield some 60 miles away.[22] The airfield operation (Objective "Rhino") was conducted by 199 Rangers parachuting from four MC-130s at 250 metres (800 feet). The fire support and Ranger force itself was overwhelming, and opposition was extremely light.[23] Simultaneously, a heliborne force landed at Omar's Palace (Objective "Gecko"), and both locations were secured in less than 45 minutes. While these were essentially hit-and-run raids conducted for psychological reasons as much as for intelligence purposes, they were also a feint designed to fix Taliban forces in the south.

Initially, the main effort was in the north, where USAF Special Operations Wings operated long-range and air-to-air refuelled MC and AC-130s to support the ground operations of the Northern Alliance and other indigenous forces. Those Afghan forces were, in turn, equipped, trained, and advised by U.S. SF battalions that deployed ODAs on the ground as early as 19 October 2001.[24] The ODAs were often accompanied by a USAF Special Tactics Squadron Combat Controller, which deployed 190 men (70 percent of their total strength) to Afghanistan in the early months of the war, directed 90 percent of all terminally guided weapons dropped, and called in over 4,400 bombs onto Taliban targets.[25] By the time Kandahar, the key Taliban stronghold, fell on 7 December 2001, there were still less than 300 U.S. SOF personnel actually on the ground in Afghanistan, but their contribution was out of all proportion to their limited numbers. As the Northern Alliance became more capable, Civil Affairs and Psychological Operations personnel moved in to support their operations. Offensive psychological operations continued throughout the war through leaflet and radio campaigns.

Once the initial campaign was won, SOF elements moved into the country to establish bases from which they continued to target al-Qaeda and Taliban leadership. A Combined Joint Special Operations Task Force (K-BAR) was deployed in Kandahar, and another (DAGGER) was set up in Uzbekistan to continue offensive operations while developing more detailed intelligence through special reconnaissance and low-level information gained from the local population. Bases were established in areas of interest, and SOF combined with military intelligence specialists, electronic warfare personnel, civil affairs teams, and tactical psychological operations teams were often co-located to provide better force protection and synergy. Small conventional forces and Afghan military forces were used where feasible to provide better security for the specialist teams. Task Force K-BAR, led by SEALs from the Naval Special Warfare Command, conducted over 75 direct action and special reconnaissance missions during 2002.[26]

Once the combat operations slowed, SOF operations continued with unconventional warfare intended to support the friendly Afghan forces, and develop better intelligence to target al-Qaeda and Taliban leadership and pockets of resistance. Where necessary mobile and fixed special reconnaissance patrols were deployed, and more specialized SOF remained on standby to conduct attacks on suspected locations. Conventional forces, used in larger numbers by this point, secured bases and conducted larger scale sweep operations. As the Afghan Transitional Authority and Transitional Islamic State of Afghanistan were established, greater focus was placed on the equipping and training the Afghan National Army. Throughout all these operations, Afghanistan "called for extensive coordination between Special Forces and paramilitary assets from the CIA."[27]

The campaign in Afghanistan has often been referred to as a special operations war, and, on the whole, that remains true. Most of the fighting during the war was either conducted by SOF, or by the USAF under SOF control. SOF provided the U.S. military with both economy of effort and precise, relevant capabilities. The SOF effort was not a force multiplier, or a tributary feeding into a larger conventional campaign. In Afghanistan, SOF was the campaign. The effort of the U.S. SOF in Afghanistan is made clear in the casualty figures. By mid-2003, 39 SOF personnel had been killed in action in Afghanistan, a reasonable figure for over 20 months of fighting. This figure represents 85 percent of the total number of American troops killed in action to that date.[28] In analyzing the lessons of the war, Norman Friedman states simply, "Special Operations Forces were essential to the war's success."[29] During Afghanistan, every U.S. Special Forces Group, all Ranger battalions, all Special Operations Aviation battalions, and all Special Tactics Squadrons rotated forces through the country. And, by the end of 2002, even the large U.S. SOF component was exhausted. Even small contributions of SOF from allies were warmly received, and, in American eyes, were essential as their own forces required replacement. Nevertheless, even the huge effort of U.S. SOF in Afghanistan seems limited when compared to their commitment to the 2003 war in Iraq.

## U.S. SPECIAL OPERATIONS FORCES IN IRAQ

If the campaign in Afghanistan is seen as either an intra-state conflict or one against non-state actors that lent itself to the use of SOF, the invasion of Iraq was quite a different matter. Large conventional forces were obviously needed to deal with Saddam Hussein's still-viable and well-equipped armed forces. Nevertheless, even in this more tradition-al, inter-state conflict between modern armed forces, SOF played a transformational role.

For SOF, the 2003 Iraq War differed in two great respects from the 1991 Gulf War. First, SOF were given a significantly greater role in 2003, and second, as observed by General Tommy Franks:

> We saw for the first time integration rather than deconfliction of forces. This integration enabled conventional (air, ground, and sea) forces to leverage SOF capabilities to deal effectively with asymmetric threats and enable precision targeting simul-taneously in the same battle space.... Likewise, Special Operators were able to use conventional forces to enhance and enable special missions.[30]

This integration was especially marked in the south, where, accord-ing to a U.S. Army report, "the heroic actions of the special operations troopers in the south stood out every day because of their close integra-tion into V Corps and I MEF [Marine Expeditionary Force] opera-tions."[31] It was in the north and the west however, where the SOF role was so markedly different than it had been just over a decade before. Part of the difference was simply the scale of SOF effort. According to a Congressional Research Unit report, 9,000 to 10,000 U.S. SOF person-nel deployed for Iraq out of an available force of 47,000, of which only 10,000 are combat forces.[32] Following the SOF successes in Afghanistan, General Franks gave SOF the responsibility for controlling and domi-nating almost two-thirds of Iraq during the war. The 5th Special Force Group were tasked to protect the Central Command left flank, control the western deserts, and prevent the Iraqis from deploying Scud missiles into the area, as had been done in 1991.[33] This task was clearly success-ful, and U.S., British, and Australian SOF in western Iraq secured over 50 targets on the first night of the operation, and 50 more the next night, while other SOF dominated potential Scud and weapons of mass destruction (WMD) sites.[34]

When Turkey denied U.S. and British basing and transit rights almost at the last minute, the whole campaign plan in the north of Iraq had to be reconsidered. In the end, Task Force Viking (under the commander of 10th Special Forces Group, Colonel Charles Cleveland) was given missions to conduct unconventional operations with Kurdish groups and to fix and destroy Iraqi forces in the north.

Although some ODAs had been inserted beforehand, the bulk of the Task Force Viking forces were inserted by MC-130 on 20 March 2003.[35] As in Afghanistan, individual ODAs operated alongside indigenous forces to conduct combat operations against regular and paramilitary opposition. While this was a normal role for U.S. Army Special Forces, during the campaign Colonel Cleveland became responsible for 80,000 troops, including U.S. SOF, Kurds, allied SOF, the 173rd Airborne Brigade (which conducted a parachute assault on 26/27 March 2003), as well as a task force from 1st Armored Division, the 26th Marine Expeditionary Unit and a battalion from 10th Mountain Division, all of which linked up with his forces during the course of the campaign.[36]

While SOF were never intended to take on Iraqi armoured forces, their success against much larger mechanized forces was impressive. At one objective in Aski Kalak on 5 April, Kurdish Peshmerga and a force of three U.S. ODAs (about 36 personnel) took on and destroyed a dug-in Iraqi armoured force protecting a key bridge. Every Iraqi armoured vehicle was destroyed by either close air support or by Green Berets armed with Javelin man-pack missile systems. As one soldier later stated, "Not a single [coalition] tank was available, nor needed."[37] Results were similar on 6 April when elements from 3rd Special Forces Group and 80 lightly armed Peshmerga were engaged by an Iraqi infantry brigade with T-55 tanks and armoured personnel carriers at Debecka Pass. This engagement was widely reported at the time because of tragic "blue-on-blue" casualties filmed by a BBC crew on location, which occurred when a close air support aircraft mistook Peshmerga and SF personnel at a disabled T-55 for the Iraqi target. In spite of the friendly casualties, and again because of the combination of fast air and Javelin missiles (described by Sergeant First Class Antenori, a participant, as "worth its weight in gold"), light forces destroyed a significant number of armoured vehicles and forced the Iraqis to abandon eight T-55s and 16 Armoured Personnel Carriers (APCs) on the battlefield.[38]

In terms of conducting operations throughout the country, SOF contributed approximately 8 percent of the combat forces initially engaged in Iraq.[39] Their operations, critical in the west and north, were no less key in the south and central sectors. In a 6 April 2003 article, written after two weeks of operations, the New York Times credited SOF with securing offshore oil platforms, rescuing Private Jessica Lynch, seizing the Haditha Dam (which had the potential to cause significant flooding), controlling the west of Iraq, seizing airfields H2 and H3 (suspected Weapons of Mass Destruction (WMD) sites), raiding Saddam Hussein's Thartar Palace, destroying 10 tanks in two convoy attacks near Ramadi, securing the north, training the Kurdish forces, and finally operating with the CIA in searching for regime leadership.[40] As Brigadier General Gary L. Harrell summarized in the same article, "[SOF were] doing things that have never been done on such a large scale and have produced phenomenal results.... The coalition is getting plenty of bang for the buck from SOF."

While not all SOF operations went according to plan — British papers claim that a Special Boat Squadron insertion into northern Iraq resulted in vehicles being captured and personnel forced to flee,[41] and at least one operation demonstrated to U.S. SOF the risks of operating without air cover[42] — on the whole, SOF played a significant role in the success of the campaign. As Cordesman notes in a section of his history of the conflict entitled "Snake Eaters with Master's Degrees": "It is already clear that at least the United States has drawn the lesson that such forces [SOF] are so valuable that they need significant expansion.... It seems likely that Special Forces are becoming a critical new element of joint warfare in an era of asymmetric warfare."[43] There is however a clear understanding throughout the U.S. military that "SOF must complement — not compete with nor be a substitute for — conventional forces."[44] In Iraq and Afghanistan, SOF have proven that they are essential forces on the battlefields of the future.

The implications for Canada are twofold. First, as SOF have proven their utility, both against asymmetric threats and as a war fighting tool, the CF needs now to consider their relevance and relative priority in our force structure. Second, SOF are unmistakably now the fourth component (in addition to naval, land, and air) in joint operations, and only those nations that provide forces to the coalition special operations component commander will be informed of the nature of theatre SOF operations. As SOF operate in politically sensitive environments, their operations will often be discreet and compartmentalized. Only a CF SOF contribution will give Canada true insight into what is actually happening behind the scenes in a theatre of operations. Canada therefore needs to consider SOF as one of four possible service contributions to coalition operations.

## EMERGING ROLES

The great theoretician, Sun Tzu, wrote, "Generally, in battle, use the normal force to engage; use the extraordinary to win."[45] By definition, SOF are required for specialized operations where there is no broad conventional force requirement. Counterterrorism has long been a specialty of SOF. Operations such as the SAS Princes Gate hostage rescue in London in 1980 demonstrate vividly the role of military forces in domestic counterterrorism. Since 9/11, this role has taken on broader meaning. In Canada, for example, the December 2001 "public security" budget allocated funds and tasked the Department of National Defence (DND) to double the capacity of JTF-2, including its capability to attack terrorists and terrorism beyond our borders.

In the U.S., countering terrorism has required specialized and often covert, discreet, or clandestine SOF capabilities specifically designed to track and attack terrorist or regime leadership targets. These forces are separate from the largely "white" or warfighting SOF referred to above. While the United States developed such special mission units in the late 1970s and early 1980s, these forces did not emerge from the shadows until the post-9/11 operations.

Not only have the forces emerged from the shadows, but their roles are being transformed.

As Canadians consider what SOF capabilities are required within the CF, we must be cognizant of the distinction between "black" and "white" SOF, and of the fact that SOF themselves are not static. We must not aim to develop capabilities based solely on yesterday's operations, but must develop relevant forces for the future.

With the recommendations of the Holloway commission, the United States created a standing counterterrorist special operations task force. Several authors have suggested that the Joint Special Operations Command took on that role,[46] although the U.S. government has never confirmed this, and even retired General Carl Stiner and Tom Clancy, in their book dealing with Stiner's role as commander of the counterterrorist task force and later of Special Operations Command, refer only to a generic Joint Special Operations Task Force (JSOTF).[47] Nevertheless, it was clear even before 11 September 2001 that U.S. special mission units would play a key role in attacking terrorism. In fact, SOF preparations began long before 9/11. According to former U.S. National Coordinator for Security, Infrastructure Protection and Counterterrorism Richard Clarke, joint special operations

222

personnel prepared a plan to capture an al-Qaeda leader in Khartoum in 1996, only to have the plan cancelled at the White House (in spite of Al Gore's reputed recommendation to "Go grab his ass").[48] The *9/11 Commission Report* also highlights the fact that in early 1998 (prior to the embassy bombings in Kenya and Tanzania) the Joint Special Operations Forces commander and the commander of Delta Force were asked to review CIA plans for an assault to capture bin Laden in Tarnak Farms (the site where four members of 3 PPCLI were killed in 2002).[49] Clearly, U.S. SOF have long had a key national interagency role that goes far beyond military joint operations.

According to several press reports, it was these specialized national-level strategic Special Operations Forces that made up a series of largely covert numbered task forces established to track and capture or kill al-Qaeda, Taliban, and later Iraqi regime leadership. According to an article in the *New York Times*, two special operations missions tasked to track "high-value targets" (Task Force 5 in Afghanistan and Task Force 20 in Iraq) were replaced in the summer of 2003 by Task Force 121, which had a broader regional mission.[50] Task Force 20 was reportedly responsible for the collation of intelligence on and the subsequent capture of Saddam Hussein's sons Uday and Qusay on 22 July 2003.

While the *Washington Post* suggested that there was a rift within the SOF community on how best to go after such targets,[51] proponents of the numbered joint task forces were vindicated when Task Force 121 captured Saddam Hussein on 13 December last year.[52] As in previous operations, interagency intelligence gathered and analyzed by the task force provided a sound basis for a successful action. According to *Newsweek*, Task Force 121, "a pure hybrid of civilian intelligence and military striking power," continued its operations into 2004 in Afghanistan tracking Osama bin Laden.[53]

It was the confidence of Secretary of Defense Rumsfeld in the ability of the U.S. Special Operations Command to create and employ such relevant, coordinated, and responsive interagency task forces that caused him to lobby for and eventually assign SOCOM an expanded role in January 2003, for the prosecution of the global war on terrorism. With this change, the Commander SOCOM now has the responsibility to conduct his own operations, rather than just support the operations of regional commanders.[54] In order to adapt SOF for this new task, a new Center for Special Operations has been created within SOCOM Headquarters to consolidate intelligence, planning, and operations functions to better track down and "destroy terrorist networks around the world."[55]

This seemingly continual change and transformation of SOF is unlikely to stop anytime soon. At a recent conference, Lieutenant General Norton Schwartz, the senior Pentagon operations officer, stated that even more, fundamental changes will be required of SOF in the future. "This community needs to morph.... We need to look more like them [terrorists] than we do like us," Schwartz stated as he argued for greater human intelligence and signals intelligence components within SOF.[56] Even greater changes may be on the horizon as the 9/11 Commission has recommended that, "lead responsibility for directing and executing paramilitary operations, whether clandestine or covert, should shift [from the CIA] to the Defense Department. There it should be consolidated with the capabilities for training, direction, and execution of such operations already being developed in the Special Operations Command."[57] While commentators such as Jennifer Kibbe have expressed concern over the legal framework for U.S. military covert operations, there does seem to be a growing support for this type of consolidation.[58]

## OBSERVATIONS ON MODERN SPECIAL OPERATIONS FORCES

This chapter has presented only a glimpse of current SOF structures, recent operations and future trends. Much has had to be left out because of space considerations and the limitations of open source references. In particular, the role of SOF in national domestic responses to terrorism, while downplayed here, is very important. In Canada, the United Kingdom, Australia, and New Zealand, SOF provide the primary national counterterrorist armed response. Even in the United States, with the legal limitations on the use of the military in the United States delimited in the Posse Comitatus Act, U.S. SOF nevertheless play important roles in concert with the Department of Homeland Security and the FBI. These domestic responsibilities of SOF are now among the highest priority military tasks.

Finally, the contributions of Canadian and Commonwealth SOF during the past few years have been glossed over. While the U.S. clearly operates on a different scale than their smaller allies, British, Canadian, Australian, and New Zealand SOF have all conducted similar types of operations. From these collective experiences we can draw some general observations. First, SOF have truly become the fourth component of joint operations. They are not solely an add-on, a force multiplier, or an optional approach. They are a critical component to success. Without them a military coalition will be less likely to win. Without SOF, and having to rely on allies for that capability, a nation is likely to be deprived of an understanding of what is happening below the surface of an operation and therefore less able to exercise its sovereignty preroga-tives during coalition operations.

Second, SOF are in demand today and for the future. All of our clos-est allies are enhancing their SOF capabilities, and yes, it is usually at the expense of other elements of their force structure. Australia rerolled an infantry battalion and allocated it to SOF, the British are reducing the strength of their infantry while enhancing SOF and, finally, the United States is placing a priority on SOF augmentation. As armed forces are reduced in strength and have to rationalize defence capabilities and spending, SOF are growing and taking a greater share of limited funds.

Third, as U.S. SOF doctrine has stated for years, "competent SOF cannot be created after the crisis occurs." It takes years to create SOF structures and to develop competent SOF personnel. The U.S. SOF community was ready to respond to 9/11 only because, as USAF General Charles Holland said in 2002, "political and military visionar-ies ... created this command to ensure the United States had a force trained, equipped and ready to combat such adversaries [terrorists] and destroy them."[59] It is clear that joint SOF structures will not be proposed by the individual services at the expense of their own core capabilities. Tough decisions must be made, and, to be ready for future threats, they must be made now.

Fourth, when used appropriately, SOF create military, diplomatic, and political successes out of all proportion to their numbers. They are cost-effective. They operate across the spectrum of conflict, understand the requirements of other government departments, and are comfort-able with tactical, operational, and strategic goals. Armed appropriately, employed sensibly, and supported by joint assets, they are high-intensity warfighters, as important a contribution to coalition operations as any other arm. They can be capable force "packages" that Canada can afford to develop to the highest world standard, and ones that allies will request in the future.

Fifth, specialized counterterrorist SOF are best used as a part of coordinated interagency teams, either conducting intelligence-led operations or conducting operations to develop intelligence. They do not and should not conduct conventional military operations. To be most effective, they must be established within coherent and ready standing formations, with all the tools necessary to function. JTF-2 provides Canada with the tip of a spear, but we cannot go searching for the shaft on the day of a crisis. What's more counterterrorist forces must not be misused. Committing JTF-2 to some SOF tasks would not only be an inappropriate use of a strategic asset, it may actually reduce that unit's ability to conduct counterterrorist operations to protect Canadians. Canada needs a range of SOF capabilities that can function in a broad spectrum of scenarios, and which can be combined when needed.

Sixth, SOF are precise, lethal, and discriminating. In preventative, conflict, and post-conflict operations, they are part of the solution not part of the problem. They can be structured so as to have knowledge of the operational locale and the language skills needed to function amongst the indigenous population, and they train to operate and fight in sophisticated and sensitive environments. Considerations of collateral damage are weighed, as a rule, not just against the military objective to be achieved, but against the political and humanitarian goals.

Finally, as seen in both Afghanistan and Iraq, all SOF are not equal. Counterterrorist forces should not be used to conduct overt unconventional warfare. Direct action units like Rangers are not suited for discriminating engagements or "hearts and minds" tasks. Just as armed forces require a range of conventional capabilities, so too, do they require a range of SOF capabilities. Particularly in a small military force, these capabilities must complement conventional forces, not replicate them. Just as all SOF are not equal, not all nations are capable of developing sophisticated and credible SOF. These are high-end forces that G-8 nations like Canada can generate, whereas many other nations cannot.

## DECISIONS FOR CANADA: STILL WING-WALKING?

This chapter began with some basic questions about defence relevance. Are the changes we have made and are making too modest and incremental? As we consider our future force structure in Canada, some hard questions must be asked about what are discretionary and non-discretionary operations. What are the military options that the CF *must* be capable of providing to the government of Canada at short notice in a crisis? Given the huge cost to the taxpayer of virtually any defence capability, we must ensure the forces we develop are relevant, robust, and ready. In coalition scenarios, they must be contributions to success, not just contributions to force size. If they can meet domestic, asymmetric, and combat threats, their relevance can only be increased. Few would dispute the claim that SOF meet the non-discretionary asymmetric threats of the future security environment.

This chapter has attempted to show how SOF either contribute to warfighting, or lead it. They are compatible with Canada's aspirations and economic realities. SOF are equally well-suited for soft-power diplomacy and capacity building, and for hard-power fighting. While a number of proposals for SOF structures have or are being proposed,[60] what is a critical first step is for the CF to acknowledge the need to transform to remain both affordable and relevant. While most officers need little convincing of the relevancy of SOF, many still believe they are unaffordable for a small force. I would suggest that in an era of sustained asymmetric threats, we cannot afford not to have a robust SOF capability to protect Canadians at home and abroad, and to engage enemies when necessary.

As our government undertakes a serious and detailed review of defence requirements, military planners will have to come up with creative options for relevant, robust, precise, and affordable defence capabilities for the future. That will require letting go of some older and less relevant capabilities developed during the Cold War. In the early 1990s, then chief of the defence staff, General John de Chastelain, proposed the "wing-walker" metaphor for Canadian defence policy. In short, as the security environment changed, our actions were akin to a daredevil wing-walker whose key to success is never releasing hold of one thing until something else is firmly gripped. For General de Chastelain, the aircraft in the analogy was our national defence policy. We are again in a situation where the security environment is changing. We now can see that capabilities such as SOF are the secure handholds that will take us through the turbulence of asymmetric threats, but we hesitate to drop the old and trusted handholds of our current force structure. If we can only look down, we will see that some of our most trusted handholds have rusted through over the years, and others are prohibitively expensive and therefore beyond our reach. Some we have not actually used for decades, yet they continue to weigh down the aircraft. Others might not even be attached to the airframe any longer. The world has changed, and we don't have a lot of money. Yes, we really do have to think.

NOTES

1.  Memo to CJCS General Richard Myers, VCJCS General Peter Pace, Deputy Secretary of Defense Paul Wolfowitz, and Under Secretary of Defense for Policy Douglas Feith, dated 16 October 2003. Accessed at *www.golbalsecurity.org/military/library/policy/dod/rumsfeld-d20031016sdmemo.htm*.

2.  After the Strategic Defence Review of 1998, the U.K. MoD published an updated white paper in 1999, a "New Chapter" to the Defence Review in 2002, a new white paper in 2003, and finally a Defence Command Paper in 2004. Each has resulted in significant changes to the structure and strategy of the MoD. Accessed at *www.mod.uk/publications/index.htm*.

3.  Eric Schmitt and Thom Shanker, "Special Warriors Have Growing Ranks and Growing Pains in Taking Key Antiterror Role," *New York Times*, 2 August 2004, accessed at *www.nytimes.com/2004 /08/02/politics/02mili.html*.

4.  Accessed at *www.johnkerry.com/issues/national_security/military.html*, 30 August 2004.

5.  Schmitt and Shanker, *op. cit.*

6.  Robert Wall, "Sharpening the Sword," in *Aviation Week and Space Technology*, Vol. 160, No. 8 (23 February 2004), 80.

7.  Accessed at *www.mod.uk/issues/security/cm6269/index.html*, 2 August 2004. Note that the United Kingdom and Australia refer to all of their Special Operations Forces as Special Forces (SF), while in the United States only the U.S. Army Green Berets are referred to as SF; the term *SOF* is used to encompass all U.S. Special Operations Command forces.

8.  Sean Rayment, "SAS Creates a New Squadron to Counter Threat from Al Qaeda," in *The Telegraph*, 7 March 2004, accessed at *www.telegraph.co.uk/news/main.jhtml?xml=/news/2004/03/07/wbin107.xml*.

9.  Sean Rayment, "Britain Forms a New Special Forces Unit to Fight the Al Qaeda," *The Telegraph*, 25 July 2004, accessed at *www.telegraph.co.uk/news/main.jhtml?xml=/news/2004/07/25/nrsr25.xml*.

10. Of note, the commander of SOCOMD (a major-general) is of equivalent rank to the chiefs of the other services. Accessed at *www.defence.gov.au/terrorism/*.

11. See speeches by senior Australian commanders at press conferences, accessed at *www.defence.gov.au/media/2002/73002.doc* and *www.defence.gov.au/media/2003/ACF17A.doc*.

12. General Henry Shelton, the past chief of the Joint Chiefs of Staff, was commander of SOCOM in 1996–97; General Peter Schoomaker, the current chief of staff of the U.S. Army, was appointed to that position after retiring in 2000, following three years as Commander SOCOM. In addition, the current J3 at the Pentagon, Lieutenant-General Norton Schwartz, has a strong SOF background.

13. Susan L. Marquis, *Unconventional Warfare: Rebuilding U.S. Special Operations Forces* (Washington, DC: Brookings Institution Press, 1997), see especially Chapter 6 — "Legislating Change." This book is of value not only to those interested in SOF history, but is also an excellent case study in capability development and institutional resistance to change.

14. Field Marshal the Viscount Slim, *Defeat into Victory* (New York: David Mackay, 1961), 99.

15. For reviews of the Iranian Hostage Rescue Mission by participants, see James Kyle, *The Guts to Try* (New York: Orion Books, 1990), or Charlie Beckwith, *Delta Force* (New York: Harcourt, Brace and Jovanovich, 1983).

16. Admiral James L. Holloway, et al., Report of the Review Group into the Iranian Hostage Rescue Operation (23 August 1980). Report accessed at *www.gwu.edu/~nsarchiv/NSAEBB/NSAEBB63/doc8.pdf*.

17. These tenets are taken from William H. McRaven, *Spec Ops: Case Studies in Special Operations Warfare: Theory and Practice* (Novato, CA: Presidio Press, 1996).

18. For a short and critical review of these operations, see Richard A. Gabriel, *Military Incompetence: Why the American Military Doesn't Win* (New York: Hill and Wang, 1985).

19. Source for the material below is primarily from the U.S. Special Operations Forces Posture Statement 2003–2004: "Transforming the Force at the Forefront of the War on Terrorism," accessed at *www.defenselink.mil/policy/ solic/2003_2004_SOF_Posture_Statement.pdf*, supplemented by various open websites, including *www.specialoperations.com* and *www.specwarnet.com*. Where possible web-based information has been corroborated.

20. In fact, the two regiments were twinned and shared very similar company-level organizations and equipment.

21. This event took place on 3–4 October and was the subject of Mark Bowden's book *Black Hawk Down: A Story of Modern War* (New York: G.K.

Hall, 2000) and the feature film of the same name. For a short review of this operation and other SOCOM operations prior to Iraq, see United States Special Operations Command, *US SOCOM History: 15th Anniversary Edition* (MacDill AFB: SOCOM, 2002) accessed at *www.socom.mil/Docs/15th_aniversary_history.pdf.*

22. See Jason Burke, et al., "US Special Forces Kill 20 in Fierce Afghan Firefight," *Guardian Observer*, 21 October 2001, *www.guardian.co.uk/waronterror/story/0,1361,578138,00.html*, accessed on 8 August 2004. Some of these claims are corroborated in Robin Moore, *The Hunt for Bin Ladin: Task Force Dagger: On the Ground with the Special Forces in Afghanistan* (New York: Random House, 2003), 28–29. For the view of Commander CENTCOM on these initial operations (which he discusses in detail), see General Tommy Franks and Malcolm McConnell, *American Soldier* (New York: Regan Books, 2004), 303–305.

23. See Dr. Richard Kriper, "Into the Dark: The 3/75th Ranger Regiment," *Special Warfare: The Professional Bulletin of the John F. Kennedy Special Warfare Center and School.* (September 2002), 6–7.

24. See the account of ODA 595 in "The liberation of Mazar-e Sherif: 5th Group conducts UW in Afghanistan," *Special Warfare*, Vol. 15, No. 2 (June 2002), 34–41 and Moore, *op. cit.*, 104, who identifies ODA 555 as the first force on the ground during the war. Although CNN and the *Guardian* claimed that U.S. and U.K. SOF had already entered Afghanistan on 28 September 2001, these claims have not been confirmed by other sources. See *www.cnn.com/2001/US/09/28/ret.special.operations/* and *www.guardian.co.uk/international/story/0,,560245,00.html.* The SOF insertions were actually planned much earlier. See Franks, *op. cit.*, 296–300 for his frustration at 10 days of delays, largely due to weather and dust.

25. Colonel John T. Carney, Jr., and Benjamin F. Schemmer, *No Room for Error: The Covert Operations of America's Special Tactics Units from Iran to Afghanistan* (New York: Ballantine Books, 2002), 274–275. For AFSOF operations, see also Michael Hirsh, *None Braver: U.S. Air Force Pararescuemen in the War on Terrorism* (New York: New American Library, 2003).

26. See *www.navsoc.navy.mil/navsoc_missions.asp.*

27. Frank L. Jones, "Army SOF in Afghanistan: Learning the Right Lessons," *Joint Forces Quarterly* (Winter 2002/3), 18.

28. Carney and Schemmer, *op. cit.*, 284.

29. Norman Friedman, *Terrorism, Afghanistan and America's New Way of War* (Annapolis, MD: Naval Institute Press, 2003), 221.

30. Presentation to the Senate Armed Services Committee, 9 June 2003, quoted in Anthony H. Cordesman, *Lessons of the Iraq War: Summary Briefing* (Washington, DC: CSIS, 15 July 2003), *www.csis.org/features/iraq_instant lessons_exec.pdf*, accessed on 24 July 2003.

31. Gregory Fontenot, Colonel (Retired) et al., *On Point: The United States Army in Operation IRAQI FREEDOM* (Fort Leavenworth: Center for Army Lessons Learned, U.S. Army, 2003), accessed at *www.globalsecurity.org/military/ library/report/2004/onpoint/ch-8.htm*.

32. Ronald O'Rourke, coordinator, *Iraq War: Defense Program Implications for Congress*, CRS Report RL31946 (Washington, DC: Congressional Research Service, 4 June 2003), 40–42.

33. Williamson Murray and Major General (Retired) Robert H. Scales, Jr., *The Iraq War: A Military History* (Cambridge, MA: Belknap Press, 2003), 185.

34. Anthony H. Cordesman, *The Iraq War: Strategy, Tactics and Military Lessons* (Washington, DC: The CSIS Press, 2003), 59. See also "Australian Forces Go Scud Hunting in Western Iraq" in *Jane's Intelligence Review* (July 2003), 20–22, and "Interview with MGen Duncan Lewis," same issue, 56.

35. For detailed chapters on Task Force VIKING, see Robin Moore, *Hunting Down Saddam: The Inside Story of the Search and Capture* (New York: St. Martin's Press, 2004).

36. Murray and Scales, *op. cit.*, 189–190.

37. Quoted in Moore, *Hunting Down Saddam*, 44.

38. Gerry Gilmore, "Special Operations Troops Recount Iraq Missions," American Forces Information Service (Washington, DC: 5 February 2004), accessed at *www.defenselink.mil/news/Feb2004/n02052004_200402057.html*.

39. Cordesman, *The Iraq War*, 362.

40. Thom Shankar and Eric Schmitt, "Covert Units Conduct a Campaign Invisible Except for the Results," *New York Times*, 6 April 2003, *http://query.nytimes.com/search/restricted/article?res*, accessed on 14 August 2004.

41. Thomas Harding, "Shake-Up in Special Boat Service over Claims It 'Panicked and Fled' in Iraq," *The Daily Telegraph*, 26 July 2004, accessed at *http://portal.telegraph.co.uk/news/main.jhtml?xml=/news/2004/07/26/nsbs26.xml*.

42. See Steve Voegel, "Far from Capital, a Fight That US Forces Did Not Win," *Washington Post*, 10 April 2003, 38.

43. Cordesman, *The Iraq War*, 364–365.

44. Joint Publication 3–05, *Doctrine for Joint Special Operations* (17 December 2003), I–1, accessed at *www.dtic.mil/doctrine/jel/new_pubs/jp3_05.pdf*.

45. Sun Tzu, *The Art of War*, translated by Samuel B. Griffith (London: Oxford University Press, 1963), 91.

46. See David C. Martin and John Walcott, *The Best Laid Plans: The Inside Story of America's War Against Terrorism* (New York: Harper & Row, 1988); and Jennifer D. Kibbe, "The Rise of the Shadow Warriors" in *Foreign Affairs*, Vol. 83, No. 2 (Mar/Apr 2004), 102–116. See also Franks, *op. cit.* in which he refers to the elite operators and special mission units of Joint Special Operations Command.

47. See General (Retired) Carl Stiner, Tom Clancy, and Tony Koltz, *Shadow Warriors: Inside the Special Forces* (New York: G.P. Putnam's Sons, 2002).

48. Richard Clarke, *Against All Enemies: Inside America's War on Terror* (New York: Free Press, 2004), 144–145.

49. Thomas H. Kean et al., *The 9/11 Commission Report* (Washington, DC: Government Printing Office, 22 July 2004), 112–113, accessed at *www.9-11commission.gov/report/911Report.pdf*.

50. Thom Shanker and Eric Schmitt, "Pentagon Says a Covert Force Hunts Hussein," *New York Times*, 7 November 2003.

51. According to Green Berets in Afghanistan, at least two high-value, senior Taliban targets were allowed to slip through their hands while distant special mission units were tasked to respond rather than SF troops already in the area. In both cases, SF personnel claimed that the slow response of the elite SOF forces resulted in the escape of Taliban leaders. See Gregory L. Vistica, "Military Split on How to Use Special Forces in Terror War" *Washington Post*, 5 January 2004.

52 See Robin Moore, *Hunting Down Saddam*, 227–256, for the most detailed account of this operation, dubbed "Red Dawn."

53. Michael Hirsh et al., "The Hunt Heats Up," *Newsweek*, Vol. 143, No. 11 (15 March 2004), 46–49. According to the article, TF 121 was at the time commanded by a Sea Air Land (SEAL) team officer, William McRaven, author of *Spec Ops* cited above, and described in the article as "the smartest SEAL that ever lived," a claim that, though possibly true, will undoubtedly bring a smile to the face of many U.S. Army SOF operators.

54. Discussions on this topic were reported as early as September 2002. See Susan Schmidt and Thomas E. Ricks, "Pentagon Plans Shift in War on Terror," *Washington Post*, September 18, 2002, A01. See also Jennifer Kibbe, *op. cit.*, 110.

55. Tom Breen, "U.S. Special Operations Command," *Armed Forces International* (July 2004), 46.

56. Quoted in Robert Wall, "Sharpening the Sword: Special Operations Clamors for Better ISR, but Cultural Change Also Deemed Critical," *Aviation Week and Space Technology*, Vol. 160, No. 8 (23 February 2004).

57. Thomas H. Hearn, et al., *The 9/11 Commission Report*, 451.

58. For useful discussions of the issues involved, see Jennifer Kibbe, *op. cit.*; Eric Schmitt and Thom Shanker, "Special Warriors Have Growing Ranks and Growing Pains in Taking Key Antiterror Role," *New York Times*, 2 August 2004; Richard Ladner, "Special Ops, CIA Mix in War Stir Legal Questions," *Tampa Tribune*, 29 February 2004; and Colonel Kathryn Stone, *"All Necessary Means" — Employing CIA Operatives in a Warfighting Role Alongside Special Operations Forces*, USAWC Strategy Research Project (Carlisle Barracks, PA: U.S. Army War College, 7 April 2003). It should be noted that *covert* has a particular meaning in the United States. Although clandestine operations intend to hide the operation prior to execution, covert operations intend to hide the sponsor, in this case the United States. While covert operations are an unlikely strategy for the government of Canada, clandestine and discreet operations are understood as a necessary part of Canadian security operations. That said, effective oversight must be considered thoroughly in any such operations.

59. Quoted in Tom Breen, *op. cit.*, 47.

60. See Major Brister's chapter in this volume; and CF Land Staff's Directorate of Land Strategic Concepts, *Future Force: Concepts for Future Army Capabilities* (Kingston: DLSC, 2003), 176–179.

# PART III

## The Way Ahead
## for Canadian Special Operations

# 11

## Putting a Square Peg in a Round Hole:
### *Finding a Special Forces Capability for the Canadian Army*

### Tony Balasevicius

Since their inception during the early stages of the Second World War, modern special operation forces (SOF)[1] have steadily grown and evolved into a key element of a nation's military inventory. In the post–Cold War period they have proven to be particularly popular with the political leadership because of their small footprint, low-visibility, and ability to accomplish a myriad of sensitive missions. They eliminate the need for larger national commitments, reducing the risk of heavy casualties or adverse political fallout.

The utility of SOF has gained increased recognition in the aftermath of the 11 September 2001 terrorist attack against the United States. The trend since then has been to enhance the capabilities and extend the employment of SOF. Evidence suggests that the employment of these soldiers will likely continue to grow in the coming years. Since 9/11, SOF have played key roles in recent operations in Afghanistan, Iraq, and the Philippines.

These well-publicized examples of SOF missions are only a small part of the ongoing and increasing SOF commitment by Western states.[2] This heavy operational tempo is not surprising given the range of their capabilities, which include long-range reconnaissance, sabotage behind enemy lines, counterterrorism, and the training of foreign military forces.

Most modern militaries now have some type of SOF capability. According to journalist and author Robin Neillands, already in 1997 over 287 SOF units were operating worldwide within 66 nations or states.[3] This number has continued to grow in the turbulent aftermath of 9/11. It is not surprising, therefore, that the Canadian Army is looking at developing an SOF capability as part of its force development review. One option under consideration is the formation of a direct action (DA) organization based on the U.S. Army Rangers.

As with any option, the potential of creating a Ranger-type unit demands some form of critical analysis to answer key questions like, how would such a capability enhance Canada's ability to respond to the various SOF contingencies? And would the formation of such a unit enhance Canadian capabilities and meet strategic goals?

Given the complexity of the subject, this chapter will focus on the Ranger concept as an SOF capability and consider its historical development and employment to determine its strengths and limitations based on operational experience. Finally, the utility of a Ranger-type unit within the Canadian context will be assessed.

As in any doctrinal construct, nations characterize special operations (SO) in different ways. For the purpose of this chapter, special operations will be defined in accordance with American doctrine and will focus primarily on American SOF models such as the Rangers that have developed within this context. According to U.S. joint special operations doctrine, SOF operations are those operations conducted in hostile, denied, or politically sensitive environments to achieve military, diplomatic, informational, and/or economic objectives employing military capabilities for which there is no broad conventional force requirement. These operations often require covert, clandestine, or low-visibility capabilities.

Special operations are applicable across the range of military operations. They can be conducted independently or in conjunction with operations of conventional forces or other government agencies and may include operations by, with, or through indigenous or surrogate forces. SO differ from conventional operations in degree of physical and political risk, operational techniques, mode of employment, independence from friendly support, and dependence on detailed operational intelligence and indigenous assets.[4]

As such, SOF units are organized and trained in nine principal mission areas:[5] counter-proliferation (CP), counterterrorism (CT), foreign internal defence (FID), special reconnaissance (SR), direct action (DA), psychological operations (PSYOP), civil affairs (CA), unconventional warfare (UW), and information operations (IO).[6] In addition to these nine principal missions, there are also a number of other tasks, commonly referred to as "collateral activities," that have been carried out by SOF and are the result of their unique skills and training. They include coalition support, combat search and rescue (CSAR), counter-drug (CD) activities, humanitarian demining (HD), humanitarian assistance (HA), security assistance (SA), and special activities.

Interestingly, many of these missions, both primary and collateral, have not necessarily resulted from an evolution of operational circumstances. "This list is a hodgepodge of conventional, unconventional and just plain odd missions, some of which are actually subsets of others," observed Thomas K. Adams, a former director of intelligence and special operations at the U.S. Army Peacekeeping Institute. This "results in part from a general willingness at the command levels of the SOF community to accept almost any mission as one in which SOF can succeed."[7] Adams adds, "There is an idea that, by accepting many missions, SOF demonstrates its fitness and remains competitive with other organizations in the struggle for a share of the diminishing military budget. This leads to the inclusion of things, which clearly is [sic] and ought to be conventional."[8]

Nonetheless, the nine principal missions and seven collateral activities have evolved from three core missions, which have, with some exceptions, developed from the capabilities established to meet specific operational requirements during the Second World War. The three core missions are direct action (DA), special reconnaissance (SR), and unconventional warfare (UW). The reason that these three missions are highlighted is that modern SOF units are generally organized, equipped, and trained to be proficient in one of these areas. Residual capabilities developed during training will allow some overlap, but it is important to understand that there is a limit on how much an SOF unit can do outside the spectrum of their core mission.

For example, DA missions can be broken down into large-scale actions carried out by units such as the British Army Commandos and American Rangers or small-scale operations carried out by a more surgical strike from smaller forces such as the Special Air Service (SAS). UW can likewise be broken down into missions undertaken by larger forces such as the former Office of Strategic Services (OSS), operational groups (OGs), and the current American Special Forces[9] or by smaller liaison teams similar to the Second World War concept of Jedburgh teams employed by the Allies.[10] Jedburgh teams were groups of three Allied agents (SOE or OSS) dropped into France prior to D-Day to assist the local French resistance. Their task was to supply the Resistance and ensure that its efforts were coordinated in the best interests of Allied strategy. Each team consisted of two officers and one NCO wireless operator, all of whom were trained in demolitions and guerrilla tactics.

Because the requirements of each core task are extremely specialized, in terms of their organization, training, and equipment, SOF units tend to focus in one area, either large-scale DA, small-scale DA and SR,[11] or UW. In the case of the Rangers, their specialization is large-scale DA missions.[12] In fact, since the inception of the large-scale DA units during the early stages of the Second World War, this capability has moved out of the purview of SOF into the domain of conventional forces.

Unfortunately, military institutions will often create these units with the mistaken idea that they can provide an SOF capability that can also be used for other, conventional tasks. This lack of understanding of SOF in general and of the large-scale DA capability in particular often leads to misemployment because military commanders do not understand the limitations of these forces.[13] The concern of misemployment is extremely relevant today as SOF are in high demand and the option to provide a quick fix with a hybrid capability such as the Rangers is a tempting one. Rangers are highly trained light infantry that have developed a very specialized mission capability that fits within the context of the U.S. Army's total spectrum dominance extremely well. When used within this limited context, such a capability can produce outstanding results. However, with few exceptions, the opportunities to employ these large DA forces in appropriate operations have thus far proven limited.

The development of a large-scale DA capability had its genesis in the creation of the British Commandos during the Second World War. One of the first SOF units to be formed by the Allies, the Commandos were conceived as "mobile and hard-hitting light troops that could raid or operate behind an enemy's lines."[14] Some 30 Commandos were eventually formed, and they were initially trained and equipped to conduct offensive operations against the German defences in Occupied Europe. These operations were designed as classic DA missions consisting of "short-duration strikes and other ... offensive actions to seize, destroy, capture, recover, or inflict damage on designated personnel or materiel."[15]

The training program developed for units to carry out these specialized missions emphasized the development of the individual soldier.

The focus was on physical fitness, weapons training (both their own and the enemy's), demolitions, orienteering, close-quarter combat, silent killing, communications, survival skills, amphibious and cliff assault, and vehicle operation. All training was extremely demanding and realistic, often employing live ammunition.[16] In fact, British experience in this area was so influential that the Americans decided to have the first group of their Rangers attend the British Commando course at Achnacarry Castle, Scotland.

The modern American Rangers were formed on 1 June 1942, when General George C. Marshall, chief of staff of the U.S. Army, directed the creation of an American commando organization. Marshall wanted a cadre of personnel with battle experience, which could be shared throughout the Army. To this end he ordered the activation of the 1st Ranger Battalion on 19 June 1942, at Carrickfergus, Northern Ireland.[17] In order to gain experience, the Rangers operated with the British Commandos. This meant that although the Rangers were equipped as an American infantry unit, they would be given additional "special equipment for amphibious landings and night attacks that included such things as collapsible rubber dinghies and life preserver vests."[18] As Commando training and operations also included individuals with special qualifications such as demolition experts, mechanics, truck and tractor drivers, and maintenance personnel, the composition of the Ranger unit reflected those additional capabilities.

Notwithstanding the excellent training and high calibre of personnel, the light scales of equipment posed a constant problem for the Rangers during subsequent operations.[19] While light holdings of equipment enhanced mobility, firepower was correspondingly reduced. This problem was not serious if engagements were short, however, if operations were prolonged or if the unit was used as conventional infantry, the limited firepower of the unit proved a major disadvantage. Ironically, this trend continued throughout the war and, as time went on, "the more the Rangers were used as conventional infantry, the more firepower they needed; and the more firepower they got, the more likely it became that the headquarters that controlled them would use them conventionally."[20]

This problem was highlighted during the North Africa campaign. In the opening stages of Operation Torch, in November 1942, the Rangers were given an appropriate DA mission to conduct a surprise night landing north of Arzew, Algeria (French North Africa), where they successfully neutralized the port's main coastal defences and captured its docks.

After this operation, the Rangers were assigned to the Fifth Army Invasion Training Center (ITC) as demonstration and experimental troops.[21] Interestingly, even commanders who understand the concept and potential of such large-scale DA forces employed the Rangers in conventional infantry missions. During the latter stages of the North African campaign, the Rangers "spent almost four times as many days in conventional combat than they did in Ranger-type operations and, in fact, spent most of their time on non-combat duties."[22]

The reason they spent most of their time on non-combat duties was that the Rangers, with their special training and capabilities, were being held back for employment on appropriate high-value operations such as the destruction of key enemy installations. As a rule, they were not employed in the line as often as conventional units, and this created the perception within the Army that these forces were a drain on the personnel pool and did not contribute significantly to the overall war effort, which was generally measured by the number of successful combat actions a unit engaged in. It was further believed that such capabilities did nothing that could not be done by well-trained infantry.[23] Of course, this logic belies the reality of the situation: These types of large DA forces are, in fact, well-trained infantry troops. Unfortunately, it is generally forgotten that, during times of conflict, the training of hastily raised infantry units in a large army to the high standards necessary to conduct these types of missions successfully is impossible.[24]

Nevertheless, a significant quandary associated with keeping highly trained DA units in reserve is the temptation to use them to fix problems more suited to conventional troops. When this occurs, higher casualty rates often result as these units are neither structured, nor equipped to endure prolonged periods of combat. A good example of such misemployment is provided by the complete destruction of the American Ranger battalions at Anzio. An official report noted:

> A botched infiltration mission on the Anzio beachhead in early 1944 completed the destruction of Darby's Rangers.... When the two battalions began their infiltration on the night of 29–30 January, the enemy quickly detected them and by dawn had surrounded them with infantry and armour just outside Cisterna. In a desperate attempt to rescue the isolated units, the 4th Ranger Battalion repeatedly attacked the German lines throughout the morning but succeeded in losing half of its combat strength in the futile effort. About noon, the remnants

of the 1st and 3rd surrendered. Only eight men escaped to American lines.[25]

Attrition resulting from conventional operations also depleted another large-scale DA unit, the First Special Service Force (FSSF) during their operations in Italy. In 1942, the British were examining the creation of a mobile commando force equipped with light over-snow vehicles for use against German facilities in Norway. After high-level discussions, the Americans and Canadians agreed to provide volunteers for a unit to carry out these missions.[26] The FSSF never carried out its original operational mission and was instead sent to Italy, where for the most part, it was used as a conventional infantry organization.[27] After two months of intensive fighting in the Italian mountains, the FSSF was reduced from its original strength of 1,800 to 400 combat-effective soldiers,"[28] a loss that proved difficult to replace. The Americans tried to solve the reinforcement problem by drawing replacements from the general infantry pool,[29] while Canadian reinforcements, had "three weeks training in US weapons and drill and Special Forces tactics."[30]

Heavy causalities, such as those suffered by the Rangers at Anzio and by the FSSF, have a tendency to create instability within the organization and generally undermine effectiveness. The loss of a significant number of highly trained soldiers and a lack of similarly trained replacements will quickly turn these units into little more than conventional infantry organizations.

However, when used appropriately, these large-scale DA units can achieve good results. During the American assault at Omaha Beach on 6 June 1944, elements of the 2nd Ranger Battalion scaled the 100-foot cliff at Pointe du Hoc and seized German artillery pieces that threatened American troops landing on the beach. Despite high causalities, the 2nd Ranger Battalion successfully held off a number of determined German counterattacks and retained the position.

Another interesting Ranger operation carried out during the Second World War was conducted in the Pacific by the 6th Ranger Battalion.[31] The unit was reinforced by members of the Alamo Scouts[32] and Filipino guerrillas, to rescue 511 Allied prisoners of war (POWs) from a Japanese internment camp near Cabanatuan in the Philippines.[33]

The preparatory planning for the operation started as the American Sixth Army entered central Luzon and involved the use of extensive map and ground reconnaissance. Once there was sufficient intelligence to confirm the location of the POWs, the mission was confirmed and detailed planning commenced. Everyone involved became completely familiar with all aspects of the plan, including "the routes to the objective, the rendezvous points and the layout of the objective."[34] In the end, the operation proved an overwhelming success and an example of what large DA forces can do when properly employed and given adequate time and resources for a specific mission. One military historian concluded:

> At a cost of two Rangers killed, the 6th Ranger Battalion (-), reinforced by Alamo Scouts and Filipino guerrillas, liberated 511 American and Allied POWs and killed or wounded an estimated 523 Japanese. The principles and techniques [utilized in the planning of the operation] were important because they contributed to the Rangers' undetected approach to the objective, their gaining complete surprise over the Japanese, their smooth assault on the compound, and their successful liberation of the prisoners.[35]

Interestingly, the 6th Ranger Battalion did not take part in any major operations after Cabanatuan. Their activities in the Philippines were limited to providing security for Sixth Army headquarters, conducting reconnaissance patrols, searching for Japanese stragglers and eliminating small pockets of enemy resistance.[36] Like most specialized units created during the Second World War, the Rangers were deactivated in 1945. But the operations at Arzew, Pointe du Hoc, and Cabanatuan proved that the capability was feasible and, if employed properly, DA units like the Rangers, FSSF, and Commandos could have a significant impact on general military operations. The difficulty was that these units were misemployed more often than not, and when in operations were used largely as highly trained assault infantry.

This is due in part to a general perception that was created within the Allied command that the limited opportunities where these forces could be employed did not justify the personnel and training that was being committed to them. The Commandos were originally raised as highly trained, flexible raiders with a range of individual skill sets. But as time passed, their role narrowed so that by the time of Operation Overlord, the invasion of Normandy in June 1944, they had effectively become specialists in amphibious assault.[37] This evolution came about because of the significant limitations of naval lift. The British discovered that even organizing a small force comprising 300 soldiers required a great deal of specialized shipping. In addition, these light forces needed significant naval gunfire and air support to have any chance of success.[38] In the end, limited employment opportunities and the level of support and protection required forced the large-scale DA unit to evolve away from the realm of the SOF and into the sphere of highly trained infantry where the Marines, airborne, and other such light forces now tend to operate.[39]

In fact, after the Second World War, the concept of employing Rangers as a large-scale DA force re-emerged very slowly and did not fully rematerialize until the early 1970s. In August 1950, 15 Ranger companies were activated during the Korean conflict. Between December 1950 and August 1951, seven of the companies saw action in the country, where they were assigned to various infantry units. Their primary tasks were to scout ahead of the main body, patrol enemy positions, conduct raids behind enemy lines, and carry out ambushes.[40] After Korea, the Rangers companies were disbanded only to be reactivated again in the late 1960s, during the Vietnam War. In the aftermath of Vietnam, the independent Ranger companies were formed into battalions, where they once again became a quick reaction light-infantry force designed to carry out larger DA missions.[41] The renaissance of a large-scale DA capability continued through the post-Vietnam era and in 1980, the Rangers started to evolve into a new role when "C" Company, 1st Battalion 75th Infantry (Ranger) Regiment was ordered to support Operation Eagle Claw, the mission to rescue the American hostages held in Iran.

The mission was primarily an SOF operation; however, the Rangers were assigned to provide security for some of the support elements while the assault forces carried out the rescue.[42] In October 1983, the Rangers re-established their large-scale DA capability in a more conventional task of airfield seizure when they led the assault during Operation Urgent Fury, the invasion of Grenada, by jumping into and capturing the Point Salinas airstrip, paving the way for the 82nd Airborne Division.[43] Six years later, in Panama, during Operation Just Cause, the Rangers were again used to secure the main airfield, at Tocumen, where they were again subsequently reinforced by elements of the 82nd Airborne Division.[44]

During the 1990–1991 Gulf War, "A" and "B" Companies of the 1st Ranger Battalion were deployed to play a supporting role in the allied mission to liberate Kuwait from Iraqi forces. The Rangers also carried out a number of raids and conducted numerous reconnaissance patrols into Kuwait to collect information for the assaulting forces.[45]

In Somalia, in the early nineties, the trend of employing Rangers to beef up Special Forces continued as soldiers from "B" Company, 3rd Ranger Battalion provided backup support to Delta Force in a series of operations designed to capture key leaders of a clan disrupting the United Nation's mission in the region.

Employing Rangers in support of SOF continued into the new millennium. In the weeks following 9/11, the Rangers assisted Northern Alliance forces that were being supervised by Special Forces during the opening stages of Operation Enduring Freedom, which was focused on destroying al-Qaeda's network and removing the Taliban from power in Afghanistan. The Rangers went into action on 19 October 2001, when a company was parachuted into a small enemy command and control compound outside Kandahar and onto a separate airfield in southern Afghanistan. During the raids, the Rangers destroyed several weapons caches and gathered intelligence. In addition to these raids, the Rangers searched various cave complexes and provided SOF with a rapid reaction force capability.

It should be stressed that these operations, carried out during the 1980s and 1990s, fit the current concept of Ranger employment envisioned by the American military. Today, Rangers are tasked "to plan and conduct special military operations ... that may support conventional military operations or they may be performed independently when conventional forces cannot be used...."[46] The Rangers are also expected to conduct what the Americans call "strike operations," which are defined as raids, interdiction, and recovery operations.[47] These strike operations are carried out to support the U.S. Army's Air Land Battle doctrine, and Rangers are integrated into an overall campaign plan to destroy, delay, and disorganize the enemy. In this concept of operations they are intended to divert the enemy's operational forces and power to their own rear area security tasks. Strike missions are also anticipated to create a suitable environment to exploit the capabilities and impacts of SOF. In addition, Rangers are expected to conduct special light infantry operations, including "many of the light infantry missions assigned to airborne, air assault, or light infantry battalions and brigades."[48] In effect, a Ranger unit can provide the same capabilities as these other light infantry units.

The Rangers' evolution from highly trained, flexible raiders with a range of individual skill sets for very specific missions in the Second World War to highly trained light infantry with a broader capability to carry out a range of missions is not difficult to understand. The limited opportunities where mission-specific forces can be employed, even during periods of international conflict such as the Gulf War, did not justify the expense of keeping them. In attempting to rationalize their relevance in a highly competitive niche, the Rangers have moved into the realm of conventional forces highlighting a more general-purpose capability, while attempting to stake a claim as the best capability to support SOF.[49]

Having examined the evolution of the American Rangers, the question must then be asked, would the creation of a Ranger capability be a suitable option for Canada? To determine the answer to this question it is necessary to first look at what capabilities the Canadian Forces (CF) anticipate needing in the coming years. According to *Shaping the Future of the Canadian Forces: A Strategy for 2020*, the CF "must evolve to meet the challenges of the future." To do this the CF must "position the force structure … to provide Canada with modern, task-tailored, and globally deployable, combat-capable forces that can respond quickly to crises at home and abroad, in joint or combined operations." More important, "the force structure must be viable, achievable, and affordable."[50]

Within the limitations of it being viable, achievable, and affordable, a Ranger capability is certainly possible. Rangers are highly trained light forces that can quickly be task-tailored and are globally deployable. The organization and training of such a force would take time but, with the exception of finding the right people, would likely present little difficulty for the Canadian Army.[51] In fact, the basic elements of Ranger training are currently provided to a select number of soldiers through the Patrol Pathfinder Course, which is run by the Canadian Parachute Centre in Trenton, Ontario.[52] This course could be easily modified to meet the requirements of a Ranger unit.

Furthermore, the Army already has a substantial light force capability (albeit lacking in coherent doctrine) with its light infantry battalions (LIBs), one of which could form the basis of a Ranger unit if necessary. For a moderate level of additional money, the conversion of a unit to this role could be completed without significant modifications to the LIB's basic structure and would thus provide a quick reaction capability to conduct strike missions and carry out the other special light infantry operations currently being undertaken by the Rangers. A significant barrier to creating this capability would be providing sufficient personnel of the quality that is needed. More specifically, will there be reasonable opportunity to employ the unit and can requirements for personnel needed to maintain the capability be sustained without jeopardizing the overall efficiency of the Army? For Canada, limited employment opportunities must be a major consideration when developing future capabilities.

Given the small size and extremely demanding operational tempo currently being experienced by the Canadian Army, it is difficult to see how a Ranger unit of 600 to 800 soldiers could be exempt from other missions such as peace support or counter insurgency operations. In recent operations, the American Rangers have been used primarily in airfield seizure and providing backup for SOF operations. In the British Army, however, conventional airborne forces have performed these same missions with very little difficulty. For example, during a hostage-taking situation in Sierra Leone, a force of about 150 British paratroopers, and members of the SAS, freed 11 British hostages. More important, paratroopers are also capable of conducting conventional missions such as peace support operations and other conventional light infantry tasks.

Although Canada does not maintain an airborne unit, each LIB has a parachute company.[53] It would be possible — given proper training, the necessary resources, and a specific mandate — for the LIBs to carry out many of the Rangers' tasks, including support for the SOF. The added benefit to such an option would be the ability to rotate the task, something that could not be done with a single-unit capability.

Another problem related to having a Ranger-type unit is that, in order to be effective, such units must remain in a constant state of high readiness for quick operational deployments. In order to be operationally ready for rapid deployment, such a unit would have to be kept free of other operational taskings so that it can focus on training and other high-readiness requirements. This is something that has not been done well in the past. The former Canadian Airborne Regiment (Cdn AB Regt) was Canada's high-readiness unit and, as such, was expected to deploy outside the country within 72 hours. However, after the unit's move from Edmonton to Petawawa in the late 1970s, the Cdn AB Regt was given a large share of the Army's individual taskings and was also deployed on UN peacekeeping missions like any other unit.

This was done because the Army was in dire need of the additional resources just to function. More important, the Army realized that even if it could maintain the Cdn AB Regt's high operational readiness posture, there was still the problem of aircraft availability within the CF to move the unit. As witnessed by the deployment of the Princess Patricia's Canadian Light Infantry (PPCLI) Battalion Group to Afghanistan in 2001, the ability to rapidly deploy units not only depends on the high operational readiness of the organization, it also depends on how quickly aircraft can be made available to move the unit, the capability to have dedicated airlift on standby to move high-readiness units in the time-frames necessary does not currently exist within the CF and would need to be addressed.

Once deployed, the basic problem facing the employment of a Canadian Ranger-type unit would be its limited tactical mobility, especially in the area of ground transport, which would make it unsuitable for most types of extended employment.[54] Recent experience with the LIBs in Afghanistan, much like the American Rangers in North Africa and Italy, has shown that significant augmentation is needed if these light forces are to provide a relevant contribution to operational requirements or, at least, when tactical mobility is necessary. This problem was clearly evident with the employment of the 3rd Battalion, The Royal Canadian Regiment (3 RCR) LIB, in Afghanistan in 2003. The unit had to be augmented with no less then two light armoured vehicle (LAV) companies from the 1st Battalion, The Royal Canadian Regiment (1 RCR), in order to properly carry out its missions.[55]

Moreover, the outstanding success in Afghanistan of the PPCLI Battalion Group, which was based on a LIB, would have been difficult without the extensive aviation support from the Americans. A Ranger unit lacks transport; if used outside the very specific mission spectrum it was designed for, it would face many of the same tactical mobility and force protection problems encountered by the RCR and PPCLI.

The issue of equipment and its impact on employment was a constant problem for the former Cdn AB Regt. "Even though the Airborne Regiment was designated the national UN stand-by force, with the exception of its deployment to Cyprus in 1974, it was never used as such," wrote Colonel Bernd Horn, a former serving member and author. He added, "It was also labelled as the nation's strategic reserve, but its light scales of equipment, particularly its shortage of vehicles, caused many to dismiss it as unemployable for anything other than a domestic context."[56] Horn explains, "Time after time, when the Cdn AB Regt received a mission it meant stripping equipment from conventional units. Each effort only reinforced the accusation that the Regiment was an anachronism and a parasite that sapped the declining resources of the remainder of the Army."[57]

Sapping the Army's declining personnel resources will be another major problem that will come with having this capability. Ranger units rely on effective leadership, the best soldiers the Army can provide, and a very high level of training to operate effectively. A Ranger capability would demand the best soldiers in the Army. One of the biggest problems faced by the Cdn AB Regt was its ability to attract and retain quality leaders and soldiers. To put this problem into better perspective, approximately 70 percent of soldiers who attend a jump course will be successful; yet, only about 50 percent of the soldiers attempting a Ranger Course will pass.[58] If the Army had trouble maintaining the Cdn AB Regt using the 70 percent who were successful on a jump course, it will have more difficulty maintaining a unit of similar size to the Cdn AB Regt,[59] which has more specialized abilities and capabilities but will accept only the top 50 percent of those who volunteer for the training.[60]

Interestingly, none of these difficulties have been acknowledged in *Future Force*, the Canadian Army's blueprint for future capabilities. As for specialized abilities and capabilities, the document states, "Although the requirement for multi-purpose forces will continue to exist within the context of the army's mandated tasks, specialization will be increasingly required to meet the growing plethora of national security risks."[61] It goes on to say, "In light of future threats, economic constraints, and political realities, the Army will have to enhance, evolve, and refine its SOF capability."[62] Although the document recognizes many of the limitations currently facing the Army, it does not take into consideration Canada's experience with maintaining large, quick reaction capabilities.

In fact, the document provides an option for an SOF organization in the future and recommends a DA unit similar in concept to a Ranger capability as part of the force structure. The difficulty with this option is that it attempts to cut and paste a model from another military, which does not fit into the limited resource realities faced by the Canadian Army. The ability to have a number of SOF capabilities, each with its own selection, training, and support capability requirements, is a luxury few nations can afford, and Canada is not one of them. If the Army is going to develop specialization in key areas, it must create an organization that can fit national requirements. Such capabilities must be selective and provide the best value for the resources expended or, as is often stated, "the biggest bang for the buck." Within the current strategic environment, the use of SOF by nations such as the United States has been extremely successful because they are highly trained, have a small footprint, low-visibility, and can accomplish a myriad of sensitive missions. Rangers do not operate within this SOF spectrum. They are not equipped, trained, or organized to generate missions such as long-range, long-duration reconnaissance. Nor are they capable of operating for extended periods without support-attributes that distinguish SOF organizations from conventional forces. Attempting to employ such a unit for SOF missions would be a mistake. Canada cannot have capabilities that cover the full spectrum of SOF missions and must explore options that give her the most flexibility regarding employment within its resource envelope. In essence, the optimal solution is one that provides the most flexibility, and therefore the most potential for employment, namely an SAS, small-scale DA, SR capability, backed by some type of conventional DA capability such as an airborne unit.

In summary, many of the strengths and weaknesses that resided in the original unit-size DA capabilities such as the British Commandos are present in the modern American Rangers and would be intrinsic to any capability the Canadian Army developed. That being said, no military capability is perfect as each has its own particular strengths and weaknesses. The question that must be asked is whether those strengths and weaknesses can fit into the specific strategic requirements of Canada. If the Canadian Army is looking for an SOF capability, the Ranger model is unsuitable. Rangers are not equipped, trained or organized to provide any type of SOF capability that Canada would need. They conduct operations in a very narrow spectrum of tasks and suffer from the limitations associated with a light infantry. Despite some spectacular mission successes, specialized DA units, such as the Rangers, have not faired well historically. This is due largely to their limited scope for employment and the substantial support necessary to allow them to carry out operations. In recent operations, the Rangers have been used primarily in airfield seizure tasks and for providing support to SOF operations.

From a Canadian perspective, creating a unit specifically to support SOF operations or to develop a very specific DA capability is wasteful. The British Army's airborne forces have adequately carried out the same tasks. In this regard, Canada would be much better served if it focused on a true SOF capability modelled on the American Special Forces (UW) or the British SAS (SR/small DA) capabilities. These SOF units have a significant operational impact, and their relative scarcity keep them in high demand. Such units demand greater effort in personnel selection and training, but they are within the Army's ability to generate and maintain. More important, they would do a better job than a Ranger unit in providing Canada with the relevant capability it is seeking.

## NOTES

1.  William S. Cohen, secretary of defense, United States, *Annual Report to the President and Congress, 1998* (April 1998), accessed at *www.dtic.mil/exec-sec/ adr98/index.html*. Special Operations Forces (SOF) are specialized military units designed to deal with a variety of situations. According to the report, "They offer a range of options to decision makers confronting crises and conflicts below the threshold of war, such as terrorism, insurgency, and sabotage. Second, they are force multipliers for major conflicts, increasing the effectiveness and efficiency of the U.S. military effort. Finally, they are the forces of choice in situations requiring regional orientation and cultural and political sensitivity, including military-to-military contacts and noncombatant missions like humanitarian assistance, security assistance, and peacekeeping operations."

2.  John T. Carney and Benjamin F. Schemmer, *No Room for Error: The Covert Operations of America's Special Tactics Units from Iran to Afghanistan* (New York: Ballantine Books, 2002), 23. "Between October 1, 2000, and September 30, 2001 ... Special Operations Forces deployed to 146 countries or foreign territories with an average of 4,938 personnel deployed each week — while also conducting 132 Joint Combined Exchange events in 50 countries, 137 counterdrug missions in 23 countries, and humanitarian demining missions in 19 countries. That represents a 43 percent increase [*sic*] in country deployments in the ten years since Desert Storm, a 57 percent increase in the number of missions undertaken, and a 139 percent increase in the number of Special Operations Command personnel serving abroad in any given week — all with essentially the same number of people."

3.  Robin Neillands, *In the Combat Zone: Special Forces Since 1945* (London: Weidenfeld and Nicolson, 1997), 320.

4.  United States, Joint Chiefs of Staff, *Joint Pub 3–05 — Doctrine for Joint Special Operations* (Washington, DC: 17 December 2003), I–1. Most allied countries, including Canada, have largely accepted this definition.

5.  *Ibid.*

6.  *Ibid.* In May 2003, changes to the SOF principal missions and collateral activities were made. Specifically, "principal missions" are now referred to as "core tasks." These include unconventional warfare (UW), foreign internal defence (FID), direct action (DA), special reconnaissance (SR), counterterrorism (CT), counter-proliferation of WMD (CP), psychological operations (PSYOPS), information operations (IO), and civil affairs operations (CAO). In addition, the Americans no longer work in terms of col-

lateral activities. Notwithstanding this change, the Americans believe SOF may be assigned one or more of these former "collateral missions" as an embedded task. For the purposes of this chapter I have remained with published unclassified material. The definition of the key tasks includes:

- Special reconnaissance (SR) — conduct reconnaissance and surveillance actions to obtain or verify information concerning the capabilities, intentions, and activities of an actual or potential enemy or to secure data concerning characteristics of a particular area.
- Direct action (DA) — conduct short-duration strikes and other small-scale offensive actions to seize, destroy, capture, recover, or inflict damage on designated personnel or materiel.
- Unconventional warfare (UW) — organize, train, equip, advise, and assist indigenous and surrogate forces in military and paramilitary operations normally of long duration.
- Information operations (IO) — achieve information superiority by affecting adversary information and information systems while defending one's own information and information systems.

7. Thomas K. Adams, *US Special Operations Forces in Action: The Challenge of Unconventional Warfare* (Portland, OR: Frank Cass Publishers, 1998), 303. Eric Morris states much the same thing in his book, *Guerillas in Uniform*: "Guerrilla units (Special Forces), once created, were desperately afraid of being left on the shelf. This made them vulnerable to a form of moral blackmail, which meant they took on tasks and missions, which they were singularly ill-equipped to handle. This was frequently the case with the Middle-East Commandos, roundly abused and misused by generals who could not, or willfully chose not to understand their tactical role." Eric Morris, *Guerillas in Uniform* (London: Hutchinson, 1989).

8. *Ibid.*, 303.

9. Office of Strategic Services (OSS) was the forerunner of the CIA, 1942–1945. Operational groups (OG) were used when missions required a more robust capability than the Jedburgh teams had. They were similar in organization to the current American Special Forces "A" Team.

10. Jedburgh teams were trained to parachute into France in the summer of 1944 to support the Normandy landings. Jedburghs joined the French Resistance organizations fighting against the Germans. Each team consisted of two officers and an enlisted man who was employed as the radio operator.

11. From the Allied perspective, the concept of SR was developed by the Long Range Desert Group (LRDG) in North Africa. Concerned about the vast unprotected desert flank west and south of Cairo, Major Bagnold proposed

the establishment of a small organization equipped with desert-worthy vehicles to travel deep behind enemy lines for extended periods and observe traffic along the coastal road in northern Libya and Egypt and, if the opportunity presented itself, to attack remote desert outposts and airfields. The proposal was eventually accepted, and the LRDG was born. Arguably, the concept of modern patrolling in order to carry out DA or SR derived from the British experience during the Malaya campaign. The experience had a significant impact on how the British trained the reactivated Special Air Service (SAS), and many armies used the SAS model to develop their capabilities. Many SOF capabilities use patrolling as a basis for SOF operations.

12. Adams, 17–18.

13. Michael J. King, *Rangers: Selected Combat Operations in Second World War* (Fort Leavenworth, Kansas: Combat Studies Institute, U.S. Army Command and General Staff College, June 1985), Introduction.

14. Wikipedia Encyclopaedia online. *British Commandos, http://en.wikipedia.org/ wiki/British_Commandos#Formation*, accessed 15 February 2004.

15. Joint Pub 3–05, II–11.

16. Peter Young, *The First Commando Raids: History of the Second World War Series* (BCE Publishing Ltd., First Edition 1966), 1–4. According to Charles Messenger, author of *The Commandos 1940–1946*, "While in very early days, emphasis was on the Commando operating as an individual, it was quickly realized that unless the necessary self- and corporate discipline was instilled, he would be of little value. The same went for basic military skills, and it was competence in these, which gave the Commando his inherent flexibility. Thus, apart from his specialist roles, he could fight just as well as an ordinary infantryman, as Crete, Tunisia, Normandy and Hill 170 showed. What marked him as different from the ordinary soldier was that he had to be physically fitter; capable of operating both as part of a large body and on his own and have a greater versatility of skills." Messenger uses the definition of the post-war Royal Marine pamphlet on Commando training to define the qualities of a Commando. He says it states that "Commandos are highly skilled infantryman who must be expert in his own branch of infantry work. In addition he must: (a) be able to move fast across any country and be independent of roads; (b) be very happy to fight at night; (c) be ready to work in small parties or on his own; (d) be able to land on coasts impracticable to normal infantry and follow up climbing leaders in cliff assaults." Messenger goes on to say the pamphlet recognized, more important than anything else was the inculcation of the right psychological attitude. This is called "the Commando spirit," which was made up of: (a) determination; (b) enthusiasm and cheerfulness, especial-

ly under bad conditions; (c) comradeship; (d) individual initiative and self-reliance. Charles Messenger, *The Commandos 1940–1946* (London: William Kimber, 1985), 410–411.

17. William O. Darby with William H. Baumer, *Darby's Rangers: We Lead the Way* (United States: Random House, 1980), 28–29.

18. *Ibid.*, 29.

19. King, *Rangers.* "Each platoon was authorized one officer and twenty-five enlisted men and was composed of a platoon headquarters and two sections. The platoon headquarters was authorized a platoon leader, a platoon sergeant, one messenger armed with a submachine gun, and one sniper/grenadier armed with a Springfield 1903 rifle. Each section was authorized a section leader, an assistant section leader, two scouts, one BAR-man, one assistant BAR-man, and five riflemen. All men in a section were armed with M-1 rifles except one of the scouts, who carried a submachine gun, and the BAR-man. Each section had, in addition, one .30-calibre M1919A4 machine gun that was held in a pool at battalion headquarters."

20. *Ibid.* The Rangers' transformation from a light force designed to conduct "special operations" into a much heavier unit capable of undertaking more conventional combat operations started prior to their first operation.

21. Darby and Baumer, 66.

22. King, *Rangers.*

23. *Ibid.*

24. Brigadier Mike Calvert, the former commander of the wartime SAS, was more direct. In his report on the value of the SAS after the war, he stated that, "Volunteer units such as SAS attract officers and men who have initiative, resourcefulness, independence of spirit, and confidence in themselves. In a regular unit there are far less opportunities of making use of these assets and, in fact, in many formations they are a liability, as this individualistic attitude upsets the smooth working of a team. This is especially true in European warfare where the individual must subordinate his natural initiative so that he fits into a part of the machine." Anthony Kemp, *The SAS at War, 1941–1945* (London: John Murray, 1991), Appendix D, 294.

25. David Hogan, Jr., *U.S. Army Special Operations in Second World War* (Washington, DC: CMH Publication 70–42, Department of the Army, 1992), 23.

26. Kenn Finlayson and C.H. Briscoe, "Case Studies in the Selection and Assessment: The First Special Service Force, Merrill's Marauders and the OSS OGs," *Special Warfare: The Professional Bulletin of the John F. Kennedy Special Warfare Center and School* (Fall 2000), 22.

27. Interestingly, the First Special Service Force (FSSF) suffered the same lift capability problem that was to plague the Commandos. See *Canadian Army Journal*, Vol. 7, No. 2 (Summer 2004), 49. The main objective of the FSSF training program during the winter of 1942–3 was to prepare for an operational deployment into Norway to sabotage Norwegian power installations. However, an alternative plan for the mission had to be developed because the planners of the mission encountered difficulty finding the number of aircraft needed to move the unit and its equipment. As a result, the unit was chosen to lead the assault on Kiska Island during the Aleutians campaign and moved to Fort Bradford to carry out amphibious training (information was taken from the Department of National Defence, Directorate of History and Heritage [DHH], "Historical Report No. 5, 1st Canadian Special Service Battalion," 13).

28. DHH, Historical Report, No. 5, 10–12.

29. *Ibid.*, 54.

30. *Ibid.*, 42.

31. The 6th Ranger Battalion was created from the 98th Field Artillery Battalion in September 1944. The men went through a very strenuous training program that was similar to what Darby's Rangers had undergone in Scotland. The unit entered combat in the Philippines, where it "successfully landed on the islands of Dinagat, Guiuan, and Homonhan on 17 October 1944, three days before the main American invasion, and destroyed radio facilities and other Japanese positions guarding the entrance to Leyte Gulf." During these operations the unit received information that POWs were being held in the area of Cabanatuan.

32. Faced with a need for reliable information in the dense jungles of the theatre, the Sixth Army activated the Alamo Scouts in November 1943. The purpose of this unit was to obtain strategic intelligence and to perform other covert operations.

33. United States, Department of the Army, *FM 78–5 Ranger Operations* (9 June 1987), Chapter 4, accessed at *www.army.mil/cmh-pg/books/wwii/70-42/70-424.html*.

34. King. The plan also detailed that the Alamo Scouts would provide surveillance on the objective. Teams "would head out prior to the operation, link up with the guerrillas where they would be joined by native guides, and then go to a position north of the objective. They would contact local guerrillas in the area and keep the compound under surveillance to determine the number of Japanese troops, who the guards were, and what the guards' routines were." The information would then be forwarded to the Rangers once they arrived in the area.

35. *Ibid.* The "Army weekly G2 report described it as 'an almost perfect example of prior reconnaissance and planning ...' It was further held up as demonstrating 'what patrols can accomplish in enemy territory by following the basic principles of scouting and patrolling, sneaking and peeping, [the] use of concealment, reconnaissance of routes, from photographs and maps prior to the actual operation ... and the coordination of all arms in the accomplishment of a mission.'"

36. *History of the Rangers*, accessed at *www.grunts.net/army/rangers.html*.

37. Adrian Weale, *Secret Warfare: Special Operations Forces from the Great Game to the SAS* (London: Coronet Books, 1997), 76.

38. *Ibid.*, 76. David Stirling, founder of the SAS, believed that Commando raids such as those conducted on German positions along the coast of Cyrenaica, in North Africa, were of little value. He felt that such operations were also extremely inefficient and argued that forces being launched from naval vessels required almost a third of the force to be first established and then defend the beachhead. He also argued that even if initial surprise could be achieved the action would result in a fighting withdrawal and heavy casualties. Stirling concluded that at best these were expensive ventures, which placed heavy demands on both personnel and resources, and delivered only a temporary inconvenience to the enemy. More important, these large-scale direct action operations had become well known to the Germans who had constructed defensive positions to mitigate the threat. Stirling reasoned that if a small force could overcome the difficulties of moving over the vast desert areas to the south it would be possible to infiltrate a force behind enemy lines and quickly move them out again. Alan Hoe and Eric Morris, *Re-enter the SAS: The Special Air Service and the Malayan Emergency* (London: Leo Cooper, 1994), 2–3.

39 It is important to note that these limitations are structural in nature and will remain with these types of units into the future. The ability to quickly deploy very light SF units is only advantageous if the mission is important, deployment is of short duration, and tactical mobility is not an issue. Longer deployments and/or the need for greater tactical mobility will

negate any advantages this capability offers and is one reason these units disappeared after of the Second World War.

40. *FM 78–5 Ranger Operations*, Appendix F, Ranger History.

41. History of the Rangers.

42. *Ibid.*

43. *Ibid.*

44. Tom Clancy and Carl Stiner, *Shadow Warriors: Inside the Special Forces* (New York: Penguin Putnam 2002), 322–324 and 352–361. The Rangers also neutralized an enemy company based at Rio Hato Military Airfield and General Noriega's fortified beach house.

45. *Ibid.*

46. *FM 78–5 Ranger Operations*, Chapter 5. It should be noted that these are tasks provided by the American Army and not what is necessarily expected from SOCOM.

47. *Ibid.*

48. *Ibid.* Rangers have some inherent limitations as well. According to American doctrine, these include a "limited capability against armoured or motorized units in open terrain, no organic transportation, a limited sustained combat capability due to the shortage of organic combat support and combat service support elements, limited organic air defence weapons, limited organic indirect fire support, no casualty evacuation capability, and significant reconstitution and retraining is needed to replace combat losses."

49. Assuming they are the best to do all these tasks, there is still the problem of a lack of employment opportunities: American Rangers have been employed on three declassified operations in support of SOF and two DA missions over the last 30 years. This figure does not include the Gulf War, 1990–1991, or Haiti, 1994.

50. Canada, Department of National Defence, *Shaping the Future of the Canadian Forces: A Strategy for 2020* (Ottawa, June 1999); and *Canadian Army Journal*, Vol. 7, No. 2 (Summer 2004), 6.

51. Soldiers must complete the following physical fitness standards if they wish to become a Ranger: (1) score 80 points for each Army Physical

Readiness Test (APRT) event and do six chin-ups; (2) pass the Ranger swimming test; (3) complete an eight-kilometre run in 40 minutes; (4) complete a 12-kilometre road march in three hours (with rucksack, helmet, and weapon); (5) meet the Army height and weight standards. If a soldier is selected, he then attends a three-week Ranger indoctrination program. This is also physically demanding and is designed to indoctrinate and teach basic skills and techniques used by the Ranger units. Training includes daily physical training; Ranger history test; map reading; APFT; airborne operation; Ranger standards; day and night land navigation; five-mile run; combative knots; combat water survival test; six-, eight-, and 10-mile road marches; driver training (DDC Card); fast rope training; and combat lifesaver certification. The program identifies and eliminates applicants who do not show dedication, motivation, physical fitness, and emotional stability. A similar program, with a leadership focus, is given to officers and non-commissioned officers who want to join the unit.

52. The Ranger leadership course, commonly referred to as The Ranger Course, must be completed if the soldier wants to become a leader in the Ranger regiment. This course is 56 days long and very similar in concept to the original Commando course with heavy emphasis on patrolling. The training is very physically demanding and teaches platoon and section commander procedures, operation orders and small unit patrol actions.

53. This organization is very similar to the Ranger battalions. Each unit has a parachute company.

54. Interestingly, many nations are currently looking at options to increase the tactical mobility of their light infantry forces in order to make them more relevant to today's operating environment. According to Dr. Roger Thornhill in an article published in the March/April 2003 edition of *Asia-Pacific Defence Reporter*, "In 1999/2000 the RAND Corporation produced a study on the effectiveness of the U.S. Army's rapid airmobile divisions (using the 82nd and the 101st divisions as case studies). It found that these land force formations were too light and in essence could only be employed as a speed hump to a determined military advance, such as that of Iraq invading Kuwait in 1990/91. The report suggested a number of ways to bolster the airborne divisions using technology."

55. The problem is not confined to the LIBs. This is indeed a much wider problem. Most missions currently being undertaken by the Army require significant augmentation to fill the need for soldiers and equipment.

56. Bernd Horn, *Bastard Sons: An Examination of Canada's Airborne Experience 1942–1995* (St. Catharines, ON: Vanwell Publishing, 2001), 265–266.

57. *Ibid.*

58. Although it should be noted that the Ranger course is a leadership course, and not all Rangers are required to attend, anyone wishing to remain with the Ranger battalions for a long period must pass the course.

59. This figure is based on a Ranger unit of about 600 soldiers. If the unit is going to be larger, the problem increases.

60. According to unclassified sources, the success rate for SAS/American SF after selection and training is about 24 percent. America's Delta Force has about 10 to 12 percent success rate, which we can assume is about the same for JTF-2. This means the Army has a potential to pick the difference between the 12 and 24 percent depending how selection is organized to create a green capability. This could provide a force of about 120 to 150 operators and would be far less than the 600 to 700 needed for a Ranger capability.

61. Canada, Department of National Defence, Directorate of Land Strategic Concepts, *Future Force: Concepts for Future Army Capabilities* (Kingston: Army Publishing Office, 2004), 172–176.

62. *Ibid.*

# 12

# The Evolving Requirements of the Canadian Special Operations Forces:
## *A Future Concept Paper*

### J. Paul de B. Taillon

All men dream, but not equally. Those who dream by night in the
dusty recesses of their minds wake in the day to find that it was
vanity: but the dreamers of the day are dangerous men, for they
may act out their dream with open eyes, to make it possible.
— T.E. Lawrence, *Seven Pillars of Wisdom*

On 1 April 2006, the Canadian Special Operations Forces (CAN-
SOF)[1] celebrates its 14th year of service in the Canadian Forces
(CF).[2] The past years have been ones of great challenges and change,
with a developing national and international reputation for professionalism, which was recently proven in joint and coalition Special
Operations Forces (SOF) work in Afghanistan. This has also been a
period of garnering military and political support.

In over a decade, the unit has gone from one that drew heavily from
the Canadian Airborne Regiment, to an organization comprising a
broad spectrum of service volunteers, including reservists. CANSOF has
performed duties in a number of countries, including Bosnia, Rwanda,
Afghanistan, and Haiti. Moreover, CANSOF operations have run the
gamut. They have undertaken protective duties for Canadian VIPs,
acted as Joint Commission Observers (JCOs)[3] in Bosnia, trained

Haitian police personnel,[4] and carried out surveillance and direct action operations in Afghanistan.[5]

In the wake of the New York and Washington attacks on 11 September 2001, the Canadian government reportedly increased CANSOF's budget by some $119 million as an integral part of Canada's participation in the global war on terrorism (GWOT).[6] The government's intent was to double the size of this unit to a reported goal of 600 personnel.[7] This is a most difficult challenge considering not only the size of the regular CF but also the demanding selection requirements for those individuals who aspire to become SOF operators. Thus, the CF may have to shift the recruiting and selection process for SOF operators, looking instead to reservists and to those Canadians who have the identified skills and capabilities. The creation of a reserve CANSOF squadron, paralleling a move a number of our allies have made, would provide a trained and operationally ready cadre of SOF operators able to augment CANSOF when required.

## SOF PERSONNEL ATTRIBUTES

An SOF operator needs to be highly motivated with a keen intellect, physically fit, psychologically stable, and resourceful and self-reliant. Moreover, an SOF operator must be able to operate alone or in a small team and possess an unflappable personality, as well as a courage that Ernest Hemingway described as "grace under pressure."[8]

In addition, tact and persuasive skills are critically important for those involved in advising and training foreign militaries; those not sensitive to the socio-cultural milieu in which they are operating will hold little local influence over foreign officers and their non-commissioned officers (NCOs), many of whom may have had more practical experience. As one Special Air Service (SAS) operator noted: "You may advise the wily Afghan how to orchestrate a better ambush, but never say that they do not have experience in conducting ambushes."[9] Any short military history on Soviet operational experience between 1979 and 1989 will quickly persuade you as to the capabilities of the Afghan fighters to inflict casualties and destruction on their opponents.[10]

## SOF TRAINING ASSISTANCE AND THE REQUIREMENT FOR CULTURAL/LANGUAGE EXPERTISE

SOF operations, by their nature, are low-visibility, using speed, surprise, audacity, and deception to minimize the associated risks and to maximize the results. These tactics, techniques, and procedures (TTPs) enable SOF forces to accomplish missions that, in many cases, conventional military forces could likely accomplish, albeit with greater difficulty; hence, they are a "force of choice."[11] Our allied forces — the United States and Great Britain in particular — have many SOF operators who have been or are geographically oriented and, therefore, culturally well-attuned and capable of communicating in the language(s) of the region.[12] This capability enables our SOF allies to acclimatize rapidly in exotic locales and undertake their missions from a standing start. Thus, our allied forces can easily employ their personnel to conduct foreign internal defence (FID) operations,[13] mobile training teams (MTT)[14] or act as advisers, not only to assist friends and allies, but also to leverage their assistance to further the foreign policy agenda of their respective governments. For the SOF personnel involved in these initiatives, such training programs improve their spectrum of competencies, while developing personal contacts and networks that could be important at a future date.

Considering that SOF and intelligence will be in the forefront in the GWOT, CANSOF is one of the three strategic military assets that the Canadian government has available.[15] In this regard, CANSOF has the capability of influencing Canada's international security agenda. The future employment of CANSOF, as a training asset to assist friendly nations, would ensure high-quality training while, at the same time, extending, and leveraging Canadian foreign policy interests and influence abroad. In addition, CANSOF conducted initiatives, while requiring a relatively small outlay in personnel and material, would have the strategic impact of contributing to nation building, democratization, and regime stabilization in nascent democracies while strengthening Canadian relations and influence in regions needing training assistance. Canadian participation in FID and military assistance programs, in conjunction with our allies, would enhance Canada's international stature while providing a viable and attractive option for those nations that may not seek assistance from our British and American cousins.

In order to address this possible future requirement, CANSOF will have to incorporate language abilities, other than the two official Canadian languages, into their skill sets. Arabic, Spanish, Chinese, and Afghan dialects are some of the languages that will likely remain necessary in the foreseeable future. In addition, our skills in French will be a great asset in dealing with Haiti, as well as African francophone nations, who may, in the future, solicit Canadian military assistance.

One way of resolving the issues of language and cultural sensitivity would be to talent spot[16] and directly recruit second-generation Canadians of various ethnic groups[17] into the CF, with the aim of selecting and assigning them for CANSOF training. The selection of second-generation foreign-language speakers, who are Canadian citizens, would be similar to the Swedish model of employing, for security reasons, only second-generation Swedish translators with their forces abroad.[18] A similar initiative would provide CANSOF selection with candidates who are not only Canadian but who have been born and raised in a multi-ethnic nation, retaining the vital skill sets of cultural sensitivity and insight,[19] in addition to having a critical language capability. Moreover, in the wake of selection and training, Canadian-ethnic operators (CEOs) should be allowed the opportunity to travel to their family homelands in order to see, firsthand, their potential area of operation and to evaluate the necessary requirements, should the time come, to undertake or assist special operations in these areas. Native speakers selected and trained as CANSOF operators who could easily blend into the environment would be a highly valuable addition to our capability spectrum.

Another way to obtain these skills is to talent spot university-level students who are studying languages of operational interest and ascertain their potential contribution to CANSOF. Such personnel, once recruited and trained, could also undertake a country familiarization visit and be provided with an opportunity to tour the country and study it firsthand, while concomitantly practising their language skills and developing cultural awareness.[20] Unfortunately, there are no shortcuts. The classroom lecture regarding the geography, people, culture, language, and terrain features of a certain country will not provide the necessary insights on issues such as the social order, the local politics and local political peculiarities, or specific eccentric social practices. Equally important, SOF operators must be capable of adapting to an indigenous lifestyle, wherever they go. This personal adaptability is not within everyone's character and makeup. However, those that are capable of adapting to foreign cultures will garner the respect of the locals and develop useful personal relationships, while expediting the mission. This falls in line with the evolving military policy of "coalition advocacy," which is the building of relationships to enable operations. The chief of the defence staff (CDS) action directive further amplifies the goals of coalition advocacy to include effective inter-operability and integration with non-traditional allies and coalition partners, critical enablers if the CF is to be capable of multinational lead-nation status in peace support operations. CANSOF could play a strategically instrumental role in this CDS initiative.

To assimilate such important, yet often overlooked, linguistic and cultural skills, the CF may have to shift their recruiting and selection procedures to initiate a new, innovative, and flexible program to talent spot, recruit, screen, select, and train these personnel, as well as oversee their administration and career development.[21] Needless to say, this paradigm shift from more traditional recruiting and selection procedures would be difficult. However, we must be willing to take innovative initiatives to meet the expectations of government. By ignoring the need to change, the CANSOF community may well lose an important means of acquiring and recruiting suitable SOF candidates, and gaining political support and credibility.

It is important to appreciate the advantages of the cultural and ethnic mosaic that now makes up Canadian society and the importance of having SOF embrace this mosaic.[22] Historical examples illustrate the importance of such advantages, such as when British Army recruiters sought out Chinese Canadians to join the Special Operations Executive (SOE) Force 136.[23] These same Canadians performed their duties in the harsh Malayan jungles in an outstanding fashion, always with the knowledge that they would be executed should the Japanese capture them. Recently, it was a lack of linguistic and cultural knowledge that dogged the Army when Canada deployed to Afghanistan as, reportedly, there was no one in the CF personnel inventory who could speak the Afghan languages. Fortunately, a Canadian intelligence officer was discovered who had the requisite language skills and was subsequently attached to the 3rd Battalion, Princess Patricia's Canadian Light Infantry (3 PPCLI) as an interpreter. This experience underscores the necessity for ensuring linguistic and cultural capabilities exist within our SOF, and our highly capable light infantry battalions.[24]

## CANSOF RESERVE SQUADRON

CANSOF has been assigned the task of doubling its operational capability. This is a difficult order to fulfill, especially given that the regular contingent of the CF numbers approximately 55,000, with a total reserve of roughly 23,000.[25] Moreover, during the recent past, SOF has lost a number of its operators and support personnel to retirement, the police world, and the private or public sectors. Considering the numbers lost, it is reasonable to assume that any future growth will be painstakingly slow. As a result of this situation, it may be appropriate to explore the creation of a reserve CANSOF squadron. The reserve squadron would be assigned, trained, and organized to conduct limited special operations, such as mobile training teams, red cells, intelligence gathering, talent spotting of linguists, and rural/urban surveillance, amongst other SOF capabilities. This new reserve SOF squadron would be comprised of former members of the unit, selected CF reservists who have specialist skills sets, and civilians who have been talent spotted and recruited for specific qualities and capabilities, as well as individuals who self-identify as having the skills required for CANSOF. All of these individuals would have to undergo a rigorous selection program, and required follow-on training. These personnel would be augmentees, similar to the Individual Ready Reserve (IRR) in the U.S. Marine Corps or the reserve status 21st and 23rd SAS Regiments (SAS[R]), consisting of British reserve Territorial Army (TA) soldiers who are prepared to undertake training and operations at short notice.[26] In the United Kingdom, the TA and regular SAS regiments have a close relationship, with members of 22 SAS routinely being attached to the SAS(R). During the 1980s, the regular force SAS established a practice where an officer or senior NCO in 22 SAS who wished to advance in rank had to serve time with the SAS(R).[27] These reservists went on to hold prominent positions at a high corporate and political level, adding a dimension that is currently missing in the CF in general and the CANSOF community in particular. For example, Sir Paddy Ashdown, a former Special Boat Service (SBS) officer, was leader of the Liberal Democrats in the United Kingdom from 1988 until 1999.[28] With individuals such as Ashdown in a position to provide peer to peer advice to their Cabinet colleagues on the capabilities and limitations of SOF troops, the high standard of politico-military cooperation and mutual understanding would be that much closer to realization.

While the idea of a reserve CANSOF squadron might be unconscionable to some in the Canadian SOF community,[29] our allies have found that they could undertake direct recruiting from the streets, as the British Army's 21st and 23rd SAS Regiments have done since their inception. It is noteworthy that the London-based Artists' Rifles Territorial Army regiment was converted to 21st SAS (Artists' Rifles) in 1947[30] and remains an integral component of the British SOF community, as does 23rd SAS. In January 2001, the U.S. Army Special Forces (SF) initiated a recruiting plan called the Special Forces Initial

Accessions Program, better known as the 18X Program. Twenty-five years ago, the U.S. Army had attempted to recruit SF soldiers directly off the streets, an initiative that was the subject of much controversy. Notwithstanding this initial problematic attempt, U.S. Army Recruiting Command began screening and selecting 18X soldiers. The scheduled training timetable for these "off the street candidates" is a two-year full-time program consisting of training at the infantry and airborne school. Once the SF candidate has undergone the first phase of training, he is posted to Fort Bragg, North Carolina. At Fort Bragg, the 18X soldier attends the Special Forces Assessment and Selection Center. If selected for SF, the candidate then attends the SF Qualification Course (SFQC). Following the SFQC, he will attend language training and the Survival, Evasion, Resistance, and Escape (SERE) course. Once these courses are completed, he is promoted to sergeant. According to Command Sergeant Major Michael S. Breasseale, "the quality of recruits is impressive and, so far, the 18Xs have exceeded all expectations."[31] Considering the British and American models noted herein, the CF may wish to study and undertake experimentation with one or both of these methodologies to ascertain if either one could address current and future Canadian SOF requirements.

The inclusion of SOF reservists in Canada, however, would require an administrative redesign, as their incorporation will necessitate a dramatic change in personnel administration and career management. On the positive side, this would provide impetus to resolve the issue of permeability and integration between regular and reserve components that, to date, has been problematic. Permeability would enable personnel to transition easily between the regular military stream and the reserves, with few bureaucratic requirements, retaining necessary security clearances, while expeditiously addressing any training or operational requirements. This would require a highly flexible and innovative personnel management system, individual training, and recruitment system. CANSOF could be the vanguard champion of the initiative of permeability between regular and reserve forces.

## SIMILAR MILITARY/CAREER JOB PARAMETERS

The CF needs to ascertain if SOF skill sets exists that align with certain civilian occupations. There are reservists who employ, on a day-to-day basis, certain skill sets that are similar to, or that parallel, some of those required in SOF units. Police officers assigned to Emergency

Response Teams (ERTs) come to mind immediately, as do demolition engineers who work on construction projects, medical attendants, professional deepwater divers, and a myriad of other civilian professional skill sets that could be easily placed under the capabilities umbrella of special operations. For example, a former American SOF officer advised the writer in June 2004 that one of the most proficient SOF units in the United States was the Los Angeles Police Department (LAPD) Special Weapons and Tactics (SWAT) team. Apparently, some American SOF operators had been sent to LAPD SWAT as observers, and to undertake courses.

The Second World War saw the creation of the British SOE and the American Office of Strategic Services (OSS) where it was demonstrated that the recruiting methodologies suggested herein are neither unique nor unusual and, indeed, have historical precedent. The multitude of psychological and physical tests available, that are specifically designed to ascertain the potential military capabilities of an individual for SOF, could be adapted to expedite the selection of direct entry candidates. Reservists have historically brought with them valued skill sets due to their occupational spectrum. They could be the vehicle for positive innovation (i.e., administrative permeability, enhanced capabilities, and cultural redesign), assist in breaking down internal barriers, and aid in the generation and cross pollination of ideas — all of which are critical for an effective and constantly evolving SOF capability.[32]

## COVERT OPERATIONS

At some point in the future, particularly should the GWOT continue unabated for the next decade, it might be necessary for Canada to develop a covert operational capability. This could be required to counterterrorist initiatives domestically or those emanating from third countries that may target Canada or Canadian interests, or those of our allies. The campaign in Afghanistan revealed certain CANSOF activities when a photograph appeared in the media of Canadian operators taking blindfolded Taliban fighters off a transport aircraft thus unveiling Canada's participation in the covert war in Afghanistan.

The future conduct of successful covert operations will require the incorporation of a competent CANSOF capability with an integrated intelligence support unit. This unit must be able to "reach back" to access all source intelligence and be capable of fusing these sources of information into coherent, timely, and actionable intelligence. The need to understand a more complex and culturally diverse enemy will increase the requirement for more sophisticated intelligence products, necessitating an intelligence support apparatus based upon an interdepartmental and interagency approach. Such an organization will likely incorporate representation from the Canadian Security Intelligence Service (CSIS) to address tactical and strategic human intelligence (HUMINT) capability, slices of the Communications Security Establishment (CSE) and the CF Information Operations Group (CFIOG) to provide an intercept capability and, depending on the situation, a policing capability from the Royal Canadian Mounted Police (RCMP).[33] Furthermore, this intelligence support unit may also take on representation from any other government department or agency, including those of allied nations, deemed necessary to meet the operational requirements of the moment. This would enhance the spectrum of capabilities available to CANSOF in an operational theatre, as well as providing an enhanced level of situational awareness on the ground.

## "GO SOFTLY SOFTLY"

Not to be critical, as all SOF units must learn from their experiences, the 2004 deployment of CANSOF operators to Haiti underscored a lack of sophistication in low-visibility, some would say covert, operations. Their deployment was uncovered shortly after their arrival when front-page photographs of very fit SOF operators, wearing trendy wraparound sunglasses and Nike baseball caps, resulted in media hype and, hence, political and public attention. Unfortunately, this incident further fuelled the media interest in CANSOF activities in Haiti and in Canada. This incident brings to mind what the late and former chief of the British general staff, Field Marshal Lord Carver, once stated regarding his reticence in employing the British SAS in Northern Ireland. It was his firm belief that "the problem with clandestine operations is that they seldom remain clandestine for long."[34] His view resonates particularly today when military activity remains under intense media scrutiny.

SOF operators must spend considerable time training and learning how to access denied areas. Parachute, swimmer delivery vehicles (SDV), boat, submarine, helicopter, scuba, and klepper (two-man kayak) operations are just some of the means available for insertion or extraction. As global populations move from rural to urban centres, SOF forces may have to seek out lower testosterone-driven techniques of infiltration and extraction. They must learn to blend into domestic and foreign populations, while fully equipped to undertake the mission at hand. This requires training in clandestine tradecraft, so that operators may move innocuously or, as the SAS would say, in a *keeni meeni*[35] fashion towards their objective and, after the mission is completed, egress the area expeditiously without a trace. Such new realities underscore the necessity of previously noted multi-ethnic recruiting policies so that SOF can operate unnoticed within the expanding mixture of ethnic and cultural environments found around the globe.

To address our lack of covert/clandestine operational methodology, CANSOF may wish to seek exchanges with our British and American allies, as do our intelligence services, in order to augment our expertise in these aspects of special operations. As well, attachments to the Royal Canadian Mounted Police (RCMP) and the Canadian Security Intelligence Service (CSIS), to learn intelligence/covert operational tradecraft, may also assist in enhancing the clandestine skill sets and capabilities of SOF operators and personnel.

## SOF COALITIONAL INTELLIGENCE REQUIREMENTS

One of the major issues evident in recent Afghanistan operations was the ongoing difficulty of intelligence sharing amongst coalition allies. It can be appreciated that intelligence sources and sensitive technology may have to be protected. However, to assign coalition allies high-risk conventional or SOF missions without providing critical all source intelligence along with the assigned target package, is arguably immoral and particularly disenfranchising. This became a serious issue within the coalition SOF community in Kabul, at one point exacerbating relations with an ally and having a deleterious effect on multinational SOF operations. Fortunately, Canadian intelligence personnel were able to intercede and address the problem. The employment of Canadian personnel to mediate this issue amongst allies ensures the necessity for a degree of tact and patience, both of which are important special operations qualities. Thus, it is vital to ensure that the SOF select and retain intelligence support personnel who are capable of operating in a joint and coalition staff, as well as working with ambiguity, prickly intelligence issues, allied/foreign SOF operators, and allied agendas.[36] Considering the critical nature of intelligence in driving SOF initiatives, it behooves the integral SOF intelligence organizations, particularly those of the traditional or special alliance comprising Canada, Great

Britain, Australia, New Zealand, and the United States, to address the issue of how to appropriately deal with SOF intelligence requirements in a coalition. This will prevent future conflict and negate any animosity that could easily arise before, during or after coalition SOF operations. By multilaterally addressing this critical, yet sensitive, issue of intelligence sharing now, our traditional and future coalition allies will be more willing to incorporate their respective SOF forces in future coalition endeavours.[37]

## INFORMATION OPERATIONS

Due to the increasing operational tempo and the focus upon effects-based operations (EBO),[38] there is a need to integrate within CANSOF an Information Operations (IO)[39] capability incorporating electronic warfare (EW), computer network operations (CNO), psychological operations (PSYOPS), as well as operations security and deception (OPSEC). In both the special operations and conventional spheres, IO is a force multiplier that can:

- Deter, discourage, dissuade, and properly orchestrated, direct an enemy;
- Disrupt the enemy's unity of command while protecting our own; and
- Protect our own plans while misdirecting the enemy.

Properly integrated information operations can enhance special operations across the operational spectrum and can also shape the SOF operational environment.[40] IO will provide, now and into the future, a vital support asset that must be encompassed by SOF and employed innovatively.

## SOF IN NETWORK-CENTRIC WARFARE

Network-centric warfare (NCW) is a relatively new approach to waging war, described by U.S. Air Force Captain Greg Gagnon as focusing "on the greater synergistic effect that can be created by networking and electronically linking geographically separated forces into one sensor-to-shooter engagement grid." It also provides the operator with enhanced situational and battle space awareness through extending the individual teams and network.[41] Gagnon argued that accessing a

271

common operating information centre could amass information, instead of combat forces, in order to effectively project combat power. All operators in the information-based network undertake their operations in accordance with the commander's intent, as well as the "rule set" governing the activities and providing "guidelines for coordinating and controlling the interactions of the network entities." The rule set will also address who is responsible for target engagement, as well as optimizing sensor coverage while de-conflicting operators. NCW's intent is to decentralize the decision-making powers and, through the access of a common operating information base, the network accelerates the Boyd cycle of observation, orientation, decision, and action cycle — better known as the OODA loop.[42] As a result, the network of operators "can engage more targets as an aggregate system that they individually can handle." Concomitantly, there is an enhanced situational awareness predicated on the rules and the commander's guidance ensuring SOF and conventional forces will not have to wait for orders.

There are a number of advantages to this network-centric capability. The ability to leverage real-time information may have organizational implications in that we may have a smaller but much more situationally aware and, therefore, more effective tip of the spear. On the other hand, the technical capability to share real time situational awareness, drawn from a common operating information base, may invite hierarchical intervention. In SOF and conventional partnering, the ability to access the commander's network enables SOF, as well as conventional forces, to extend their combat reach with access to faster, longer-range weapon systems within our inventory.

Network-centric special operations will, theoretically, both enhance battle space and situational awareness, and expedite the decisions-making cycle, thereby increasing our combat effectiveness. Considering the theoretical benefits of network-centric warfare and its possible future application, it behooves our CANSOF, and perhaps our light forces, to join with our allies, as well as the academic community, to explore the potential impact and what it will mean to future light infantry/SOF operations.[43]

## INTRODUCING SOF TO MILITARY EDUCATION

The impression held by many staff officers is that SOF operators are "Rambo"-like personnel in uniform. Moreover, many officers in core staff and command positions are not well versed in the capabilities of and requirements for SOF operations. In addition, there is little appreciation that SOF is a "high-value, low-density" national strategic asset. It is, therefore, incumbent upon the Canadian Forces Staff College system and the staff training systems of our close allies to introduce courses that familiarize future staff officers with SOF and include them in exercises, particularly scenarios incorporating a domestic and/or foreign counterterrorist situation, in a similar vein to that currently done at the U.S. Army Command and General Staff College, employing a Commander Joint Special Operations Task Force (CJSOTF) in Combined Joint Task Force (CJTF) exercises. This will ensure that aspiring SOF staff officers garner an appreciation of how a joint and coalition staff would employ these assets (integration of capabilities), as well as understanding some of the real issues that coalitions have with SOF and how to remedy them. Our educational institutions should also encourage studies in the history of SOF operations, their requirements, lessons learned, et cetera, so students acquire an understanding of SOF special requirements and operations in the political and military context. Such studies will assist future staff officers in understanding what SOF represents, what they can achieve when given the resources and opportunity, and what the political risks are in conducting SOF missions.

It is also vital for planning staffs to be aware of the SOF skills available within our traditional coalitions and to partake in exercises incorporating SOF as a main player and not just an ancillary asset.[44] Such initiatives will assist in embedding SOF in our contingency planning and establishing, within our staff officer cadre, means of employing their special skills while ensuring that these high-value, low-density resources are employed in an appropriate manner. This could necessitate the creation of a separate career field for SOF officers and non-commissioned members (enlisted) personnel.

Furthermore, education for SOF personnel should be expanded to increase the depth of their knowledge of the history of SOF, enhance their understanding of the political and military implications of SOF forces in peace and war, and give them a deeper appreciation of their role in conventional and unconventional operations. Selective SOF courses and case studies are currently offered by the Royal Military College of Canada in Kingston, Ontario, and could be expanded by the addition to the War Studies Department of a Special Warfare Studies Centre (SWSC), staffed by academics who study this field and by SOF experts. Continuous experience with SOF operations will also be an important learning tool for the operators, their commanders, and the staff that support them. It will be important to maintain a reasonable operational tempo to gain experience with, and learn from, SOF operations. This may mean partnering with our allies to conduct joint SOF operations on a routine basis to detect and disrupt terrorist cells and other threats to our national interest worldwide. CANSOF cannot be allowed to be placed on permanent stand-by as a type of national SWAT team, otherwise their skills and equipment will quickly become obsolete. To maintain an SOF capability, you must "use it or lose it."

## RE-ALLOCATING NON-SOF TASKING

A number of tasks that are currently undertaken by SOF could be re-allocated to our light infantry battalions. Such duties, although well within the scope of our Canadian light infantry capabilities, could be viewed by some observers as degrading their "conventional" force capabilities. On the other hand, Canada may wish to make our conventional light infantry more SOF-like, enabling it to undertake certain traditional SOF tasks, such as FID. The non-combatant evacuation operation (NEO), and the close personal protection (CPP) roles are two tasks that, arguably, could be more appropriately assigned to selected individuals within our highly trained light infantry battalions that are better suited to undertake to them. This creates a capabilities triangle. At the apex are SOF such as American Army and Navy counterterrorist forces, the Counter-Revolutionary Wing (CRW, formerly known as the Pagoda Team of the SAS), and CANSOF. Beneath the apex are SOF capable of conducting strategic reconnaissance, direct action operations, foreign internal defence, et cetera. The base of the triangle consists of light infantry that are highly trained and skilled in airborne, airmobile, raiding, patrolling, and traditional light infantry operations.

The light infantry represents a feeder organization for CANSOF, where young soldiers have an opportunity to develop a spectrum of leadership and soldiering skills that will give them a solid base from which to move into the next level in the SOF triangle. CANSOF selection will take them to that stage, where they are monitored for their skill sets and mentored for their development. Canadian light infantry battalions should be seen as a logical intermediary step, for those inclined to undertake CANSOF selection. Should that become the case, the light infantry battalions would be able to assume, due to the high quality of their personnel and their training, the traditional Ranger/Commando operations that fall into the wider range of what are known as grey SOF tasks. Arguably, Canadian light infantry should be capable of conducting normative roles expected of a highly trained unit of this type, as well as becoming counter-insurgency specialists able to conduct operations of this nature utilizing all manners of surveillance, tactics, PSYOP, and civil-military cooperation (CIMIC). The designation of a light infantry unit as a Special Operations Direct Support Unit (SODSU), like the 1st Battalion, The Parachute Regiment, or the 75th Ranger Regiment, could undertake similar selection/training to that of a traditional Ranger or Commando unit and be able to support CANSOF operations.[45] As historical experience demonstrates,[46] the SODSU must be an integral component of the CANSOF community and, ideally, be co-located with CANSOF to facilitate planning and integrated training, both of which are vital for operational effectiveness.

Counter-insurgency operations (COIN Ops) have historically improved the quality of light infantry. They exercised junior leaders at all levels, as well as developed and honed combat skills such as tracking, instinctive shooting, small unit patrolling, and tactics, survival, navigation, intelligence, and situational awareness. The British experiences in Malaya and Borneo demonstrated the advantages derived from this sort of demanding training. In Borneo, the SAS absorbed members of the Guards Independent (Pathfinder) Company of the Parachute Brigade, as well as a number of individuals from the 2nd Battalion, The Parachute Regiment, all of whom were selected for their finely honed light infantry and operational skills.[47] Hence, our light infantry battalions could become leading-edge counter-insurgency experts,[48] as well as a stepping stone for those interested in becoming CANSOF operators. In short, we should consider making our high-quality, non-SOF forces more SOF-like, not only in the context of our light infantry but across the combat arms spectrum.

## CONCLUSION

The intent of this chapter was to underline a number of issues that will likely have some impact on the evolution of the Canadian SOF. It must be kept in mind that Canada does not have the 60-plus years of experience of our Commonwealth and American allies. Moreover, we are a conventional force steeped in a conventional military culture, with its attendant views and opinions. However, it is vital that we learn from the past — our own and the pasts of other nations — and aggressively pursue the skills that our allies have within their respective SOF communities in order to develop and expand our own capabilities for future SOF operations/coalitions. Thus, the CANSOF community should consider:

- Development of a CANSOF force structure to include specialized tasks, skills, and training for a reserve CANSOF squadron;
- Development of CANSOF linguistic and cultural skills;
- Encouragement of unorthodox approaches and unconventional techniques;
- Development of flexible thinking and innovation in addressing unconventional security threats;
- Investment in academic expertise, science, and technology, using academics and technologists as force multipliers;
- Promotion of a CANSOF capability for forward-basing, rapid deployment, regional adaptability;
- Development of regional orientation of CANSOF.

CANSOF has strategic utility that is invested in two qualities that run sublimely through this chapter. They are economy of force and the expansion of strategic choice that CANSOF offers senior government and military decision makers. If properly staffed, trained, equipped, and deployed, CANSOF can offer the prospect of a favourably disproportionate return of the military investment.[49]

However, it is important that Canadian decision makers understand that there are four simple yet self-evident truths coined by our American colleagues, which are fundamental and underline aspects of the issues discussed in this chapter and apply to all SOF. They are:

- Humans are more important than hardware;
- Quality is more important than quantity;
- Special Operations Forces cannot be mass-produced;
- Competent SOF cannot be created quickly after emergencies occur.[50]

Utilized correctly, SOF truly becomes the force of choice for the complex future security environment.

## NOTES

1.  Refers to the Joint Task Force Two (JTF-2) in both their original and evolved forms.

2.  The term *Special Operations Forces (SOF)* is used to incorporate all special operations capable and direct support elements. Canada has a rich yet largely unmined history in the field of special operations, dating back to the French colonial period. Arguably, one of the first special operators was Pierre Boucher (1622–1717), a *coureur de bois* (clandestine fur trader) who was a student of the Iroquois art of war. His knowledge and insights of the Iroquois warfighting techniques enabled him to write the book *Histoire véritable et naturelle des moeurs et productions de la Nouvelle-France vulgairement dite le Canada* (Paris, 1664). In this treatise, Boucher discussed Iroquois tactics and operations and, concomitantly, offered insights into their behaviour, the use of scouts, their preference for raids and ambushes, and their use of terrain. He argued that the French could only counter these small, mobile raiding parties if they could master the ability to move efficiently through the woods and adapt to the environment. In turn, the French needed to become an effective counter-insurgent force, capable of operating effectively against the Iroquois by adopting their capabilities, methods, and tactics. In the course of his life, Boucher was a governor, soldier, and author. He also founded the city of Boucherville in Quebec. See Michel Wyczynski, "New Horizons, New Challenges," in Bernd Horn, ed., *Forging a Nation* (St. Catharines, ON: Vanwell Publishing, 2002), 15–42.

3.  JCOs were employed in Bosnia by commanders in order to garner "ground truth" in the never-ending quest for certainty. These trusted personnel existed outside the chain of command, acting as the eyes of the commander, and reported findings from their observations of various units and/or operations. Lieutenant-Colonel Gary B. Griffin, *The Directed Telescope: A Traditional Element of Effective Command* (Fort Leavenworth, KS: Combat Studies Institute, 1991), 1.

4.  David Pugliese, "Elite Canadian Commando Force Planned Attack on Peru Terrorists," *Ottawa Citizen*, 4 November 1998.

5.  Stephen Thorne, "JTF2 in High Gear in Afghanistan," accessed at *http://cnews.canoe.ca/CNEWS/CANADA/2005/09/16/1220529-cp.html*, 16 September 2005; and "JTF2, Canada's Super-Secret Commandos," accessed at *www.cbc.ca/news/background/cdnmilitary/jtf2.html*, 15 July 2005.

6.  Canada, Department of Finance, "Enhancing Security for Canadians, Budget 2001," accessed at *www.fin.gc.ca/budget01/bp/bpch5e.htm*.

7. Interestingly, in the British experience, a unit of 600 operators would realize a total size of approximately 3,600 personnel. For every badged Special Air Service (SAS) operative, it was estimated that approximately five support staff maintained equipment, boats, planes, helicopters, stores, catering, ranges, research and development, intelligence, and training. It was noted that a well-functioning infrastructure would go a long way to recruit and retain operators. Discussion with a former senior SAS operator, Toronto (27 August 2005). It should also be appreciated that the recruiting issues faced by CANSOF are reflected in the Canadian Forces. A Queen's University study noted that "the Canadian military will be hard pressed to raise anywhere near the 8,000 additional recruits it hopes to attract over the next five years." Stephen Thorne, "Military Recruiting Goals Too High, Report Says," *Globe and Mail*, 26 September 2005.

8. John Collins, "Why Special Operations Forces Are Special," *Special Forces Study Group* (Washington, DC: 15 June 2004).

9. Discussion with an SAS officer who was operating in Afghanistan in 2001–2002, London, England, 1 November 2004.

10. The losses incurred by the Soviet forces included 118 jets, over 333 helicopters, 147 tanks, 1,314 armoured carriers, 433 mortars and artillery pieces, over 1,338 command and control vehicles, over 11,369 trucks, and 510 engineering vehicles. Soviet troop strength never really rose above 104,000 personnel. M.Y. Nawroz and Lester Grau, "The Soviet War in Afghanistan: History and Harbinger of Future War?" *Military Review* (September-October 1995). It should be appreciated that 75 percent of these troops were assigned to defend cities, base camps, and lines of communication. The situation was more problematic than it seemed at first as these units were not up to full strength as 25 to 30 percent of Soviet personnel were stricken with a number of diseases, including malaria, dysentery, typhus, and hepatitis. Of the 642,000 Soviet personnel who rotated through Afghanistan during the decade of war, the number of dead was reportedly 15,000, a number viewed as a gross underestimation by many analysts. Some experts argue that at least 40,000 to 50,000 Soviet forces were killed, while some 415,932 troops fell victim to disease, 115,308 suffered infectious hepatitis, and 31,080 had typhoid fever.

11. Bernd Horn, J. Paul de B. Taillon, David Last, eds., *Force of Choice: Perspectives on Special Operations* (Kingston: McGill-Queen's Press, 2004).

12. As Major-General James W. Parker, commandant of the U.S. Army John F. Kennedy Special Warfare Center and School stated, "It is imperative that our SF soldiers learn to communicate with the populace of the regions in which they will operate. It has always been the hallmark of SF soldiers that they possess warrior skills and cross-cultural communication skills, as

both are necessary in the performance of SF missions. Warrior skills alone will not be enough for SF soldiers who need to work by, with, or through indigenous forces or who need to train host-nation forces. They must have the language skills and the cultural sensitivity that will allow them to communicate and build rapport with members of other cultures." Major-General James W. Parker, "Foreword," *Special Warfare*, Vol. 18, No. 1.

13. FID operations consist of "organizing, training, advising, and assisting host-nation military and paramilitary forces to enable these forces to free and protect their society from subversion, lawlessness, and insurgency." Bernd Horn, "Special Men, Special Missions," in Bernd Horn, J. Paul de B. Taillon, David Last, eds., *Force of Choice*, 9.

14. The Canadian experience has been to employ our highly trained conventional forces to undertake MTTs, as we have done in Afghanistan. It may be advantageous to run a CANSOF training team in parallel with a "green army" (i.e., conventional army) task to give conventional forces exposure to SOF troops who can take advantage of a situation to conduct recruiting while gaining exposure to an operational area. Discussions with a former senior SAS operator, Toronto, 29 August 2005.

15. The other strategic assets are our four submarines and the CF Reserves.

16. *Talent spot* is intelligence tradecraft jargon used to describe the search for *talent*, in other words, likely candidates for recruitment. In this case, the intent is to seek out personnel who have certain personal or professional skills that may be of use to CANSOF. See definitions for *spotter*, *talent spotter*, *agent spotter* in Leo D. Carl, *CIA Insider's Dictionary* (Washington, DC: NIBC Press, 1996).

17. Issues of social cohesion and social inclusion are becoming more important, especially given that Canada's population growth will be "driven by visible minorities — defined as 10 groups, including Chinese, South Asians, Filipinos, and Latin Americans — through immigration and higher fertility rates." By 2017, Canada will have between 6.3 to 8.5 million people of visible minorities. Jill Mahoney, "Visible Majority by 2017: Demographic Balance in Toronto, Vancouver Will Tip Within 12 Years, Statscan Says," *Globe and Mail*, 23 March 2005. This initiative would also reflect the intent by the CF to recruit visible minorities. Mike Blanchfield, "Forces Hiring to Mirror Canada's Diversity: Defence Chief Hillier Promises New Vision for Country's Military," *Ottawa Citizen*, 15 April 2005.

18. Discussions with Swedish officers, 1st Mech Infantry Bde HQ, Pristina, Kosovo,15 May 2002. These linguistic and cultural skills have not been lost on the terrorists. In the declassified study by the Canadian Security Intelligence

CASTING LIGHT ON THE SHADOWS

Service, "Sons of Fathers: The Next Generation of Islamic Extremists in Canada," it was noted that "these individuals have been raised in an atmosphere of strict, extremist Islam within the general Canadian mosaic. They represent a clear and present danger to Canada and its allies and are a particularly valuable resource for the international Islamic terrorist community in view of their language skills ... and familiarity with Western culture and infrastructure." Stewart Bell, "Jihadists Being Raised in Canada," *National Post*, 23 April 2005. This obviously raises the importance of a highly effective security screening program to ensure all personnel selected as CEOs are cleared before any enrolment. The British Secret Intelligence Service (BSIS), better known as MI6, has understood the operational requirement to attract ethnic minorities and women: reportedly 9 percent were from ethnic minorities and 41 percent women. Michael Evans, "MI6 Drops Secrecy Over Spy Jobs," *Times*, 9 August 2005.

19. The importance of cultural sensitivity is often overlooked due, in part, to our own cultural arrogance. T.E. Lawrence understood this as he developed and led an Arab guerrilla force against the Turks in the First World War. As advised by Lawrence in article 15 of the *27 Articles of T.E. Lawrence*, "Do not try to do too much with your own hands. Better the Arabs do it tolerably than that you do it perfectly. It is their war, and you are to help them, not to win it for them. Actually, also, under the very odd conditions of Arabia, your practical work will not be as good as, perhaps, you think it is." This wisdom is easily applicable to other countries and cultures. For an excellent insight into the requirement for cultural awareness, see George W. Smith, Jr., "Genesis of an Ulcer: Have We Focused on the Wrong Transformation?" *Marine Corps Gazette* (April 2005), 29–34; and David P. Fitchitt, "Raising the Bar: The Transformation of the SF Training Model," *Special Warfare: The Professional Bulletin of the John F. Kennedy Special Warfare Center and School* (February 2005), 2–5.

20. Other countries do this in Canada. China, for example, sends students here to study and spy on the West. "Defectors Detail China's Global Espionage Operations," *NSI Advisory* (August 2005), 8. During the Cold War, Spetsnaz operatives travelled extensively in other countries under the guise of an athletic team. Our main challenge as a nation would be to overcome any ethical concerns presented by such activity. Robert S. Boyd, "Spetsnaz: Soviet Innovation in Special Forces," *Air University Review* (November-December 1986).

21. This initiative does not argue for lowering the rigorous standards of selection; however, it may entail adjustments in selection with respect to mentoring candidates and disabusing them of the "myths" that surround the selection process.

22. This cultural and linguistic appreciation is underlined in the new U.S.-based initiative called the "Pat Roberts Intelligence Scholar Program" (PRISP), which is a three-year pilot program that grants up to $50,000 per student studying the language and culture of a "critical area" such as the Middle East. The program is described as a way "to provide the Intelligence Community (IC) with an enhanced means to recruit intelligence officers with critical skills that the labor market does not readily provide." This could also be applied to SOF. Russell Cobb, *The Daily Texan*, 20 April 2005. This issue is also important in regards to interrogation techniques and strategies. For an explanation of this, see Stephen Budiansky, "Intelligence: Truth Extraction," *The Atlantic* (June 2005).

23. For an overview of special operations experiences by Canadian military personnel, see Roy MacLaren, *Canadians Behind Enemy Lines 1939–1945* (Vancouver: University of British Columbia Press, 1981).

24. As one senior American SOF operator advised, the capacity to understand the culture of the area of operations is a strategic necessity. This facilitates the development of non-lethal strategies, such as advising the tribal chief or village elders that men from their village are dallying with nefarious elements that bring shame on the village. Expending certain monies to facilitate the building of rudimentary housing could make marriage an option for young men, taking many out of the influence of Islamic extremist recruiters. As a result, there is a need for socio-anthropologists who are target area specialists and can assist in providing a broader strategy against violent extremism. See Susan B. Glasser, "Review May Shift Terror Policies," *Washington Post*, 29 May 2005. This could also refer to the British experience in Northern Ireland where 14 Intelligence Company and police undercover assets made extensive use of native-born Ulstermen to successfully penetrate IRA cells. This resulted in a breakdown of the IRA's intelligence network, which ultimately led to peace negotiations. The Protestant paramilitaries were far easier to penetrate and defeat as the under cover operatives used were mostly Protestants themselves and were more easily assimilated into loyalist cells for cultural reasons. On 14 Intelligence Company see James Rennie, *The Operators: Inside 14 Intelligence Company — The Army's Top Secret Elite* (London: Century, 1996). On the undercover war in Northern Ireland, see Jack Holland and Susan Phoenix, *Phoenix: Policing the Shadows, the Secret War Against Terrorism in Northern Ireland* (London: Hodder and Stoughton, 1996).

25. Due to the small number of regular and reserve personnel that comprise the CF, to enlarge the volunteer pool for SOF, there is a need to talent spot potential candidates outside of the military stream.

26. The IRR of the USMC and the reserve SAS provide individual replacements to their regular counterparts and can be employed to expand their

depth of capabilities or provide specialist skills as required.

27. During the 1980s, the SAS director, Brigadier Peter de la Billière, established a rule that an officer or senior NCO in 22 SAS who wished to gain rank had to serve time with the SAS(R). General Sir Peter de la Billière, *Looking for Trouble: SAS to Gulf War* (London: HarperCollins, 1994), 160–161.

28. "Shadowy Sister of the SAS," *BBC News* (20 September 1999).

29. Some observers have argued that the requirements for creativity and innovation in SOF operations are qualities that may be more prevalent in the reserve than in the regular Army.

30. J. Paul de B. Taillon, *The Evolution of Special Forces in Counter-Terrorism: The British and American Experiences* (Westport, CT: Praeger, 2001), 28.

31. CSM Michael S. Breasseale, "The 18X Program: Ensuring the Future Health of Special Forces," *Special Warfare* (May 2004), 28–31; and Lieutenant-Colonel David P. Fitchitt, "Raising the Bar: The Transformation of the SF Training Model," *Special Operations Technology* Vol. 3, No. 3 (2005), 13–14.

32. It should be noted that Britain has formed a new regiment to be called the Special Reconnaissance Regiment (SRR). This unit will recruit men and women from the various branches of the armed forces, especially those of Middle Eastern or Mediterranean appearance, as well as other ethnic minorities. Such an initiative is highly supported by this chapter. Sean Rayment, "Britain Forms New Special Forces Unit to Fight Al-Qaidah," *Sunday Telegraph*, 27 July 2004; and "New Regiment Will Support SAS," *BBC News* (5 April 2005).

33. The RCMP has a role in future counter-insurgency operations by assisting with training, as well as advising foreign police in law-enforcement operations. Moreover, criminal networks continue to support terrorist operations through drug-trafficking and smuggling, as well as other criminal ventures, and these must be dealt with by an effective police force.

34. Field Marshal Lord Carver, letter to author, 24 December 1985.

35. *Keeni meeni* is a Swahili phrase used to denote extremely dangerous undercover work. It refers to the sinuous movement of a deadly snake in long grass.

36. For an interesting discussion on this, see Jon-Paul Hart, "Killer Spooks: Increase Human Intelligence Collection Capability by Assigning Collectors to Tactical-Level Units," *Marine Corps Gazette* (April 2005).

37. For an interesting insight on intelligence issues, see Lieutenant-Colonel Lester W. Grau, "Something Old, Something New, Guerrillas, Terrorists and Intelligence Analysis," *Military Review* (July–August 2004).

38. EBO: The integrated application of all relevant instruments of government and military power under common strategic aims and objectives to achieve desired operational outcomes through the coordinated achievement of military and non-military effects.

39. IO: Information operations are actions taken in support of national objectives that influence the adversary's decision making by affecting their information and information systems while exploiting and protecting your own and allied information and information systems. IO is an overarching strategy for the coordination of military capabilities and operations. It enables commanders to protect their information assets and decision-making processes while affecting the adversary's information and decision-making process. It creates synergies in support of strategic, operational, and tactical objectives.

40. Lieutenant-Colonel Bradley Bloom, "Information Operations in Support of Special Operations," *Military Review* (January-February 2004).

41. The Canadian Forces, particularly the Army, have not had access to the spectrum of information management means available to their American counterparts. The focal point for the Canadian Army and for CANSOF has been the development of human-centric networks that incorporate technology, a niche capability that is done well by both the Canadian Army and CANSOF. See Howard G. Coombs and General Rick Hillier, "Command and Control During Peace Support Operations: Creating Common Intent in Afghanistan," in a currently untitled collaborative manuscript from the CF Leadership Institute and Defence Research and Development Canada in Kingston, Ontario, to be published by the Canadian Defence Academy Press in 2006.

42. Colonel John Boyd was a United States Air Force (USAF) fighter pilot who made a lasting impact on pilot training, fighter design, and military theory and doctrine. Boyd's major contribution to military theory is what is known as the Boyd cycle or the OODA Loop. The Observation, Orientation, Decision, and Action Cycle Loop, while seemingly simplistic, is a complex analysis of military decision making before and during a blue-on-red encounter (real battle), positing that the side proceeding through the decision-making cycle the fastest will be the winner. The ability to predict what the enemy is going to do implies an understanding of his decision cycle and an ability to anticipate his moves. Robert Coram, *Boyd: The Fighter Pilot Who Changed the Art of War* (Boston: Little, Brown, 2002).

43. For an excellent article on this topic, see Captain Greg Gagnon, USAF, "Network-Centric Special Operations: Exploring New Operational Paradigms," accessed at *www.airpower.maxwell.af.mil/airchronicles/cc/gagnon.html*.

44. Steven P. Schreiber, Greg E. Metzgar, Stephen R. Mezhir, "Behind Friendly Lines: Enforcing the Need for a Joint SOF Staff Officer," *Military Review* (May-June 2004).

45. In May 2005, the Canadian Forces announced that the Army would be creating a strike force of highly trained "Ranger" troops to assist in operations with CANSOF. It was estimated that this force would be brought into being within five years. Chris Wattie, "Ranger Troops to Replace Airborne as 'Pointy End' of Canadian Forces," *Ottawa Citizen*, 3 May 2005.

46. Operational experiences underline the necessity for close coordination between SOF units and a SODSU. The ill-fated attempt to rescue American nationals from Tehran in April 1980 (Operation Eagle Claw) employed American SOF with a Ranger force in direct support. The Battle of Mogadishu in October 1993 employed American SOF supported by a Ranger force. In Sierra Leone in September 2000, an SAS squadron supported by the 1st Battalion, The Parachute Regiment (1 PARA), rescued 11 British soldiers who were held prisoner by a group calling itself the West Side Boys. This last experience brought home the need for a designated SODSU and subsequently saw the British Army designating 1 PARA to support future British SOF operations.

47. During the Borneo conflict, the SAS trained the Guards Independent (Pathfinder) Company of the Parachute Brigade to undertake SAS-type operations. In 1966, before the conclusion of the Borneo campaign, G Company 22 SAS was formed from the ranks of this Guards formation and volunteers from the 2nd Battalion, The Parachute Regiment. Steve Crawford, *The SAS Encyclopedia* (London: Simon & Schuster, 1996), 45.

48. We must develop our CANSOF, as well as our light infantry, to be capable of operating in ethnically complex, cross-cultural environs. As noted previously, this initiative does not exclude the other combat or support arms.

49. Colin S. Gray, "Handful of Heroes or Desperate Ventures: When Do Special Operators Succeed," *Parameters, US Army War College Quarterly* (Spring 1999), 2.

50. Joint Special Operations University pamphlet. Undated.

# 13

## Canadian Special Operations Forces:
### *A Blueprint for the Future*

### Bernard J. Brister

If you cannot attack your enemy, you should attack the friend
of your enemy.
— Ramzi Ahmed Yousef, 1993 World Trade Center Bomber[1]

The security environment within which Canada must exist for the
foreseeable future is characterized by global dominance exercised by
the United States.[2] This dominance is, however, likely to be challenged
periodically by transnational groups and non-state actors who will
employ asymmetric tactics and strategies to achieve their goals and
objectives, groups that will not necessarily be constrained by funding or
technology, or western morals and ethical standards.

Within the global family, Canadians tend to see themselves as
champions of human security, individual rights, and peacekeeping.
However, the reality is that Canada is a wealthy, Western democracy
closely identified geographically, culturally, and socially with the United
States. Canadians could thus be at risk by virtue of our proximity to the
Americans from groups and factions intent upon forging a new world
order, or simply destroying the one that now exists. If, as Canadians, we
attempt to deny this reality of our situation and refuse to take the necessary measures to protect ourselves, we may well become the target of

an attack. It is an unfortunate fact of life that refusal to acknowledge a threat or to defend adequately against one will attract rather than deter those bent on mischief.

Canada has a well-established tradition of multilateralism in world affairs, which includes its military contributions to international security. The concept of assisting in the maintenance of international security with our friends and allies by means of expeditionary operations within a coalition is one of the basic precepts of our defence planning. Within the context of the *1994 Defence White Paper*, Canada committed itself to the maintenance of a general-purpose military force capable of a broad spectrum of tasks and missions in defence of the nation and of Canadian interests worldwide. In recent years this has been interpreted as providing forces that are interoperable with our most probable ally — the United States. But one of the stark realities of the modern economic and security environment is the prohibitive cost of manning and equipping a modern military force. Despite careful budgeting and spending practices, it is thus unlikely that Canada will have any more success than our traditional allies, the United Kingdom, Australia, and New Zealand, in fielding a general-purpose force with the same or similar technologies and capabilities as those of the United States.

Given this, Canada might want to consider the development of certain "niche capabilities." These capabilities must, of course, fit within the general concept of domestic operations, and, at the same time, be capable of contributing effectively to an international coalition employing state of the art equipment and tactics. If this position is accepted as being reasonable, the question then becomes, "what niche capabilities should Canada focus upon?" A detailed analysis of just what this focus could entail is beyond the scope of this article. However, by way of background, it may be instructive to note the results of an earlier study conducted by this author[3] and the emphasis placed upon the use of Special Forces (SF)[4] and of Special Operations Forces (SOF)[5] by the United States, the United Kingdom, Australia, and New Zealand in the most recent campaigns in Afghanistan and Iraq.

If SOF are a viable contribution to coalition expeditionary operations by Canada, the next question to be asked is: "What exactly should Canada focus on in terms of the type, nature, and capability of an SOF contribution?" That question will be the main focus of this chapter. The identification of capabilities will be based upon recent coalition experience in Afghanistan and Iraq. A hypothetical organization and structure for this force, including command and control, will then be presented, using the examples set by Australia and Britain as the basis for discussion. Finally, a Canadian SOF capability and a methodology for its development will be proposed as a possible blueprint for future Canadian contributions to international security.

## SPECIAL FORCES CAPABILITIES

The modern approach to SOF coalition warfare involves the designation of a "Lead Nation" for a given operation or campaign. That nation provides a major force contribution, as well as the nucleus of the command and control, staff, and support infrastructure. The Lead Nation is also expected to provide or assist in the provision of key capabilities, known as "enablers," to the other contributing nations, such as strategic and tactical airlift or logistic support. The combined (multinational) and joint (multiservice or component) nature of the coalition concept extends down to the individual National Task Group level. There is no integration of national forces or components below this point, and the guiding principle being observed is "unity of command along national lines."[6]

Despite a Lead Nation's obligation to provide strategic and operational enablers to contributing nations, the realities of defence budgets, even amongst those nations capable of acting as Lead Nation in a coalition, quite naturally limits the amount of assistance that can be provided. Thus, the extent to which any participating nation can contribute a stand-alone strategic and operational-level SOF capability will determine the relative value of that contribution to the coalition's overall goals and objectives. Those nations that contribute the most capable SOF task forces will possess capabilities at the strategic and operational levels that will earn them significant influence over the conduct of activities. This influence will exist, not only with respect to issues concerning the actual conduct of coalition military operations, but also in the international political and diplomatic processes surrounding those operations.

Special Operations Forces are differentiated from one another on the basis of an assessment of the quality and the scope of their capabilities. Those organizations possessing the highest quality skills, expertise, and professionalism, and the broadest scope of capabilities, are categorized as *world-class* or *Tier 1*, terms used both formally and informally.[7] The key characteristics that generally define a Tier 1 SOF organization are as follows.

## Power Projection

The organization must be able to project itself strategically into a theatre without assistance from or reliance upon the resources of the Lead Nation. Operationally, the National Task Group must also have the resources to move itself about the theatre with the necessary national air, land, or maritime resources, such that it does not have to draw upon the resources of the Lead Nation other than for very unique situations or missions.

Strategic lift is extremely expensive for any nation to acquire and maintain, and this type of transport is in chronically short supply among nations requiring a global or strategic reach for their forces. In a time of a crisis that would generate the requirement for a coalition, each nation's lift capability would likely be committed entirely to moving its own forces to and from an operational arena. Thus, the requirement for a contributing nation to provide its own strategic lift, either organic or contracted, is essential if its SOF are to be considered a Tier 1 organization.[8]

Tactical or operational mobility in the theatre of operations is also a critical prerequisite of an effective SOF contribution. As with strategic lift, there are few nations capable of fielding sufficient operational and tactical lift to fully support their own forces. The ability of a nation to deploy fixed-wing aircraft with specialized navigation and defensive suites, combined with an air-to-air refuelling capability, would help to ensure that national forces have the support they need to conduct the missions for which they have been deployed. Having to rely on other coalition nations to provide this type of assistance is an uncertain option at best, since that lift support will, in all likelihood, be addressed only after the other nations have met their own requirements. Similarly, having helicopters with the same specialized equipment, including an air-to-air refuelling capability, provides greatly increased flexibility for the execution of the SOF mission.

Taken together, the possession of sufficient strategic, operational and tactical airlift by a nation deploying an SOF task force will help categorize its SOF within the Tier 1 community, and place it on the list of preferred military coalition partners.[9] On the other side of the coin, without mobility at the strategic, operational, and tactical levels, regardless of the quality of the personnel and equipment deployed, an SOF task force will be of limited value in most coalition situations.[10]

### Command and Control (C2)

The C2 capability of the SOF task force should include strategic, operational, and tactical communications, and a stand-alone intelligence capability that could include signals, electronic, imagery, and human intelligence assets, as well as linkages to other government agencies. It should also include a full-spectrum planning capacity, and sufficient resources to exercise positive command and control during the execution of all operations. The SOF task force must have the resources to plan and conduct operations while keeping the national chain of command and the coalition fully apprised of the situation. The value of the national SOF contribution to the coalition can be enhanced by the addition of national specialty skills to the overall coalition capabilities, such as intelligence collection and analysis.[11]

### Operational Flexibility

A national SOF contribution must have the resources and capabilities to operate as a discrete force in the execution of its missions. It must also be able to incorporate and effectively use attachments from each of the national land, sea, and air components. And it must have the ability to function effectively within a joint force construct, either as part of a national task force, such as the British campaign in the Falklands, or as a member of a combined SOF coalition, as in Iraq and Afghanistan.

### Tactical Capability

A national SOF must have the capability to execute a broad spectrum of high-order missions. These could include strategic reconnaissance, conducted either on foot or with vehicles; direct action assaults on enemy strong points and sensitive site exploitation tasks requiring precision entry and shooting skills; and the pursuit and recovery of high-value targets associated with an opposing force or regime. These missions are generally associated with the ability to conduct sustained operations over a lengthy period (low intensity, long duration) combined with an ability to transition, with little or no notice, to a high-energy response or manoeuvre (high intensity, short duration).[12]

*Specialist Support*

The contributing nation must be able to tailor support to its SOF as required by the operational environment. Well-trained and capable specialist support, such as airborne, commando, or Ranger-type units, must be available if necessary. These types of units could perform security tasks in support of the main effort, or act as a quick reaction force to assist in the extraction of SOF elements from their mission areas. Another type of specialist support that should be made available, if it is not organic to the SOF, is a chemical, biological, radiological, and nuclear response team. The importance of such a unit for survey, detection, analysis, and exploitation of situations that may involve those types of weapons or threats has been highlighted in both the Afghan and Iraqi campaigns.[13]

The common theme of the argument presented above is that the most effective national SOF niche capability to contribute to a coalition is a high-quality force capable of supporting itself at the strategic, operational, and tactical levels. These capabilities are neither inexpensive, nor rapidly developed in time of need. The development of a Tier 1 SOF organization requires sustained funding over a significant period. Failing to provide a force with all fundamental Tier 1 capabilities will limit the effectiveness, and, therefore, the value of the SOF contribution.

## FORCE STRUCTURE MODELS

The structure of a national Tier 1 SOF capability usually follows one of two models. The first model is best described as the "centralized" approach, where all the required units or sub-units, equipment, capabilities, and groupings are organic elements, and it is, in essence, a separate component of a national military capability, a force unto itself. As a stand-alone organization, it is funded as a separate entity and competes with the other components for defence dollars. Although this provides a welcome degree of independence, it also puts the Tier 1 SOF component into what could be unhealthy competition with the other service components for funding.

## The Australian Model

A number of nations, including Australia, have adopted the centralized model. Prime Minister John Howard has come to rely upon the Australian Special Air Service Regiment (SASR) as his force of choice when there is a military aspect to the achievement of Australian foreign policy objectives.[14] The increased employment of SF and SOF, as opposed to conventional military forces, to deal with post–Cold War security issues prompted a review of the structure of the Australian military and how it is postured to address security threats. The process culminated in early 2003 with the establishment of Special Operations Command Australia (SOCOMD), which, in its end-state, will consist of approximately 2,000 soldiers and will be considered the fifth component (along with Army, Navy, Air Force, and Logistics elements) of the Australian Defence Forces.[15]

The centrepiece of the new component is the Special Air Service Regiment, which will have the capability of executing all Tier 1 SOF missions, including long-range reconnaissance, special reconnaissance, and direct action, as well as special recovery operations associated with counterterrorism and hostage rescue situations.

Supporting and augmenting the SASR is the 4th Battalion, Royal Australian Regiment (Commando). This unit performs roles typical of a airborne, commando, or Ranger-type unit — raids and "point of entry" seizure-type missions. It has also duplicated the domestic counterterror-ism capability that had been the sole province of the SASR. Following the events of 11 September 2001, it was determined that a timely response to domestic incidents of terrorism required the positioning of a counter-terrorism, hostage rescue capability on each of Australia's west and east coasts. Consequently, the battalion was tasked to establish Tactical Assault Group East, a mission that fits into its high-intensity, short-duration task mandate. In addition to its domestic counterterrorism role, the unit will continue to be employed in conjunction with the SASR as a quick reac-tion force, or in an outer cordon role during the deployment of national SOF assets. It will also serve as a high-quality recruitment reservoir for the Special Air Service Regiment.[16]

Another significant component of the Australian model is the Incident Response Regiment (IRR), an engineer-based organization comprised of specialist response groups, such as explosive ordnance dis-posal (EOD), and chemical, biological, radiological and nuclear (CBRN) analysis, survey, and consequence-management groups. Combat service support will be provided to all elements of the command by a dedicated group focused on the unique support requirements of the full range of special operations missions. Recruitment and initial training of applicants to all these special operations units will be coordinated through a Special Forces Training Centre, which will directly support unit training and doctrine requirements.[17]

Strategic, operational, and tactical air and aviation lift is being addressed with a hybrid solution. The strategic movement of SOF resources will be accomplished by means of priority taskings to the Royal Australian Air Force (RAAF). Once in theatre, the RAAF will also provide operational or theatre-level support with C-130 Hercules aircraft manned by specially trained crews flying aircraft with specialized self-defence and low-level navigation/terrain avoidance suites. These specialized capabilities will be developed and maintained by the RAAF, working in conjunction with Special Operations Command.

Tactical lift support will be provided by the Australian Army with a squadron of special operations SA-70 Blackhawks, operated by specially trained crews. Other aspects of aviation support will likely be provided by CH-47 Chinook helicopters, several of which were fitted for Persian Gulf operations with an enhanced suite of self-defence and low-level navigation/terrain avoidance equipment similar to that used by the RAAF.[18]

It should be noted that the capabilities planned for Special Operations Command have not yet been fully funded, developed, or fielded, and this is unlikely to happen for several years. Despite this fact the Australians are included in the very select grouping of international Tier 1 SOF organizations, based upon their past accomplishments and future capabilities. Their achievements in the coalition operations "Enduring Freedom" (Afghanistan) and "Iraqi Freedom," even with an SOF capability still in its embryonic stage, and because of demonstrated governmental will to employ these forces, have already paid considerable political and economic dividends for Australia.

### The British Model

The British Special Forces organization provides an example of the second or "decentralized" model. Commanded and controlled at the national level by the Ministry of Defence through the Directorate of Special Forces, British Special Forces consist only of the Tier 1 organizations themselves. The front line commands of the conventional armed forces provide all the support organizations and attachments that are required for force employment, and they combine with the Tier 1 unit to form the national SOF. These commands task and tailor the support organizations and attachments to the needs and requirements of the Special Forces, based upon the type and nature of the mission under consideration.

The front line commands contribute to British Special Forces with some of their best personnel, and with significant funding. As such, they have a vested interest in ensuring that the forces are used to best effect. The day-to-day support for Special Forces operations within the U.K. defence community is enhanced by the placement of Special Forces staff in key positions throughout the Ministry of Defence. In addition to providing the front line commands with a return on their personnel investments in British Special Forces, this policy also serves to engender a greater level of understanding and acceptance of the roles and missions of these specialized forces within the military framework.

The end result of this method of organization is that the British Special Forces are viewed as the "jewel in the crown" of Britain's military capability, and not as a separate and possibly threatening entity by the other service components. All components contribute to their quality and capability. Similarly, all components benefit from the development of these capabilities. Controlled at the national strategic level, British Special Forces are tasked with discrete missions in the national interest or as part of a joint operation working in conjunction with one or more of the other components in order to achieve a stated goal or objective. They can be employed jointly with any one or any combination of the other services to enhance and reinforce their mission capabilities. The use of Special Forces in joint operations of this nature also forms part of the return on investment to the components for their contributions to developing and maintaining this capability.

## COMMAND AND CONTROL

The development of a Special Operations Force is an evolutionary process that requires time to mature. Regardless of the force structure adopted, be it a centralized Special Operations Command organization similar to the Australian example, or a decentralized structure such as employed by the British, the creation of a Tier 1 SOF organization in Canada or elsewhere requires more than just the allocation of personnel, funding, resources, and time. It also requires significant amounts of operational experience and acumen. Thus, to reach its full potential as quickly and as effectively as possible, a Tier 1 SOF organization requires the synergistic learning effect of working and associating with allied Tier 1 SOF organizations that have similar roles, responsibilities and capabilities.

Tier 1 SOF missions are tactical actions that achieve strategic results. That is not to say that SOF will not or should not be employed for operational or tactical results on occasion; they should indeed be deployed wherever and whenever their unique skills and capabilities can be used to effect in the attainment of national goals and objectives. Retaining command and control of SOF resources at the national strategic level, however, achieves what is arguably the most important aspect of the command and control of SOF resources. It ensures that a mechanism is in place at the highest level to make an overall assessment of where and when the use of SOF best serves the national interest.[19]

Operations in Afghanistan provide evidence that the struggle to maintain control of SOF operations at the strategic level has in some instances failed. In that theatre a number of contributing nations deployed with SOF elements attached to their conventional formations for use as reconnaissance troops — tactical tasks with tactical effects. In effect, this indicated a failure of the organizations involved to transition from a Cold War perspective on the role of SOF. In circumstances where most nations can afford only a small SOF organization, placement of these specialized forces within component commands interferes with their most effective employment at the national level for strategic effects.[20]

The American case is somewhat different, in that their SOF community is sufficiently large and diverse to function at several levels simultaneously. It does, nonetheless, demonstrate that the employment and focus of SOF is a function of where it is placed in a nation's order of battle. The American model parcels out slices of SOF around the globe, and then, following a request for forces, places them under the operational control of one of five regional or theatre command headquarters.[21] At the same time, the Americans retain SOF organizations for strategic applications at the national level. Thus, in the American case, the sheer size of their military assets permits the employment of SOF at both the national strategic and operational levels in several theatres of operation.

The balance of evidence would indicate, however, that most nations, constrained as they are by economics, would only have the resources to maintain an SOF capability that is relatively small in comparison to American capabilities. In these instances, nations are probably best served by retaining command and control of their SOF at the national or strategic level. If SOF are retained as a force provider at the national level in conjunction with the land, air, and maritime components of a nation's military, they can be utilized at all three levels as situations dictate. This will enable a "god's eye" evaluation of opportunities for the employment of SOF, such that their eventual employment should always reflect national strategic priorities and concerns.

The British case provides an example of the benefits to be derived from the retention of command and control at the national level. The British SOF can be employed as a discrete force on strategic operations, or as part of a joint force in combination with the other components of the armed services. As they are controlled at the national level, their employment will always tend to be strategic in nature, but they will remain available for operations with the other components as circumstances dictate. The optimum employment for British SOF strategically, operationally, and tactically is always determined at the strategic level, and from a strategic perspective.[22]

The Australian case is in a state of transition. At present, their Special Operations Command is subordinated to the land component. However, over the next several years, the four component commands, as well as the Australian Defence Force's operational headquarters and Special Operations Command Headquarters, will be concentrated in the capital, Canberra, bringing all key operational and component headquarters into close proximity.[23] This will have the effect of establishing Special Operations Command as the fifth component of the defence forces in all but name. This concept is reinforced by the fact that the Special Operations commander holds a rank equivalent to that of the other service chiefs. He is already included as a key member in most, if not all, senior military and government decision-making forums. Clearly, the trend in Australia is to move its SOF resources from the component level to the national strategic level for more effective allocation and employment of these resources. This trend will bring the Australian Defence Forces into line with the same SOF command and control philosophies espoused by Canada's closest allies, the Americans and the British.

## THE CANADIAN BLUEPRINT

After having examined and considered the experience and practices of some of Canada's closest allies with respect to SOF capabilities, what direction should Canada follow? If one considers, as stated in the introduction to this article, that such a capability could be the nation's most effective option in providing an expeditionary contribution to international security, what specific form should this capability take? What follows is an outline concept for such a capability that might provide for Canada its most effective contribution to international security, and, concomitantly, recognition of that contribution internationally.

### Force Capabilities and Force Structure

Government spending priorities and budget constraints will require that any Canadian contribution be small but effective. Within these parameters, there is choice between providing a vertical, or full capability, "slice" of SOF, or a horizontal "slice" — a partial capability but of greater strength — to a coalition. The recommended solution, elaborated below, will be a full capability, stand-alone SOF grouping, because of the generally greater value of such a contribution to any coalition, and because of the increased national recognition that such a contribution would generate.

At the core of this hypothetical Canadian SOF niche capability would be Joint Task Force Two (JTF-2), a Tier 1-capable unit, acknowledged by the chief of the defence staff as a counterterrorism and special operations unit capable of deploying abroad for the conduct of special operations in support of national political and military objectives.[24] Three company-sized light infantry sub-units of approximately 180 personnel each, with specialized parachute, Ranger and commando skills, would provide essential tactical support to JTF-2, both domestically and internationally. They could reduce the tasking load for JTF-2 personnel on other than clearly defined Tier 1 missions, and could also provide a pool of training and experience for the core unit to draw upon for replacements and reinforcements. Specialist support groupings would include company-sized elements proficient in explosive ordnance disposal and chemical, biological, radiation, and nuclear survey and exploitation. A dedicated combat service support grouping would provide logistic support.

Strategic lift would be provided by existing or enhanced Air Force resources assigned on a priority basis to the missions. Operational or theatre level air support would also be provided by the Air Force with specially trained crews and C-130 Hercules aircraft modified with enhanced self-defence and low-level navigation/terrain avoidance suites. Tactical lift would be supplied by leased or purchased medium lift helicopter resources, crewed by the Air Force and equipped with the same defensive and navigation/terrain avoidance capabilities as the Hercules.

The mechanics of raising, training, and deploying the SOF as a whole would be left with the air, land, and sea components, similar to the British model. JTF-2, as the core Tier 1 SOF unit, should be a stand-alone fighting force complete with its operational and tactical level command and control groupings and indigenous combat service support capability. Specialist groupings and the individual specialist components of the intelligence, and command and control functions would remain with their parent component for normal operations and training, but would receive funding from the SOF budget to maintain a required level of capability and expertise with respect to their SOF-specific tasks and responsibilities. They would be required to train with the SOF on a regular basis and remain on-call for SOF operations at a heightened state of readiness.

The lift capabilities at the strategic, operational, and tactical levels would be funded by SOF. They would reside with the Air Force but be subject to minimum training and exercise requirements with the SOF, and to short notice recall for SOF missions. The total complement of the entire Canadian SOF capability would not likely exceed 2,000 personnel.

### *Command and Control*

As is the case with Australia and Britain, it should be anticipated that the Canadian SOF assets would be very much in demand across the spectrum of military tasks, especially in those situations requiring an operational response on short notice. In order to ensure that the SOF elements are employed to the greatest effect, command and control of these forces should be retained at the highest, strategic level. To do otherwise would risk the misemployment of these assets on tasks achievable by other forces, while higher national priorities requiring SOF-specific capabilities might be overlooked. Command, therefore, must continue to be exercised by the CDS through the deputy chief of the defence staff.

### CONCLUSION

The use of niche military capabilities is both a viable and cost-effective means for governments to make meaningful contributions to international security at the times and places of their choosing. Within the category of niche capabilities, the use of SOF task groups is one such contribution that provides a particularly high "payback" in terms of influence and recognition among members of the international community. When faced with the range of options available to Canada in the provision of such a capability, one's attention must gravitate naturally towards the option that provides the greatest return for the dollar in terms of influence with our allies and partners. Thus, a full-capability or Tier 1 SOF grouping becomes an excellent choice for expeditionary contributions to be made by Canada in the interests of international security.

This SOF contribution can be quite small relative to those of our friends and allies. It is important, however, that the contribution be a stand-alone component fully capable of deploying itself, conducting operations at the highest level and with the greatest skill for extended periods of time, and returning home unassisted when the assigned task is completed. The resources comprising the contribution should raised, trained, and sustained by the subject matter experts in each specialist area, but retain the capability to gather and deploy quickly for operations. Lastly, control of this asset must be retained at the national strategic level to ensure its most effective use and employment in the national interest.

In conclusion, it must be clearly understood that while SOF has an extraordinary ability to deliver effect and capability, a number of prerequisites must be met before this can happen. First the nation must be willing to invest sufficiently in its creation, development, and upkeep. And this investment must be done in a timely manner, since the creation of an SOF organization cannot be initiated when a crisis is looming. Further, the nation must be willing to invest sufficient funds to ensure that the best personnel have the required equipment to achieve the greatest effect with the smallest numbers, since large SOF components are fiscally and practically unrealistic. The nation and the military must also be willing to commit their best personnel to this force, as only the best are likely to be guarantors of success under the situations and circumstances in which this force would, in all likelihood, operate.

Once the investment has been made, the national political and military leadership must be willing to use the SOF in the pursuit of national political and military goals and objectives. It must be seen as a precision tool to be used in special circumstances to achieve very specific and well-defined effects under a variety of difficult and demanding circumstances. It must also be viewed as a means of mitigating high-risk situations to achieve substantial gains and successes out of proportion to the resources employed. Developed and employed in this manner, this force could become a blueprint for Canadian success as an internationally respected Special Operations entity possessing very credible and significant capabilities.

NOTES

1. Words of convicted 1993 World Trade Center bomber Ramzi Ahmed Yousef. Benjamin Weiser, "Two Convicted in Plot to Blow Up N.Y. World Trade Center," *New York Times*, 13 November 1997.

2. Directorate of Strategic Analysis, *Strategic Assessment 2002* (Ottawa: Department of National Defence, 2002), 11.

3. Bernard J. Brister, "The Role of Special Forces in the Execution of Canadian Foreign Policy," paper presented at the 2nd Special Operations Symposium Royal Military College of Canada, Kingston, Ontario, 7 March 2002.

4. For the purposes of this chapter, Special Forces are defined as those forces specifically selected, trained, equipped, and tasked with a range of missions outside the spectrum of conventional military operations. Adapted from Thomas K. Adams, *US Special Operations Forces in Action: The Challenge of Unconventional Warfare* (London: Frank Cass, 1998), xxiv, xxv, and 5–7.

5. Again, for the purposes of this chapter, SOF are defined as those elements of a task force, military, paramilitary, and civilian that are assigned to support a Special Forces task group in the execution of a mission outside of the spectrum of conventional military operations. Adapted from Adams, xxiv, xxv, and 5–7.

6. Interview with a senior officer, British Special Forces, 25 April 2003.

7. Interview with a senior officer, Australian Special Air Service Regiment (AS SASR), 27 March 2003. It is important note that the use of Tier 1 in this chapter, based on the Australian input, differs from the standard breakdown of SOF Tiers, which are normally based on selection criteria and mission capability.

8. Interview with a senior officer, British Special Forces, 25 April 2003.

9. These assets, along with their highly trained crews, will also generate an increase in a nation's strategic reach, and therefore, its influence, which will pay significant if subtle benefits on the political and diplomatic fronts. The ability to quickly project power in support of allied nations, large or small, close to home, or far away, generates a tremendous amount of appreciation and cooperation. Interview with a senior officer, AS SASR, 27 March 2003.

10. *Ibid.*

11. Areas where a specific nation may have developed an intelligence capability over and above the standard of other contributing nations might include, but would not be limited to, imagery analysis, signal intelligence, and intelligence gathering from human sources. Interview with a senior officer, British Special Forces, 25 April 2003; and interview with senior officer, AS SASR, 27 March 2003.

12. Interview with a senior officer, British Special Forces, 25 April 2003 and Interview with a senior officer, AS SASR, 27 March 2003.

13. Interview with a senior officer, AS SASR, 27 March 2003.

14. *Ibid.*

15. Discussion with a senior officer, AS SASR, 9 July 2004.

16. *Ibid.*

17. *Ibid.*

18. *Ibid.*

19. Interview with a senior officer, British Special Forces, 25 April 2003.

20. Interview with a senior officer, AS SASR, 27 March 2003.

21. Adams, 7.

22. Interview with a senior officer, British Special Forces, 25 April 2003.

23. Discussion with a senior HQ AST staff officer, Sydney, Australia, 8 August 2003.

24. *A Time for Transformation: Annual Report of the Chief of the Defence Staff 2002–2003* (Ottawa: Department of National Defence, 2003), 5.

# AFTERWORD

## Bernd Horn and Tony Balasevicius

Since their inception, modern SOF have steadily grown and evolved into a key element of a nation's military inventory. This growth has been particularly evident in the post–Cold War period where they have proven to be particularly popular with the political leadership because of their small footprint, low-visibility, and ability to discreetly accomplish a myriad of sensitive tasks. As a result, they often eliminate the need for larger national commitments, thus, reducing the risk of heavy casualties or adverse political fallout. SOF is able to operate in this narrow spectrum of high-risk military activity because its soldiers possess the skills necessary to operate comfortably in ambiguous situations and this allows them to successfully navigate through complex missions. This agility is the direct result of the quality of soldiers that SOF selects. It also derives from the employment concept, organization, and training programs that have been developed by the respective organizations. These factors have allowed SOF to transform specialist-training competencies into relevant skill sets that have thus far proven sufficiently adaptive to meet the changing threats and challenges posed by the twenty-first century.

The utility of SOF's flexibility has been especially recognized in the aftermath of the 11 September 2001 terrorist attack against the United

States. In fact, internationally, the trend since then has been to enhance the capabilities and extend the employment of SOF. Furthermore, evidence suggests that this trend, at least in the short term, will likely continue to grow. Given the apparent benefits derived from employing SOF it is not surprising, that the Canadian Forces (CF) is now developing a significant SOF capability of its own. The creation of Canadian Special Operations Forces Command (CANSOFCOM), which stood up in February 2006 as part of the CF's ongoing transformation process will provide Canada with new capabilities and a potent weapon when dealing with asymmetric threats. However, it will also fundamentally change the dynamics within the CF.

When fully operational, CANSOFCOM will likely comprise over 2,000 highly trained soldiers that will be employed within one of the various units that will make of this new command. These units will include: JTF-2, the Canadian Special Operations Regiment, a special operations tactical aviation squadron, the joint nuclear, biological chemical (JNBC) company along with a formation headquarters and various support organizations. The task of consolidating the newly created CANSOFCOM into a functional organization, fully integrated into the CF, will be an arduous task and one that will be fraught with difficulty and risk.

The difficulty and risk inherent in standing up this capability is due, in part, to the fact that SOF has never been an integral element of Canada's military capability and the CF's experience in SOF operations outside the narrow spectrum of hostage rescue is extremely limited. Colonel Taillon aptly highlighted this immaturity in his discussion of the 2004 deployment of CANSOF operators to Haiti. More importantly, the CF has had little or no experience in dealing with or coordinating numerous SOF units each with its own capabilities, selection processes, training, and support requirements and there is virtually no experience in synchronizing SOF activities with conventional military forces. As a result, mistakes will likely occur and in some respects must be expected as both CANSOFCOM and the CF undergo an initial period of development and adjustment. That being said, mistakes can be greatly mitigated if there is a general understanding of the dynamics that SOF will bring to the CF's force structure. Key to this is a detailed knowledge of the strengths and limitations of this capability.

In seeking to understand the strengths and limitations of SOF, it is important to realize that these capabilities evolved from specific operational circumstances that existed during the early part of the Second World War when dedicated units were raised to carry out specific missions that included direct action, special reconnaissance and surveillance, and unconventional warfare missions. These missions were very specialized and had a significant influence on the organization, training, and equipment of the units that undertook them. Thus, the first step in understanding CANSOFCOM is to comprehend the missions each unit in the Command is capable of undertaking and how these missions influence the organization, training, and potential employment of specific units. This is important because although, SOF units are not limited to one mission, there is a limit to what they can do. Therefore, care must be taken when assigning these units tasks.

There is a common misconception that any SOF unit can do any SOF task. Nothing could be further from the truth. Although SOF units share a number of similarities, there are significant differences between them and these disparities make it difficult, if not impossible to produce a "one type fits all SOF capability." To this end, commanders and staff responsible for the planning and employment of CANSOFCOM must base their employment decisions on the skills sets available to each unit, which ought to match the criteria needed to successfully carry out the mission.

In order to educate officers in the CF about the character, capabilities, and limitations of SOF in operations two things need to be accomplished. First, it is important that SOF doctrine be produced in sufficient detail to provide the necessary information for the effective employment of this very important resource. Second, the course content of all command and staff training in the CF must incorporate a study of SOF doctrine and capabilities. Education, that highlights the significance of SOF as a force multiplier, will become important especially as CANSOFCOM begins to draw significant resources from the established Commands in an effort to meet its operational commitments.

During the initial phase of its development CANSOFCOM will have to draw off resources from the current establishment but particularly from the Army, which will have to provide the bulk of the best soldiers for JTF-2, the Canadian Special Operations Regiment, as well as the various command and support elements. This drain becomes important when one considers that SOF soldiers need to be physically fit, self-reliant, highly motivated, intelligent, resourceful, and psychologically stable. Moreover, an SOF operator must be able to operate alone or as part of a small team. These are qualities that are possessed by a select few. In fact one of the biggest problems faced by most premier SOF organizations is their difficulty in attracting and retaining quality leaders and soldiers. According to unclassified sources, the success rate for Special Air Service (SAS)/American SF after selection and training is about 24 percent. America's Delta Force has about a 10 to 12 percent success rate, which one can assume is about the same for JTF-2. Also assuming the Canadian Special Operations Regiment has similar requirements to the American Rangers we can expect a success rate of only about 50 percent of the soldiers attempting to join that unit. This means that 1,500 to 2,000 of the top 50 percent of the Army's best soldiers, NCOs, and officers will be aggressively sought after by CANSOF-COM. To put this problem into better perspective, approximately 70 percent of soldiers who attend a jump course will be successful. So, if the Army had trouble maintaining the Canadian Airborne Regiment, a unit of 601 soldiers, using the 70 percent who were successful on a jump course, it will have more difficulty in supplying the significant needs of CANSOFCOM, which has more specialized capabilities and a much larger force structure to feed, but theoretically will only be accepting candidates from the top 50 percentile of those who volunteer for training. Finding suitable volunteers is not the only issue that will confront CANSOFCOM in the coming years. The command is standing up at a time when many in the SOF community are revaluating current force structures and the future direction of SOF.

The organizational model being used by Canada's new SOFCOM is loosely based on the American's USSOCOM, which will be adjusted to fit the limited resource realities faced by the Canadian military. The American model is almost 20 years old and was designed when the Cold War was still the main focus of the American military and the main task of SOF was to provide supporting functions. USSO-COM now has the lead in the American war on terror, which by most accounts is stretching resources and capabilities. Not surprisingly, the command is now looking at ways to transform. A fact, acknowledged by General Peter J. Schoomaker, a former commander of USSOCOM. "And the truth is," he asserted in 1998, "business as usual will not provide the capabilities we need to deal with the transnational and asymmetric opponents of tomorrow. A rapidly changing world deals ruthlessly with organizations that do not change — and USSOCOM is no exception. Guided by a comprehensive, enduring vision and supporting goals, we must constantly reshape ourselves to remain relevant and useful members of the joint team. As the president of AT&T once said, 'When the pace of change outside an organization becomes greater than the pace of change inside the organization, the end is near.'"[1]

What role CANSOFCOM will play in the transformed CF of the next few years is still very much an evolving concept. However, to prepare for this future, CANSOFCOM will have to focus on providing Canada with traditional SOF capabilities, while structuring itself to quickly readjust to emerging missions and the challenges that lie ahead. The question then is what emerging challenges will CANSOFCOM likely face as it evolves into Canada's SOF capability.

First and foremost it must be remembered that SOF soldiers and their leaders will remain essential to SOF's future success. As a result, these warriors must continue to be selected and trained to very high standards. In this regard, trends indicate that training alone will no longer be sufficient to allow these soldiers to deal with the uncertainties of the complex environment they will be expected to deal with. Training focuses on producing a predictable response to a predictable event and SOF does not always operate in this environment. SOF soldiers must often balance the needs of soldiering, cultural awareness, and political sensitivity with the operational requirements of their mission. The proper focus on education will allow SOF to develop the best solution for a situation that deals with multiple variables and interdependencies, and providing this education to SOF will allow them to better deal with uncertainties they face. However, this means that the development of the future SOF soldier must be focused on providing a balance between education and training, and it will require more development time. On top of this, if SOF wishes to remain a full-spectrum capability they will have to develop additional competencies that will allow them to transition into the network-centric dynamics of warfare in the Information Age.

Network-centric warfare is based on the concept of information superiority that generates increased combat power by networking sensors, decision makers, and shooters to achieve a shared awareness. In essence, it translates information superiority into combat power by effectively linking knowledgeable entities in the battlespace.[2] Thus far, SOF has been slow to adapt their force structure to become a player in this key area of emerging military activity. Not only will they be required to develop new capabilities to remain relevant they will also have to learn to operate with others more effectively, something SOF has not emphasized in the past.

A key aspect of warfare in the twenty-first century has been the migration of strategic assets such as satellite imagery, strategic bombing capabilities, and the use of SOF down to the operational and, at times, tactical levels of war. If CANSOFCOM is to remain relevant to CF needs, it will have to operate effectively in joint, combined, and interagency environments at all levels of war. As Schoomaker points out, "SOF face two major challenges: They must integrate — with conventional forces, other U.S. agencies, friendly foreign forces, and other international organizations [i.e., United Nations and the International Committee of the Red Cross] — yet they must preserve the autonomy necessary to protect and encourage the unconventional approach that is the soul of special operations."[3]

Historically, the concept of SOF was moved forward because SOF leaders were able to provide a more flexible approach to military operations by using unconventional methods. More important, their success has been based on their ability to adapt to the changing circumstances they have had to confront. Although in some respects the times have changed, the future for the SOF still depends on its ability to adapt and think outside the box. To be successful in this new environment CANSOFCOM will have to become and then remain an adaptable and relevant organization. Moreover, CF leadership must take an active role in guiding the development of CANSOFCOM and integrating into the current force structure. If this is done correctly CANSOFCOM will become a potent capability within the CF, otherwise CANSOFCOM will be at risk of becoming another bastard son.

## NOTES

1. United States Department of Defense, *Defense Issues: Volume 13 Number 10 — Special Operations Forces: The Way Ahead* (statement presented by General Peter J. Schoomaker, commander, U.S. Special Operations Command, to the members of the command).

2. Office of the Assistant Secretary of Defense for Networks and Information Integration/Department of Defense Chief Information Officer Checklist (12 May, 2004), Version 2.1.3.

3. *Defense Issues.*

# GLOSSARY

## of Acronyms and Abbreviations

| | |
|---|---|
| APFT | Army Physical Fitness Test |
| APRT | Army Physical Readiness Test |
| | |
| C2 | Command and Control |
| CANSOFCOM | Canadian Special Operations Forces Command |
| CAO | Civil Affair Operations |
| CBRN | Chemical, Biological, Radiological, and Nuclear |
| CDS | Chief of the Defence Staff |
| CENTCOM | Central Command |
| CEO | Canadian Ethnic Operator |
| CF | Canadian Forces |
| CFIOG | CF Information Operations Group |
| CIA | Central Intelligence Agency |
| CIDG | Civil Irregular Defence Group |
| CIMIC | Civilian Military Cooperation |
| CJSOTF | Commander Joint Special Operations Task Force |
| CJTF | Combined Joint Task Force |
| CNO | Computer Network Operations |
| COHQ | Combined Operations Headquarters |
| COIN ops | Counter-Insurgency Operations |

| | |
|---|---|
| CPP | Close Personal Protection |
| CRW | Counter-Revolutionary Wing |
| CSAR | Combat Search and Rescue |
| CSE | Canadian Security Establishment |
| CSIS | Canadian Security and Intelligence Service |
| CT | Counterterrorism |
| | |
| DA | Direct Action |
| DND | Department of National Defence [Canada] |
| DoD | Department of Defense [U.S.] |
| DRMLA | Democratic Revolutionary Movement for the Liberation of Arabistan |
| | |
| EBO | Effects-Based Operations |
| EOD | Explosive Ordnance Disposal |
| ERT | Emergency Response Team |
| ESI | Escadron Special D'Intervention |
| EW | Electronic Warfare |
| | |
| FID | Foreign Internal Defence |
| FSSF | First Special Service Force |
| | |
| GIGN | Groupe d'Intervention de la Gendarmerie Nationale |
| GROM | Grupa Reagowania Operacyjno Mobilnego |
| GSG 9 | Grenzschutzgruppe-9 |
| GWOT | Global War on Terrorism |
| | |
| HAHO | High Altitude High Opening |
| HQ | Headquarters |
| HUMINT | Human Intelligence |
| | |
| IRA | Irish Republican Army |
| IRR | Incident Response Regiment |
| ITC | Invasion Training Centre |
| | |
| JCO | Joint Commission Observers |
| JTF-2 | Joint Task Force Two |

| | |
|---|---|
| LAPD | Los Angeles Police Department |
| LAV | Light Armoured Vehicle |
| LIB | Light Infantry Battalion |
| LRDG | Long Range Desert Group |
| LRRP | Long Range Reconnaissance Patrol |
| | |
| MACV | Military Assistance Command Vietnam |
| MND | Minister of National Defence |
| MOS | Military Occupation Specification |
| MTT | Mobile Training Team |
| | |
| NATO | North Atlantic Treaty Organisation |
| NCO | Non-Commissioned Officer |
| NCW | Network-Centric Warfare |
| NEO | Non-Combatant Evacuation Operation |
| NVA | North Vietnamese Army |
| | |
| OG | Operational Group |
| OODA | Observation, Orientation, Decision, and Action [Cycle] |
| OPEC | Organization of the Petroleum Exporting Countries |
| OpSec | Operational Security |
| OSS | Office of Strategic Services |
| | |
| PCO | Privy Counsel Office |
| PMO | Prime Minister's Office |
| PoW | Prisoner of War |
| PPCLI | Princess Patricia's Canadian Light Infantry |
| PRT | Provincial Reconstruction Team |
| PSYOPS | Psychological Operations |
| | |
| RAAF | Royal Australian Air Force |
| RCMP | Royal Canadian Mounted Police |
| RCR | Royal Canadian Regiment |
| | |
| TTPs | Tactics, Techniques, and Procedures |
| | |
| SAS | Special Air Service |
| SASR | [Australian] Special Air Service Regiment |

| | |
|---|---|
| SBS | Special Boat Service |
| SDV | Swimmer Delivery Vehicle |
| SEAL | Sea Air Land |
| SERE | Survival, Evasion, Resistance, and Escape |
| SF | Special Forces |
| SFAS | Special Forces Assessment and Selection [Course] |
| SFG | Special Forces Group |
| SFQC | Special Forces Qualification Course |
| SO | Special Operations |
| SODSU | Special Operations Direct Support Unit |
| SOE | Special Operations Executive |
| SOF | Special Operations Forces |
| SOG | Studies and Observations Group |
| SR | Special Reconnaissance |
| SWAT | Special Weapons and Tactics |
| SWCS | Special Warfare Center and School |
| | |
| U.K. | United Kingdom |
| UN | United Nations |
| U.S. | United States [of America] |
| USASOC | United States Army Special Operations Command |
| USSOCOM | United States Special Operations Command |
| UW | Unconventional Warfare |
| | |
| VC | Viet Cong |
| | |
| WMD | Weapons of Mass Destruction |
| | |
| 3D | Defence, Diplomacy, and Development |
| 9/11 | 11 September 2001 (Terrorist Attack) |

# CONTRIBUTORS

**Major Tony Balasevicius** is an infantry officer and member of The Royal Canadian Regiment. He has served as a platoon and company commander and in various positions with the Canadian Airborne Regiment. In 1995, he took over responsibility for the Army's interim parachute capability, and in 1998, he was posted to Ottawa. In 2002, he became the deputy commanding officer of the 1st Battalion, The Royal Canadian Regiment, and was subsequently posted to the Directorate of Land Requirements in Ottawa. Major Balasevicius is currently on staff at the Department of Applied Military Science at the Royal Military College of Canada.

**Major Bernard J. Brister** is a tactical helicopter pilot with overseas tours of duty in Germany, Haiti, Bosnia, and Afghanistan. His most recent operational experiences were undertaken over the course of a five-year assignment with the former Directorate of Counter-Terrorism and Special Operations. He is currently completing his PhD in the fields of Canadian/American foreign policy and international terrorism prior to taking up a teaching position at the Royal Military College of Canada.

**Colonel Bernd Horn** is the director of the Canadian Forces Leadership Institute. Dr. Horn is an experienced infantry officer with command experience at the unit and sub-unit levels. He was the commanding officer of the 1st Battalion, The Royal Canadian Regiment (2001–2003); the officer commanding 3 Commando, Canadian Airborne Regiment (1993–1995); and the officer commanding "B" Company, 1st Battalion, The Royal Canadian Regiment (1992–1993). Colonel Horn has authored, co-authored, edited, and co-edited 14 books and numerous articles on military affairs and history. He is also an adjunct associate professor of history at the Royal Military College of Canada.

**Lieutenant-Colonel Jamie W. Hammond** is a serving officer in the Canadian Forces and a part-time doctoral candidate at Carleton University in Ottawa. Hammond has operational experience in Bosnia and Afghanistan and was most recently employed as chief of staff transformation in the newly formed Canadian Special Operations Forces Command. He is currently the commanding officer of the Canadian Special Operations Regiment being established in Petawawa, Ontario.

**Dr. Michael A. Hennessy** is the chair of the history department at the Royal Military College of Canada and member of the International Institute of Strategic Studies, a research fellow with the Canadian Forces Leadership Institute, and a member of the editorial boards of the *Canadian Military Journal* and the journal *Defense Studies* (London).

**Dr. Sean M. Maloney** is from Kingston, Ontario, and served in Germany as the historian for 4th Canadian Mechanized Brigade, the Canadian Army's contribution to the North Atlantic Treaty Organisation during the Cold War. He is the author of several works dealing with the modern Canadian Army and peacekeeping history, including the controversial *Canada and UN Peacekeeping: Cold War by Other Means 1945–1970*, *Chances for Peace: The Canadians and UNPROFOR 1992–1995*, and *Enduring the Freedom: A Rogue Historian Visits Afghanistan*. Dr. Maloney has extensive field research experience through duty in the Balkans, the Middle East, and Afghanistan. He currently teaches in the war studies program at the Royal Military College of Canada and is a senior research fellow at the Queen's Centre for International Relations.

**Colonel J. Paul de B. Taillon** is the director, review and military liaison, at Canada's Office of the Communications Security Establishment Commissioner. Formerly an intelligence officer with the Canadian Security Intelligence Service, he has written extensively on terrorism, low-intensity operations, and special operations. Two of his books concern terrorism and special forces, while another, which he co-edited, is about special operations. A Canadian Army Reserve colonel who has served with the British and American SOF, he is a graduate of the U.S. Marine Corps (USMC) Amphibious Warfare School and USMC Command and Staff College, and is currently a student at the U.S. Army War College, class of 2006. Until recently he was a directing staff at the Canadian Forces College. Dr. Taillon is an adjunct professor at the Royal Military College of Canada where he teaches terrorism, irregular warfare, intelligence, and special operations in the War Studies MA program. He is also a senior fellow at the Joint Special Operations University, Hurlburt Field, Florida. Dr. Taillon has an MA in international relations from the Norman Patterson School of International Affairs, an MA in war studies from the Royal Military College of Canada, and a PhD from the London School of Economics and Political Science, University of London.

# INDEX